A curriculum for life

Schools for a democratic learning society

John Quicke

Open University Press
Buckingham · P

Open University Press
Celtic Court
22 Ballmoor
Buckingham
MK18 1XW

e-mail: enquiries@openup.co.uk
world wide web: http://www.openup.co.uk

and
325 Chestnut Street
Philadelphia, PA 19106, USA

First Published 1999

A catalogue record of this book is available from the British Library

ISBN   0 335 20297 7 (pb)   0 335 20298 5 (hb)

Library of Congress Cataloging-in-Publication Data
Quicke, John, 1941–
   A curriculum for life : schools for a democratic learning society / John Quicke.
      p.   cm.
   Includes bibliographical references (p.   ) and index.
   ISBN 0-335-20298-5
   ISBN 0-335-20297-7 (pbk.)
   1. Education–Great Britain–Curricula.   2. Curriculum change–Great
Britain.   3. Democracy–Study and teaching–Great Britain.   I. Title.
   LB1564.G7 Q85 1999
   375'.000941–dc21   98-33198
                                                                            CIP

Typeset by Type Study, Scarborough
Printed in Great Britain by St Edmundsbury Press Ltd, Bury St Edmunds, Suffolk

Contents

Acknowledgements   v
Preface   vi

1   Introduction: the curriculum and reflexive modernity   1

2   Education for self-identity   18

3   Becoming a 'good' learner   34

4   Towards a collaborative culture of professionalism   50

5   Pupils' cultural practices and collaborative group work   68

6   Teaching for cultural pluralism   81

7   Gender politics and school achievement   96

8   On learning and democracy in families   113

9   Reworking the work ethic   129

10 Science and the risk society   145

11 Schools for a democratic learning society   160

References   170
Index   179

Acknowledgements

I should like to offer my thanks to all those colleagues, friends and acquaintances who have discussed education and, indeed, many other aspects of life with me over the years. They are too numerous to mention and it would be invidious to single out one or two for special thanks. However, since the book in part has its origins in my experiences of teaching on educational studies courses for master's degree students in the Department of Educational Studies at the University of Sheffield, I must acknowledge the contribution of all those students and colleagues in the Department who, through discussing their ideas with me in a teaching context, have helped me to develop my thinking. Thanks must also be expressed to Andrew Pollard for his helpful comments on the manuscript, to Jean Booker for her careful typing of part of the manuscript and to Sage Publications for permission to use material in Chapter 3 taken from an article which appeared in *School Psychology International*, Vol. 15(3), pp. 247–60.

Preface

In England and Wales, it is evident that there is growing support for a National Curriculum review which will be more comprehensive than any undertaken previously. Since the introduction of the National Curriculum in 1988 there have been several minor modifications and one fairly substantial review carried out by Sir Ron Dearing in 1993–94, but nothing as wide-ranging as the one envisaged by the government's Qualifications and Curriculum Authority (QCA). According Nick Tate, chief executive of the QCA, there will be a revision of the curriculum in the year 2000 which will not only spell out what was left implicit in the current National Curriculum but will go beyond subject disciplines and the basics and begin with 'first principles', a 'statement of what society values' and recognition of 'the importance of the many aspects of pupils' personal, spiritual, moral, social and cultural development' (*Times Educational Supplement*,13 February 1998). The initial soundings of the QCA's consultation exercise suggest that there is a great deal of support for a curriculum that includes these latter elements, and for a discussion about how and why they should be taught.

Although couched in the language of 'consultation', of which teachers and other educationalists have grown suspicious in recent years, the pronouncements of the QCA do seem to suggest there may now be a real opportunity to open up a genuine debate on the curriculum. For many, like the author of this book, such a debate is long overdue and cannot come too soon. It has been a very worrying feature of the educational system in England and Wales that, despite the extensive reforms of the post-war period aimed at making 'education for all' a reality, the one element which has never been properly discussed is the curriculum itself, and this arguably is one of the main reasons why the system continues to be divisive and unjust. Despite the efforts of various curriculum reform movements, particularly in the 1970s and 1980s, the traditional curriculum, which was devised for grammar schools nearly a hundred years ago, has remained largely intact. The

Education Reform Act (1988), with its list of core and foundation subjects, merely reaffirmed this state of affairs.

The purpose of this book is to contribute to the debate that hopefully will be generated by this renewed interest in the purpose and content of the curriculum. The central question addressed will be: what kind of curriculum do we need for life in the twenty-first century? At the present time there is much talk about the society we live in being a learning society; this is often used as a description of what in large measure is apparent in current conditions but is also prescriptive of the kind of development which many educators would want to encourage. From an educational perspective, it is certainly a seductive idea. As Hyland (1994: 138) points out, it comes with all the 'positive connotations associated with learning and development'. It conjures up images of a society which is open, democratic and forward looking, where citizens are provided with opportunities at any stage of life to acquire the knowlege and skills for self-development as well as for the benefit of others; and of organizations which are adaptable and innovative and which treat their employees as persons to be developed rather than resources to be exploited. Moreover, it is an idea which appears capable of generating a new consensus about the aims and purposes of education by breaking down the barrier between the world of work and the world of education. Many of the key goals of liberal democratic education – autonomy, respect for others, the development of critical capacities – are now seen to be more compatible with the kinds of 'competences' required by the polity and the economy.

But why the learning society? What are the concerns of the present-day world which the idea of a learning society seeks to address? What kind of 'solution' does the learning society propose? How these questions are answered will, of course, vary according to our different understandings of present society and our different interpretations of the 'good' society and the best way to achieve it. And it is here the debate must start. The proposals in this book are based on a particular vision of the 'good' society which I shall refer to as a *democratic learning society*. Most of the discussion will revolve around questions to do with how such a society might be realized through education – what are the positive features of the current context, those which in specific areas prefigure this particular ideal of a learning society, and what are those aspects which hold back developments in this direction; and how do we teach about these things?

The book's challenge will be to relate these wider societal aspects to educational practice, particularly in schools, which will be regarded as having a key role to play, even in a society where learning will be conceived as a life-long pursuit and an out-of-school and post-school as well as in-school activity. The need for such a book arises because one anticipates the perspective which informs it will not be well represented in curriculum debate. It is already the case that much of the literature on the 'future curriculum' is one-dimensional and simplistic. Much of it is populist futurology which is not based on any serious analysis of present or future times. Labels like 'the information society' and 'the post-industrial society' are bandied about but with no systematic attempt to identify their defining characteristics. Social change is usually under-theorized – it is typically viewed as a 'fact of life' to which schools and other institutions are supposed to adapt. There is a lot of talk about the learning society but little discussion about how this idea relates to the 'good society'. In contrast, the author's intention in this book is to ground the discussion of a 'new curriculum' in a more thoroughgoing analysis of people's experiences of life in contemporary society and a more critical engagement with moral and political issues.

John Quicke
University of Sheffield

1 | Introduction: the curriculum and reflexive modernity

Introduction

The purpose of this book is to present and critically examine proposals for a curriculum which would enable all citizens to construct 'good lives' in the twenty-first century as members of democratic learning societies. A curriculum provides a framework for learning. It suggests that of all the things that could be learned these particular things have the most value; and it does this with reference to the educational needs of the students to be taught and the social and political context in which teaching and learning take place. In its broadest sense, the curriculum includes the 'how' and the 'what' of learning which occurs formally and informally inside educational institutions as well as outside such institutions. All societies have their curricula and in a sense all societies are learning societies, but in the era in which we live the term 'learning society' is used to describe a new kind of society where every citizen is and should be more reflexive about the processes of learning and more aware of the need to engage actively in the construction of 'good' learning communities.

In terms of its actual content, the curriculum for a 'good' life can and should be specified. It is a 'curriculum for all' which should create, confirm and develop our common sense of purpose, but which should also enable each of us to realize our potentialities as an individual. Our thinking has to take account of many aspects of a complex world, one which is changing so rapidly that questions about 'what to teach' are obsolete almost as soon as they have been asked. In embarking upon this quest for a 'curriculum for life' one begins, therefore, with a sense of foreboding that the ideas and arguments presented here will quickly be overtaken by events. Yet, at the time of writing, one writes in hope! The story told here does not pretend to be a 'grand narrative', a total 'world view' which underpins all other stories about the world, but a narrative with a limited range which is clearly of its time and for its time. Nevertheless, I would want to claim for it more staying power than some of the fashionable futuristic accounts which seek to crowd our thoughts at the beginning of the new millennium.

Starting points

In thinking about a curriculum for a democratic learning society we need to begin by considering two interrelated aspects. The first is our philosophical position, which following Bocock (1986), I shall define as a moral-political philosophical perspective; in this instance, one which assumes consonance between a moral philosophical position where human beings are seen as capable of making moral choices, and a political philosophy where ideas such as liberty, equality, justice and democracy are a central concern. The second is the theory of society assumed – in particular, what is assumed about the way society is changing at the present time and what changes need to occur if the appropriate moral and political values are to be realized. Both these aspects are important and necessary to each other – the latter, if not grounded in a framework of moral and political values, will be directionless and incoherent; and the former without the latter will be abstract and in danger of being seen as utopian and thus unconnected to concrete social circumstances. I shall consider both in turn.

A moral-political perspective

The moral-political perspective adopted here is one involving an understanding of individualism as conceptually related to the political ideas of equality and liberty. As Lukes (1973) has shown in his detailed historical and philosophical analysis of individualism, the four basic ideas of individualism – respect for human dignity, autonomy, privacy and self-development – are linked to each other but are also 'essential elements' (Lukes 1973: 125) in the ideas of liberty and equality. For instance, the idea that human beings should be respected because they have an inherent dignity is egalitarian since it asserts that persons are worthy of respect not because of some special talent or characteristic they may possess but purely and simply because they possess human characteristics. The three other ideas are related to liberty or freedom. Persons are said to be free when their actions are self-determined rather than the result of the decisions and choices of others. Freedom also involves being in a position where one is not interfered with or put upon by others; where one has sufficient personal space or privacy to carry out one's own projects without disruption. The third idea is to do with self-development. Persons are also free to the extent to which they can realize their potentialities and have control over the process which enables this to happen.

It will further be assumed that the kind of political system which is both informed by and facilitative of the realization of such values is democracy along 'classical' lines in the sense used by Carr and Hartnett (1996). In this version of democracy, the emphasis is on democracy as a 'way of life' where individuals realize their potentialities through active participation in the life of their society, and '[a] democratic society is thus an educative society [a 'learning society'] whose citizens enjoy equal opportunities for self-development, self-fulfilment and self-determination' (1996: 41). It is contrasted with a 'contemporary' conception where democracy is a 'representative system of political decision-making' (1996: 40) involving competition between political parties for the votes of a largely passive electorate, a system which 'resonate[s] closely with the principles and methods of a *laissez-faire* market economy'(1996: 42).

'Classical' and 'contemporary' are formal categories which highlight differences between systems in terms of central values and assumptions rather than being descriptive of any actual working models of democracy, but they help to clarify the different approaches to education which relate to different political ideologies. The appropriate form of education in terms of the contemporary model is one which is dominant at the present time. It involves a system characterized by the selection and differentiation of pupils leading to the reproduction of inequalities; a form of teaching and learning which is competitive and hierarchical; a way of organizing schools which is undemocratic; and the embrace of an instrumentalism which harnesses education to the economic goals of society.

By contrast, an education for a modern version of classical democracy is one which provides equal opportunities for all students to realize their potentialities as individuals and as citizens of a democratic society. The educational principles deployed are those consonant with and historically related to the formation and reproduction of the 'good' individual life and the 'good' society, which in classical democracies gives rise to a view of education as both *person-centred* and *community-oriented*. The learner in the democratic learning society is constituted as a person – someone who actually or potentially has the capacity to make moral choices, act autonomously and think rationally – and learning is about the development of persons as unique individuals through being active participants in democratic learning communities. Such participation empowers them to act upon the world around them and transform it, and to act upon themselves in the same way. The more autonomous a person becomes, the more they are able to make use of what they know to create and achieve self-originated goals and the more they will play a part in the development of their own capacities and the development of the learning communities to which they are committed. The type of community I have in mind here is of the kind referred to by the philosopher MacIntyre as a 'practice'. For MacIntyre (1981: 187) a practice is

> any coherent and complex form of socially established cooperative human activity through which goods internal to that form of activity are realized in the course of trying to achieve those standards of excellence which are appropriate and partially definitive of that form of activity, with the result that human powers to achieve excellence, and human conceptions of the ends and goods involved are systematically extended.

The 'goods' (that is, what is valued) thus have a social dimension which is inextricably bound up with the dimension of the self. Participation in practices is empowering for individuals and potentially autonomy-enhancing, since it involves 'participating in the attempts to sustain progress and responding creatively' which enables the individual to discover 'the good of a certain kind of life' (MacIntyre 1981: 190); that is, to find a morally worthy identity as an active, creative agent. Individual identities are fostered through participation in these historically located communities of practice.

Political education will always be a central feature of this form of education because students will need to develop a critical awareness of the ways in which society fosters and, as it is currently constituted, also frustrates democratic aspirations. These social and political processes can be examined on a number of levels – the personal, institutional and societal – and democratic educators would therefore have to deploy a concept of the political which was broader than is conventionally understood in contemporary democracy. Ideal relations within communities at all levels must be relations between persons where reciprocity implies concern for the freedom of the other to participate fully as an active agent in the social life of the community. One is reminded here of an earlier account of the morality of persons-in-relation: 'My care for you is only moral if it includes the intention to preserve your freedom as an agent, which is your independence of me. Even if you wish to be dependent on me, it is my business, for your sake, to prevent it' (Macmurray 1961: 190)

Reflexive modernity: dangers and opportunities in 'new times'

In explicating the second aspect referred to above, the theory of society, it will suffice, for the purposes of this introductory chapter, to identify briefly what we might take to be certain key defining characteristics of contemporary society. It is by all accounts a rapidly changing society, but what exactly is the nature of this change and how do we evaluate it? Given that the changes have been radical enough to justify describing the present period as 'new times' (see Hall and Jacques 1989), what precisely do we mean by this description? What are 'new times'? They have been characterized in various ways, but in this book it is assumed that crucially they revolve around the idea of *reflexivity* – the process whereby individuals, groups and organizations 'turn round' upon themselves, critically examine their rationales and values, and, if necessary, deliberately reorder or reinvent their identities and structures. It is now necessary to do this in a more regular and self-conscious way than previously because of the sudden and often quite dramatic changes which occur with increasing frequency as part of a new mode of life. But from the outset I want to suggest that these changes are understood as a development of modernity rather than as a break with modernity of such proportions that it is now more appropriate to speak of postmodernity. The times we live in, the 'new times', are still modern times, albeit a new form or phase of modernity, which might be called *reflexive modernity*. They can only be conceived as postmodern by identifying discontinuities and repressing continuities; a postmodernist discourse on equality of opportunity, for example, would be a contradiction in terms, since the very notion of equality of opportunity is part of the modernist project.

Of course, it could be argued that one of the most significant continuities between all forms of modernity is the reflexive nature of its practices. All modern societies are discontinuous with pre-modern societies in the way the relationship between the individual and society is conceptualized. George Mead, one of the main architects of a social psychology for modern times and, along with John Dewey, a member of the influential Chicago school of pragmatic philosophy, distinguished between conduct in traditional societies where moral compulsion did not come from the individual but 'impressed' itself upon the individual from an external force as custom was strictly adhered to; and modern society where individuals were more aware of their own agency (see Mead 1934).

On this view the self in modernity is thoroughly social, since in Meadian terms the ability to become a person is dependent on the capacity to 'take the role of the other' and thus to share meanings with others, but the individual is also a creative constructor of society and an agent of social and psychological change in its own right. The self is also therefore thoroughly reflexive in that all existing roles in institutions, structures and practices can be reflected upon by the individuals who inhabit them, and thereby acted upon by the self in accordance with its socially constituted interests and concerns.

If reflexivity distinguishes the modern from the traditional, what can be said of it with respect to the distinction between earlier and later forms of modernity? Clearly, all forms of modernity – even what Lash (1994) describes as *simple modernity* – have involved reflexivity in the sense described above. However, one might take the view – as I do here – that such a descriptor serves to highlight the difference between a period when modernism did not carry through the logic of its own revolution from one where it is, so to speak, back on track. In the period of simple modernity reflexivity or 'individualization' largely broke down traditional structures – the extended family, the church, the village community – only to replace them by new structures and practices – the state, the nation, the nuclear family, the capitalist economy, science – which themselves became reified forms, oppressive in their impact on the lives and subjectivities of individuals, and leading to technicist and bureaucratic institutional forms. But in the later period, reflexivity reasserts itself – the dynamic process of reflection on self and institutions continues and the agent is once again 'freed' to deconstruct all aspects of the social world through which it was constituted.

This so called 'freeing' of agency from structure is compatible with educational principles (those derived from our moral-political perspective) in so far as it celebrates and fosters a form of individual autonomy involving a release of creative energy directed in a positive, democratic-enhancing way at existing forms and structures, and helps to establish the social conditions for the realization of human potentialities, the flowering of new communities and the enrichment of life for all. But there is a darker side to the process which stems from the way people, organizations and governments have reacted to changes. The 'new times' have given rise to a new language of oppression, one that is heavily disguised in the vocabulary of legitimate community and democratic practice. Beneath the rhetoric, old structures of inequality and oppression have remained and continue to be influential despite denials to the contrary by liberal commentators who see only discontinuities rather than continuities with the negative aspects of the past.

Constructing a curriculum for 'new times'

In constructing a curriculum for 'new times', we need to acknowledge both the dangers and opportunities afforded by the changes that have taken place. There is a continuing need for critical engagement with institutionalized forms and structures which have always acted as a constraint on the development of democracy and continue to do so, albeit in new guises. It is in relation to these anti-democratic aspects of the past that the new curriculum needs to be discontinuous and transformational – aspects associated, for example, with ideologies and practices perpetuating bureaucratic organizational forms, the class structure, racism, patriarchy, economic fundamentalism and scientism. But the curriculum needs to be reproductive as well as transformational – the latter in that it will seek to identify and counter oppression from all sources; the former in so far as it supports and develops those elements of democracy which are an established part of the culture.

Second, we will need to identify the most salient areas of experience in the phase of modernity in which we live, namely reflexive modernity, with its warts and all. Clearly, this is not an easy task; there are many ways to describe and categorize experience, and many views on what should be prioritized in a new curriculum agenda. However, the hope is that issues can be identified which most people will agree are of vital concern in the current period, even if they disagree on the best way to address them. This concern will stem from an understanding of the fact that, in certain key areas, life has become more complex, differentiated, variable and unpredictable, and an awareness that these areas are important because they involve 'hotspots' of contestation which are particularly relevant for the realization of a democratic society.

The areas of experience which seem to me to be of most concern in this respect (and, of course, these may change in the future) revolve around several themes where the tensions between progressive and regressive elements are especially acute. The first relates to the need for the individual to find an identity in a complex, increasingly differentiated, pluralistic and rapidly changing world. At all stages of life there is a universal need for a more explicit form of self-understanding which enables people to think reflexively, critically and imaginatively about their life projects and *self-identity*. In 'new times', the foothold in reality is to be found within the self rather than outside the subjective realm of identity, since in this new world 'the individual's experience of himself becomes more real to him than his experience of the objective social world [*sic*]' (Berger *et al*. 1973: 74). Giddens (1991), however, warns of various dilemmas of the self which affect most people in the conditions of reflexive or high modernity. The problem here for the self is the protection and reconstruction of 'the narrative of self identity' – of understanding the self as a 'unitary subject' (Kitwood 1990) and attempting to live life as a morally coherent and consistent project in the face of constant pressures to fragment and decentre.

Self-identity is tied in with the second theme, which might be described as *collaboration*. In the circumstances of late modernity a commitment to collaborative, democratic relationships is of great value to the self because it anticipates social arrangements in the wider community which ensure space for autonomy-enhancing practices. These relationships should be characterized by equality, negotiation, symmetrical power relations, transactionality and mutual trust where all participants retain their autonomy and sense of self-worth. It is a commitment involving the realization of virtues and qualities, but it is provisional and revocable like all commitments and is reflexively monitored on a continuous basis. Like democracy itself it functions as a social imaginary (Mouffe 1993), and the perfect collaborative relationship is something which is constantly referred to but can never be realized in practice. It involves more dialogue between self and another than any other kind of relationship and therefore connects readily with the dialectic of reflexive self projects.

As the old bureaucratic structures of simple modernity are deconstructed the way is open for the emergence of more democratic and more collaborative organizational forms, which facilitate the development of learning communities. One would anticipate a flowering of such communities in the conditions of reflexive modernity. Organizations such as schools and colleges would be more open, more innovative and more generative and supportive of a variety of diverse selves and cultures. However, the notion of collaboration can be interpreted in ways which do not challenge the antidemocratic features of bureaucratic organizations. It is easy to underestimate the capacity for the bureaucratic mode of thought to undermine democratic ideals and to prevent the emergence of genuinely collaborative organizational cultures. In the post-war period, many of the state's legitimacy problems have allegedly stemmed from its adherence to this outmoded conception of organizational structure. Policy implementation has involved a 'top-down' approach which has ridden roughshod over emerging identities in a complex and multicultural society, and led to programmes of action, particularly in the field of welfare, which have deviated markedly from their original intentions.

A third theme is the *family*, since even the 'structures of intimacy' amongst persons in 'close' relationships are open to revision and reconstruction in the light of changing perceptions of the self and the social world. The family is a particularly important structure partly because it provides the first or primary identity for a 'new' member of society and one which is likely for some time to act as a reference point for self-reflection, and partly because it is an institutionalized form which has been and continues to be an object of attention for agencies which have an interest in the development of certain kinds of subjectivities. Like other structures, the family has felt the impact of 'new times'. In her review of recent research in this area, Fox Harding (1996) concludes that there have been fundamental changes in people's attitudes towards formal marriage and related aspects such as divorce, cohabitation, the single-parent family and reproduction outside marriage (see also Haskey 1991; Kiernan and Wicks 1990). There are now many more choices and 'possibilities for disengagement' (Fox Harding 1996: 103) from traditional forms brought about by a whole host of technological, economic, cultural and legal changes. However, it is evident that there is an ever present danger of traditional familial ideology continuing to structure family relations, even if its form may change. Democratic aspirations fostered by pervasive social and personal reflexivity are held back by a restorationist agenda drawn up by those, like neo-conservatives of the New Right (see below), who want to shore up traditional asymmetries of power.

Another important characteristic of contemporary society is its increasing cultural diversity which gives rise to the fourth theme of *cultural pluralism*. Modern societies have always had to accommodate cultural differences – whether these derive from identification with an ethnic group or some other kind of minority – but in the contemporary context cultural identities become less fixed and are more open to revision and development. As the scope for cultural interaction increases in a multiplicity of contexts via new communication systems, so the opportunities for experimentation and negotiation give rise to an increasing diversity of new cultural forms, each wanting recognition as an authentic expression of its own uniqueness (see Taylor 1992). But the increasing pluralism and diversity of society brings with it a number of dangers. Tensions between groups can easily be exacerbated by racism, chauvinism, patriarchy and other anti-democratic and socially dysfunctional elements. We ignore signs of continuities with the past at our peril. Racism has been a potent force in people's lives throughout the twentieth century and is likely to continue to be so. As Solomos and Back (1996: 206) acknowledge, in recent years 'we have seen . . . the growth and genocidal impact of new forms of racial and ethnically based ideologies in many parts of the globe, including most notably in the 1990s in both Western and Eastern Europe and parts of Africa'. It could be that in a world where there is so much uncertainty racism often presents people with simple concepts for understanding the world and their place within it. Undoubtedly the erosion of the autonomy of the nation-state will contribute to these developments, although the consequences of this aspect are difficult to predict.

As for patriarchy, although changes in relations between the sexes have undoubtedly taken place, it is evident that deeply held beliefs about gender support social and economic structures which continue to be oppressive for many women. The labour market still remains highly segregated, and this is closely related to inequalities in working conditions and job prospects, despite the opportunities that have been opened up for women in recent years, particularly in the area of part-time work. Changes in family life have made a difference, but there is evidence that the traditional division of domestic labour and the values that underpin it are extremely durable (MacEwen Scott 1994).

However, it is in the economic sphere perhaps that some of the most important changes have taken place. Here capital accumulation could not occur without 'agency' freeing itself from the 'rules' of mass consumption and 'Fordist' structures of production. Previous forms of monitoring of workers are displaced by self-monitoring, and the systems of rules and resources which constitute the means of production also become the object of reflection by agency (see Lash 1994: 119). The need to explore new, highly specialized, niche markets has become 'fundamental to survival' (Harvey 1989) in highly competitive conditions. New production technologies and new organizational forms have reduced turnover time, but this has had to be accompanied by a reduction in turnover time in consumption. Flexible accumulation has therefore gone hand in hand with accelerated changes in taste and fashion which themselves are a function of self-reflexivity and the opportunities for differentiation and diversity that this implies. Consumption has become as important as production for the construction of identity.

A fifth theme is therefore *work and economic life*. The new opportunities to which these developments give rise have been highlighted by writers such as Schlechty (1990) who regard the types of persons and relationships required by the 'new' economy as similar to those which would be developed and supported in democratic educational institutions.The 'new' workers would need to be adaptable and flexible, but also capable of seizing opportunities to develop their skills, to be creative and to take responsibility for their own work in a way which maximized the scope for self-regulation and personal autonomy, and minimized the need for constraints imposed by management. However, the extent to which the new technologies and new work organization have generated a highly-skilled, reflexive workforce have been exaggerated (see Green 1994). What has emerged in recent years is a social differentiation which looks like a new class structure rather than one where difference merely reflects diversity of occupation and lifestyle. Workers may need to have higher skills and to be more cognitively engaged than previously, but they have less security and less opportunity for being 'critical'. The majority still have little control over the production process and their scope for reflexive decision-making is limited.

Finally, as indicated above, reflexivity on structure takes place against a background of increasing complexity and uncertainty. The growth of diversity and of agency, plus the greater contact of belief systems due to the development of global communication systems, has led to a more critical appraisal and testing out of 'expertise' the truth of which was previously taken for granted. The grand narratives – those totalizing stories about the world which purported to be grounded in universal, proven truths – have fallen into disrepute as their provisionality, non-neutrality and fallibility have become increasingly recognized.

From an epistemological viewpoint, there have been changes in the way we typically understand the nature of knowledge and what it means to know. That most prestigious form of knowledge, scientific knowledge, has become less secure. Like all knowledge, it is located within a paradigm or 'language game' which has its own discourse rules and truth criteria. The 'symbolic representations' and models of science are constructs which involve an interpretation of nature rather than a theory-free description of 'what is' in nature. 'Doing science' is about looking at and thinking about the world in a particular way, developing shared meanings in a specific context and participating in scientific communities. The 'old truths' about science have given way to doubts and anxieties about the contribution of natural scientific knowledge to human well-being. Nowhere is this more evident than in concerns about the environment and the contribution of science and technology to environmental degradation and ecological disaster. What was once considered a 'source of safety' has now become a 'source of risk' (see Beck 1994; Irwin 1995). In pursuing the sixth and final theme, *science in a risk society*, learners need to develop their capacity to evaluate expertise and think rationally about appropriate courses of action in conditions of risk and uncertainty.

Other approaches to curriculum reform

To recap: in putative democratic societies, what is required is the development of a curriculum grounded in a moral-political perspective where individualism is linked with the democratic values of liberty and equality, and in a view of society as a current phase of modernity which might appropriately be described as 'reflexive modernity'. Some of the most significant characteristics of this new period have been briefly identified with particular reference to the opportunities they represent for the development of a genuinely democratic learning society, as well as the constraints on such development.

However, there have been many other interpretations of the changing society, which, although taking account of similar phenomena, such as the new structures of production and the changing role of the family, have given rise to different views on 'what needs to be done' and have resulted in a range of different proposals for curriculum reform (for a summary, see Nixon *et al.* 1996). In order to clarify the distinctive approach of this book, it will be useful to examine the policies and proposals derived from two responses to change in England and Wales which have made a significant impact in recent years.

Restoring the traditional academic curriculum

As we know from recent history in England and Wales, one response by government has been to re-establish the traditional academic curriculum as part of a package of reforms designed, amongst other things, to restore the authority of the state and with it the authority of institutions such as the family and the school in the face of a crisis of legitimacy brought about by what has been interpreted as disorderly and dysfunctional social change. Unsurprisingly, this policy has largely failed to produce the right kind of curriculum since it merely involves trying to put the clock back rather than being a genuine attempt to address current concerns. What has been restored, of course, is not an academic curriculum consisting of communities of practice in MacIntyre's sense, but precisely the kind of curriculum which negates such communities. It comes with a whole baggage of beliefs about the nature of human society and the distribution of human intelligence associated with an elitist curriculum in which learners are positioned in ways which reflect the external influences of power and status rather than their orientation to the intrinsic 'goods' of the subject defined as a practice.

The Education Reform Act of 1988 has been the centrepiece of this largely unsuccessful strategy. Despite references in its first section to the spiritual, moral, cultural, mental and physical development of pupils, in practice it has not resulted in the development of a curriculum which can meet the needs of young persons at the end of the twentieth century. Although the system might be thought of, rather generously, as having the aim to empower young people through immersion in a broad and balanced range of various traditions of thought and enquiry, this purpose is undermined by the conception of these traditions as largely coterminous with traditional school subjects, understood unproblematically as 'expert systems' aimed at fostering reflection only in the limited sense of critical reflection within the confines of the subject. To be of any value to the emerging reflexive and collaborative self, the curriculum must provide the experience of 'commitment' and be linked explicitly to the self-identity work of young people.

The National Curriculum is woefully inadequate in this respect. It bears all the hallmarks of what Bernstein (1975) described as a 'collection'- as opposed to an 'integrated'-type curriculum. The collection-type curriculum involves the reification of subjects, strong boundaries between courses and highly ritualized and hierarchical teacher–learner relationships. Far from being involved personally, learners are confronted with an 'impersonal' subject, the 'ultimate mystery' of which can only be 'revealed' after an apprenticeship stretching long into the future, and attainable only by those who stay the course and can properly access the subject. The result is that the majority of young people derive no benefit in terms of personal and social development from studying these subjects. Moreover, since the current National Curriculum is rooted in a social organization of knowledge which historically has been part of a system designed to bolster an elite and exclude the majority, it is scarcely surprising that a disproportionate number of these non-beneficiaries are likely to come from the lower classes and other marginalized groups (Goodson 1994).

Even this, I feel, understates the degree to which the National Curriculum fails to facilitate the enhancement of personal autonomy and social commitment for all. It is rare for even those pupils who are 'successful' in the system to experience studying subjects as involvement in practices which foster their self- and social development, except in a very limited way. Pupils' approach is basically instrumental. By passing exams they have made more options available in terms of life planning, but this is confined to only one area of planning – planning for a future occupational career. All other possibilities which could have been opened up by personal engagement in a range of subjects (for example, 'careers' as people who identify themselves as having an interest in maths, geography, science and so on) are not really available. Most pupils do not, in fact, have 'academic selves' in any subject, despite 11 or more years of schooling.

Finally, it is important to note that this approach to the curriculum has been linked with a political ideology, namely New Right ideology, which was dominant in many countries in the 1980s and early 1990s, and the essential ingredients of which arguably still hold sway in Britain in the late 1990s, despite the change of government. This is a particular species of conservatism which combines free market and social authoritarian approaches. The potentially contradictory notions of 'freedom' and the market on the one hand and 'authority' and the nation on the other have been welded together under the arch of an agreement about the restoration of state authority and the celebration of value in national culture. The policy agenda is dominated by an ideology of restorationism which 'speaks' both the language of individual freedom and that of 'community'.

As far as education is concerned, the New Right's agenda is clearly flawed. Its fundamentalist, retrogressive approach to personality, community and the nation is incompatible with the ironic and exploratory stance towards understanding and constructing identity required in 'new times'. The kind of identities and communities we need to foster for our own and society's well-being in this era cannot be produced merely through a process of teaching facts about the 'cultural heritage'. Encouraging people to challenge their prejudices and initial framework of assumptions becomes much more difficult in a situation where certain prejudgements are associated with a cultural essence. Moreover, the New Right's embrace of the free market has resulted in too much emphasis on the competitive economic self which, once 'unleashed', so to speak, has tended to undermine the aim to restore community through the reinforcement of a nostalgic national identity. In the words of a popular folksong, 'money knows no home or nation'. The market mechanism has not provided educational opportunities for all or fostered active participation in or allegiance to a national community. If anything it has worked in a way which has systematically disadvantaged certain groups, reinforced the class-divided society and restricted rather than increased the scope for public deliberation, choice and action which is the hallmark of a democratic community (see Jonathan 1990; Ranson 1993; Gewirtz *et al.* 1995).

Modernization, vocationalism and the enterprise economy

An alternative to the restorationist strategy of the 'New Right' is one which seeks to modernize the curriculum by making it more consonant with the needs of an enterprise economy. As I have acknowledged elsewhere, this 'new vocationalist' approach was not incompatible with traditionalism at the level of practical politics (Quicke 1988a: 15), but at the level of principle it was grounded in a philosophy which was far more explicitly utilitarian.

For K. Jones (1989) the 'modernizers' represented a third tendency within Conservatism which, in contrast to the cultural restorationists and the free marketeers of the New Right, sought to intervene in many areas of social and economic life, particularly in matters to do with economic regeneration and the creation of a new culture of enterprise. Modernizers have advocated a complete break with the anti-industrial values of the old academic tradition and have asserted the need for a more relevant, student-centred, practical and vocationally oriented curriculum, exemplified in England and Wales in the 1980s by the 'new learning' rhetoric of the Technical Vocational Education Initiative (TVEI).

In the 1990s these ideas found expression in England and Wales through the work of bodies like the National Commission of Education (NCE) whose 1993 report, *Learning to Succeed,* claimed to be 'a radical look at education today and a strategy for the future'. The NCE's vision of the future is grounded in a view of the changing nature of the economy and the organization and technology of work, where the development of new knowledge and skills becomes 'central to economic success and personal and social well being' (NCE 1993: 43). As the NCE (1993: 33) puts it: 'In an era of world-wide competition and low-cost global communication, no country like ours will be able to maintain its standard of living, let alone improve it, on the basis of cheap labour and low-tech products and services'. What is true of England and Wales is also true of many other established and aspiring modern economies. All countries need to recognize that, since the essential ingredient in economic success is knowledge and applied intelligence, education and training systems will have to focus on the production of 'knowledge' workers, those who have the appropriate high-technology skills for wealth creation in the 'information society'.

The NCE's vision also recognizes the threat to social cohesion of the possible widening gap between those who achieve success as 'knowledge' workers and those who are excluded because they have been denied the appropriate education. For the sake of social stability as well as for economic reasons, therefore, it will be important to make sure that an education and training system is developed which is suited to the capabilities of all members of society rather than just those of an academic elite. Moreover, the system will have to be improved for all regardless of age because, as the NCE (1993: 38) puts it:

> In an era in which change takes place so quickly continuous learning is an essential at work. The need is obvious enough for professionals . . . It is no less true of other workers as new technology, innovation and changed work patterns are introduced. Constant adaptation to change is the order of the day and will remain so in the future.

Although economic goals underpin prosperity and thus our ability to improve the quality of life for everybody, the NCE accepts that material

rewards are not the only goals of education. It will also be important to promote the spiritual, moral, cultural, mental and physical development of
pupils in schools and young people generally and to foster an active commitment to and understanding of democratic society and the rights and
duties of citizen.

The problem with this approach (which is similar to that of the current
Labour government in the UK) is that it is derived from a view about the
nature of work in our society and the role of further and higher education
which is too one-sided. It is based on a technocratic model which assumes
that economic prosperity is produced and sustained by the development of
'skills' in the population and, in particular, the skills of an increasing number
of high-technology, flexible workers who are committed to lifelong learning.
But this fails to recognize the realities of the relationship between edu-
cation/training and the economy, and the persistence of gross structural
inequalities. Whilst there has been some upskilling, one of the paradoxes of
investment in a high-technology economy is that it often creates very few
high-quality jobs and in many countries goes hand in hand with an increase
in structural unemployment. As Coffield (1997) points out, in the UK and
USA, for example, policies and programmes which focus on developments
in the quality and quantity of skills in the workforce to create a thriving
economy overlook the fact that there is in both these countries a low
demand for high-quality skills. He draws attention to the creation of new
occupational groups differentiated by types of qualification and new combi-
nations of skills which gives rise to the new class system referred to above.

The continuing influence of class-based strategies, and thus of an education and training system where democratic citizenship goals play second
fiddle to economic goals, is reflected in a new divided curriculum where
students selected for vocational programmes are provided with an impoverished curriculum, which the skills-oriented rhetoric of organizations such as
the NCE only serves to reinforce. The skills-based curriculum in fact does as
much to disempower as empower the student (see Chapter 9). There is a tendency to regard skills as abstracted from practices and as accomplishments
of individual students or workers, whose learning is assessed in terms of their
performance in relevant skills and the capacity for learning new skills. The
idea of the flexible learner with a 'toolkit' of skills has a certain appeal but it
underplays the extent to which learning is an interactive process. The skills-
based curriculum is a nonsense because it puts the cart before the horse.
Skills have to be situated in the purposive context of learning communities
of practice and cannot be selected prior to a clarification of this context, since
there would otherwise be no way of ascertaining which skills should be
taught out of the many hundreds that could be taught. Even so-called generic
skills are taught with a finite range of practices in mind, though these may
not be made explicit at the time of teaching. Moreover, conceiving learners
as nothing but 'bundles' of skills – whether these are defined narrowly (for

example, information technology skills) or more broadly (for example, personal effectiveness or thinking skills) – is based on a highly reductive and technicist notion of the individual, which is out of kilter with the aim to produce critical, morally engaged, independent-minded, self-reflexive agents who actively participate in society as workers and citizens.

An alternative curriculum

An alternative to the traditional academic and the vocationalized curricula described above would involve the consolidation, development and integration of their respective strengths. Thus the idea of learning as involving critical participation in communities of practice would be retained but this would entail an induction into 'open' rather than 'closed' systems of knowledge, practices which were not influenced or 'corrupted' by power or status, and practices which were relevant. The 'know-how' approach of the vocationalized curriculum would be acceptable, provided it was recognized that individual skills and abilities could only be realized through participation in these communities of practice.

Which practices will be selected as the main foci for curriculum development will depend on a variety of factors – the concerns and priorities of society at a particular point in time; the immediate concerns of the local community; the social and cultural preoccupations of the particular students being taught. The relevance and meaning of any specific practice will, of course, vary from one person, one group, one culture to another. However, in the present circumstances and in the light of the above analysis, it seems hopeful to argue for the attainability of a consensus on a curriculum which revolves around the themes identified above – self identity and reflexivity, collaboration in organizational contexts, family life, cultural pluralism, work/economic life and science in a risk society.

The traditional subjects of the academic curriculum (such as maths and geography) would not necessarily be dropped, but their content would be reviewed with respect to their relevance in relation to these themes. Those which were not considered essential for the common core might be included as options in the full curriculum, depending on the specific needs of individuals and localities. The likely outcome, however, would be a complete reconstitution of the organizing categories of the curriculum, which would in any case be broadly interpreted to include the informal and formal features of the institutions in which learning took place. Whether a topic relating to a theme was taught formally or informally or both would depend on the circumstances. In schools, for example, at certain ages it might be thought more appropriate that understandings about 'collaboration' were taught by example than by formal teaching, although ultimately such understandings would need to be made explicit if they were to be reflected upon.

The following chapters will each focus on a specific curriculum theme, although some overlap will be unavoidable. It will be assumed that the themes themselves would be regarded as relevant by most people, but that the teaching approaches to each would be contested. The challenge of each chapter is to demonstrate how we might need to think about each theme for pedagogical purposes if the educational goals of a democratic learning society are to be realized. Participation in the curriculum should be fostered in all parts of society: in learning which takes place in schools, colleges, universities, homes, offices or factories; in relation to paid or unpaid work; and in the activities of people of all ages – children, young people and adults. However, most of the actual discussion will be school-focused, the assumption being that school, despite the importance of post-school and out-of-school learning, is still a crucial phase for the development of citizens who will be taking up the challenges of 'new times'. But the dominant themes of the new common curriculum – education for self-reflexivity, for family relationships and so on – will be treated as central to the idea of a 'curriculum for life', not as 'subjects' that are dropped as soon as the school phase has ended. Schooling will have failed if students do not continue to develop their knowledge and understanding in these areas after they have left school.

In most chapters, links will be made to topical interests (for example, the so-called gender gap in achievement in Chapter 7) so that, although the aim is to construct an alternative curriculum, the discussion in each chapter should connect with an existing concern. The themes of self-identity and reflexivity, collaboration and cultural pluralism will have two chapters devoted to each. In Chapter 2 the first theme will be addressed via an analysis of issues in teaching about autobiography and self-narrative, whilst in Chapter 3 the focus shifts to a particular aspect self-identity – the self as a 'good' learner. In Chapter 4 collaboration will be examined in the context of teacher and school culture, whilst in Chapter 5 this theme is taken up in a discussion of collaborative group work and pupil culture. The educational implications of cultural difference and diversity will be discussed in Chapter 6 with particular reference to anti-racist teaching strategies, and in Chapter 7 the politics of gender and school achievement will be explored. Chapter 8 will focus on the family and the ideas and assumptions which should underpin the curriculum for family life, and Chapters 9 and 10 will do the same for work/economic life and for science and the risk society, respectively. In Chapter 11 the book concludes with some tentative proposals for school reform.

2 | Education for self-identity

Introduction

> ... the crisis of modern identity becomes manifest. On the one hand, modern identity is open-ended, transitory, liable to ongoing change. On the other hand, a subjective realm of identity is the individual's main foothold in reality. ... Consequently it should not be a surprise that modern man is afflicted with a *permanent identity crisis*, a condition conducive to considerable nervousness.
>
> (Berger *et al.* 1973: 74)

These words are taken from a celebrated book called the *The Homeless Mind*. They describe a dilemma of the human condition with which many people today are only too familiar. Making sense of ourselves and the world we live in is a constant imperative, not something we can shrug off once we have reached some mature state of adulthood having left behind an angst-ridden period of storm and stress called adolescence. Feelings of 'homeless-ness', of belonging nowhere, of having no identity are a possibility at any stage of life in 'new times'.

The curriculum for self-identity addresses the question of how people should be educated who are going to have to create their own 'meaning of life' and their own meaning of their own life. This curriculum should facilitate a particular kind of critical reflection, namely that involving reflection on the self as a biographical project. In the circumstances of reflexive modernity, where the individual is confronted with so much change and uncertainty and such a diversity of possible 'ways to live', self-reflection becomes a prevailing mode of thought. The questions arising require a perspective on self-understanding which treats the self as something to be 'worked on' like a project. It involves biography because the process is one of constructing a narrative which makes sense of the many experiences and actions attributable to the self.

My self-identity will be of concern to me. If I can live with the stories I create about myself, I may feel life is worthwhile and 'good'. But clearly there is also the likelihood of 'in between' periods or 'crises' when I am likely to feel insecure and anxious. I may learn to love myself but I may also learn self-hatred. Thus, there is always a moral dimension woven into the process of constructing a self-narrative. It is an expression of what Charles Taylor describes as the 'second axis' of our lives as moral beings, and one that is particularly significant in the age we live in. The first axis involves the familiar constellation of beliefs around the notion of 'respect for others' and the third beliefs about the dignity of the individual, whilst the second is to do questions about 'how am I going to live my life?' which touches on the question 'what kind of life is worth living? . . . what kind of life would fulfil the promise implicit in my particular talents . . . what would constitute a rich and meaningful life?' (Taylor 1989: 14).

For many teachers and learners this focus for education in the contemporary world will be consonant with their own understandings. They may not use terms like 'biographical project' or 'reflexivity', but much of what they typically say about the aims of education amounts to the same thing. Most teachers in educational institutions will be familiar with the notion of 'careers education'; they will know that it involves encouraging pupils and students to think about themselves, their strengths and weaknesses, likes and dislikes, and to make choices informed by this self-knowledge, coupled with knowledge of the opportunities available. The self-identity curriculum involves an elaborated version of this. It interprets career widely to include not only career as paid worker but also as unpaid worker, as citizen, as male or female, as consumer, as learner, as friend, as child in the family as well as pupil in school and so on, but above all a career is viewed in its 'totality' as it pertains to the self-identity work and the life goals of particular individuals.

The self-identity curriculum

The peculiarities of the self in 'new times' have to be taken into account in the construction of a curriculum which will enable the achievement of autonomy and 'personhood'. In general, the task is similar to the one identified by Pring (1987: 18). The challenge for educationalists of the greater focus on the person is to articulate and foreground

> the qualities that enable young people to act responsibly, autonomously and with respect for other persons in a world where new and unpredictable problems are arising, where the past is not in many cases an adequate precedent for future cases and where different perceptions of the problems and their solutions will need to be tolerated and respected.

But in the current period there would need to be a particular emphasis on the young person's emerging capacity to reflect on the totality of their qualities and commitments and make judgements derived from reflexively interpreted accounts of what kind of person they were, who they wanted to be and what kind of life they wanted to live.

The self-identity curriculum would be a practice in MacIntyre's sense (see Chapter 1) but would involve reflection upon the practices in which one was immersed with a view to developing awareness of values or qualities and their coherence or lack of it in constructed narratives of the self. It might therefore be better described as a metapractice, one which involved a linguistic differentiation of the 'I' and the 'me' enabling a 'way of thinking' about identity as self-identity, and which included the imperative to understand oneself as a 'whole person' and as a continuity across practices and across space and time. It would promote a certain disengagement from commitment to a practice and enable us to review this commitment with a view to ascertaining its place in the kind of life which we perceived as the 'good life' for us. The discourse of the self-identity curriculum would therefore involve an ethical language which identified the qualities or virtues across a range of practices as characteristics of the person, one might say the character of the person. Thus self-identity would be signified in terms of moral qualities such as compassion, constancy, courage, honesty and generosity as well as intellectual virtues such as creativity, imagination and capacity for cogent argument. Crucially, however, what would be fostered in the self-identity curriculum is the capacity for critical reflexivity – the capacity to reflect about priorities amongst values; about the nature and application of moral qualities in one's own life; about how to improve one's own life; about one's situation and the constraints on one's self-development that existed 'externally' in the environment (for example, the bureaucratic imperatives of school life) or 'internally' within the self (for example, inhibition or lack of self-confidence).

Interpreting pupils' self-portraits

In helping pupils with their self projects, autobiographical writing has an important role to play. Writing an autobiography is a process which involves working to produce a coherent narrative of the self rather than having the aim of faithfully recording what the 'real' nature of the self is. It is itself part of an ongoing process of self-formation, serving as a vehicle for articulating, reflecting upon and analysing the various threads of experience which we associate with ourselves. It would, of course, be written from some vantage point within the existing structure of the self and its experience and understanding of the world, but this reference point would not be fully articulated in advance and the purpose of the writing would be to clarify it. The whole process would be negotiated within the social context of its production; that is as, say, a school-based endeavour, it would be mediated through the ongoing structuring of identity in schools.

In exploring these matters further, it will be helpful to take a look at some of the typical ways pupils' self-portraits have been interpreted in this context. When asked to write about themselves, what do pupils write about and how is it interpreted by teachers? Wilkinson (1986) provides evidence that when given the title 'Myself' young writers give three kinds of information: first, the formal sort that might be required on an official form, such as name, age, address, members of the family; second, information about actions, such as going to school; and third, information about dispositions, such as temperament, character and personality. Amongst young children lists of likes and dislikes are such a typical feature of their writing about the self that they can almost be regarded as a separate category.

When it comes to interpretation, Wilkinson deploys a *developmental model*, a key aspect of which is the identification of an emerging 'objectivity' about the self, so that by the age of 10 or so pupils are likely to show an awareness that others might have an opinion about the writer which the writer might not agree with. The writing contains more comments that are self-critical and is generally less egocentric. Pupils are more willing to suggest bad as well as good points about themselves. Wilkinson gives the following examples:

> I am Alan Bader and aged 11. A bad point about me is I don't fit into the person my family would like me to be, my parents would like me to be a president or prime-minister but I would like to make a living as something dangerous or adventeres like a stuntman or actor. Another bad point is I lie to get out of situations I don't like. A good point about me is I am very careful about what I say & what I do and I always chose my own desitions
>
> (Wilkinson 1986: 50)

An older boy aged 17 writes:

> I believe I have my bad points like stubbornness and on some occasions a short temper. But I also have my good points. I have a sense of humour and an opinion on life which is farly elastic, and I also believe in other people. Some people of my age believe the world rotates round them.
>
> (Wilkinson 1986: 51)

Another related aspect of the developmental model revolves around the psychoanalytic notions of 'defending' and 'coping'. To put it simply, defending means avoiding the problem, whereas coping means coming to terms with it. In less mature forms of writing, writers shows no awareness of the distinction between these two modes of functioning. They do not attempt to distance themselves from the situation they are describing and tend to identify in an uncritical way with the definition of the problem as seen by themselves as the main protagonist in the account. More mature writers are aware of the distinction and are able to identify the various defence mechanisms deployed by themselves and others.

It is a common criticism of such theories of development that if they are followed too closely they can be more restricting than enabling, generating pseudo-insights which bend the 'facts' and the experience to fit the model. They should be looked upon as resources which, in so far as they are consonant with educational values, have a part to play in the development of pupils towards the kind of maturity which the self requires in order to realize its projects in a democratic society. 'Coping mechanism' is a shorthand way of describing what is a more desirable mode – the autonomous self needs to be capable of distancing itself from emotions generated in certain conflict situations. In defending rather than coping, learners have no conscious knowledge of their feelings or desires and therefore do not resolve conflicts but merely 'dam them up' by using one or more defence mechanisms – for instance, by projecting the conflict on to someone else or denying its existence altogether. The strength of this idea is that it introduces us to the notion that desires might be hidden and not readily available to consciousness. We do not necessarily have to go along with the rest of psychoanalytic theory (for example, that desires are always of a particular kind and related to unresolved conflicts in early childhood) to see the possibilities this opens up for developing insights into the self and how it operates. Desires might be so submerged in the psyche that they are rarely available to consciousness; on the other hand, they might just be conveniently forgotten or deliberately hidden.

Education for self-identity would require pupils to become more conscious of their desires, how desires may conflict and how some are prioritized and realized (or not, as the case may be) in their day-to-day living. Self-understanding, however, in relation to desires is not an all-or-none thing. The sum total of an individual's experience is ever changing and can never be grasped in its totality at a conscious level. Desires change and so do the relationships between them. In any particular situation one is not always aware of all one's desires, and part of what it means to know oneself is knowing this. Developing reflective knowledge of the self mainly involves coming to understand one aspect of the 'whole' self a little better. As John White (1990: 90) puts it:

> As one proceeds through life, occasions for particular self knowledge multiply. One reflects on this desire, now on that. A person who 'really knows himself' is someone who has had many experiences of this kind, has clarified different desires and their relationships on innumerable occasions. But he may well not be able to give you a description of his value hierarchy in general.

But educators are concerned with evaluation as well as clarification of desires. Charles Taylor (1985) distinguishes between two forms of self-evaluation – one 'weak' and one 'strong'. In the first sense, evaluation involves weighing two desires to determine which is more convenient or how to get the most satisfaction overall. A person may have a liking for both net-ball and squash. She appreciates the finer points of each and enjoys playing both equally. Ideally she would like to pursue both sports and she tries to arrange her life in a way that enables her to do this, but sometimes she has to choose to play one or the other. There are things to weigh up here – whether either match can be rearranged and whether she has the power to do this, for example – but what is not in question is the 'worthiness' of each activity as far as she is concerned. That she desires to play both is acknow-ledged; and that it is 'good' to do both is also accepted. In 'strong' evalu-ation, however, the desire is acknowledged but is not assumed to be 'good'. Indeed, on reflection, as Taylor (1985: 18) puts it, some desires 'can be judged as bad, base, ignoble, trivial, superficial, unworthy and so on'. All this may seem obvious, but it is crucial to understanding what it means to reflect on the self evaluatively.

For Taylor two different kinds of self are involved here. The first is a weak evaluator. Such an evaluator is reflective and does not just follow her desires willy-nilly. She does evaluate to a degree. She chooses between preferences using utilitarian criteria, but a crucial aspect of personhood is missing, namely that which we often describe using the metaphor of 'depth' expressed in the kind of language used when considering alternatives . When describing what is 'good' about two different desires, she often resorts to the inarticulate notion of 'feel' – this course of action 'feels' better than that. The strong evaluator uses an altogether richer vocabulary of qualitative contrast – for example, some course of action is courageous, another is cowardly. Some actions are experienced as more uplifting and meaningful than others.

The deconstructionist critique of autobiography

In teaching for self-evaluation, however, it will be important not to lose sight of the idea that the self is a socially constituted entity and that the language used to tell stories about the self is socially and culturally embedded. This does not mean self-reflection is a meaningless or impossible activity, but it does mean that the words deployed in self-analysis have to be recognized for what they are – context-bound vocabularies which are part of a wider dis-course of meaning inhabited by the individual. To explicate this further, let us take a look at a critical perspective which starts from the same point.

Nick Peim (1993), in his account of how critical theory might be applied to the teaching of English, contrasts the idea of writing as creativity and 'the idea of writing as produced meaning according to its ready established structures of form and meaning' (1993: 124). In contrast to conventional wisdom about how writing is produced, deconstructionism asserts that what

> it is possible to write is largely determined by the predominant forms of writing, by predominant images and ideas. The writing subject can only reconfigure these already existing identities ... Words used by the writer, the meanings, the ideas, the values they convey are not determined by the writing subject – just as the way they are put together is not and cannot be.
>
> (Peim 1993: 124)

Thus, the individual subject as creative agent is something of a fiction since much more is determined than the uncritical English teacher imagines. The same applies to the individual's response to literature. The model that most English teachers have is of the pupil as an autonomous 'subject', who has personal opinions which should be valued since they reflect a unique interpretation.

But this is an illusion because we all know that in practice there are many constraints operating and, either directly or indirectly, it will be communicated to pupils that there are set procedures for reading and responding. Once they have learned these, pupils' responses might almost be said to have been programmed in advance. This applies to autobiographical writing or any other form of writing as much as it does to reading. Peim argues that the very idea of autobiography in conventional terms is grounded in the traditions of liberal progressive English which regards writing as individual self-expression and draws together notions about the self, about identity and about writing under a similar ideological framework. Yet the issues raised by this form of writing have rarely been fully explored. For instance, in what sense is an autobiography 'auto' when the form and structure of it have already been determined? As Peim (1993: 144) points out: 'From background, through early memories, to hopes and fears for the future – this progress is presented simply as *the* shape of a life's experiences, rather than the shape of a particular form of writing.' What is not usually discussed is the problematic nature of the relationship between the writing and the life. The autobiography is structured by a particular discourse of identity-as-narrative which structures the form and a great deal of the content.

One can see what Peim is getting at here, but I think there are two issues which need to addressed. First of all, autobiography as narrative may be a restricted definition but in practical terms in asking pupils to write their life stories there is much that can be made problematical without spending time on the deconstruction of the narrative form *per se*. The very idea of narrative seems to me to be consonant with the aim of fostering personal autonomy, since it implies an attempt to give some meaning and coherence to a life experienced in time and space across a range of contexts. There is no implication, however, that the narrative of a life is the 'truth' about that life or that it is more than a partial and selective view influenced by the current interests and self-perceptions of a 'situated' writer. It can quite easily be demonstrated to pupils that what they wrote on one occasion is likely to differ from what they wrote on another because they themselves have changed; that autobiography is a reflection of the self they have constructed or are in the process of constructing, and indeed is an important part of that process; that autobiography is in a sense expressed in all the writing, and indeed speaking and reading, that they do; and that there are other ways of looking at the self, other stories to be told.

Second, despite Peim's insistence that the 'writing subject' is largely determined by the discourses in which he or she is located, he still seems to give some 'life' to the subject as a socially constituted agent. There is a problematic here which Peim does not himself explore. According to his 'alternative account', the problem with liberal English is that it does not treat writing as 'discursively prestructured'. The possibility of individual expression is never really questioned, but it is in fact a 'tenuous' notion – the individual only becomes an 'I' in the writing. Yet if this is so, what are we to make of his statement about the form of autobiography – that it is a narrative form which acts as 'a kind of strait-jacket preventing certain important aspects and ideas of the self from being expressed, and that the general cultural form of autobiography positions and defines the self in a limiting kind of way – in relation to important cultural notions of identity and personal history' (Peim 1993: 139)? Clearly, there is an imposition involved here, but why should it be any more limiting – or enabling, for that matter – than any other discourse of autobiography? What aspects and ideas about the self may emerge? In what sense might these be seen as 'important'? If they are not restricting because they are not a 'strait-jacket', in what sense might they be 'releasing' or 'liberating'?

Peim's challenge to the discourse of English is certainly far reaching, but in my view is still well within the parameters of the liberal discourse. What he seems to be arguing for is a more open conception of the self rather than the abolition and erasure of the idea of the self altogether. The self is a unique entity even if it is constituted by socially given identities grounded in discursive practices. The idea of emancipation or liberation – the classic concern of liberalism – lurks behind Peim's formulation of the argument about narrative and identity. In any case, the whole social and cultural milieu which encourages students to question existing forms and propose alternatives is itself nested within a discourse, or perhaps a kind of metadiscourse, where such questioning is valued. Critical awareness and independence of thought are intrinsic to the liberal discourse. They certainly need to be interpreted afresh in the light of what we know about how the self is constructed, but are not to be abandoned altogether.

The values associated with liberalism as a moral discourse are evident in

Peim's suggestions on teaching about autobiography. Thus students are asked to respond to statements gleaned from interview reports; statements such as 'she doesn't think she has been loved or in love', 'someone she loves dying would hurt her more than dying herself', 'she takes great pains to be liked and to be genuine'(Peim 1993: 148–9). But Peim writes about these things as if they could be tackled without reference to the moral framework in which he and liberal progressive teachers are both located. Thus the statements are to be dealt with by looking at whether or not the truth or reality of each statement is decidable, what grammatical structure is used and what context and discourse of personality are at work. The crucial omission here is awareness of the process of deliberative judgement – everything is decidable although not with certainty; some decisions are better than others, some discourses of personality are more 'liberating' than others. The discourse of liberalism includes an imperative about the use of power – it has to be used in the interests of all – and thus liberal-minded 'subjects' who hold linguistic power will seek to construct the discourse in non-hierarchical ways.

The significance of narrative

In the light of the deconstructionist critique, however, we certainly need to clarify our understanding of all human life as 'enacted narratives' (MacIntyre 1981: 211). The idea of narrative is not so determining that autobiography or biography always has to have a particular form and content. It does not have to treat early childhood as particularly significant or to assume that there are no contradictions or tensions between different conceptions of the self in the same person or that the story of a life can be told unproblematically as a linear sequence. At times, particularly in a complex modern society where the self is so 'open' and life so full of uncertainty and ambiguity, it may seem that the quest for a 'good' and coherent self-identity is doomed to failure. Nevertheless, time and time again – whether we are trying to understand our own lives or those of others, in whatever situation, whether we are watching a film on television, reading a newspaper or gossiping or working with others, whether the action is thought to be factual or fictional – we resort to narrative in order to explain why things happened as they did and why people took certain actions and thought certain things and not others. When considering any piece of human action, we all have this tendency to place it in the context of narrative histories both of the individuals involved and the social and historical context in which they were operating. A story is not just something which is told after the event, however; we live out our lives in narrative and understand our own lives in terms of the narratives that we live out. An account of self-identity can thus only be given against the background of a story or stories – narratives which inevitably give some kind of unity to the character of the self, otherwise they would have no sense. This narrative concept of selfhood requires that I am a *'subject* of a history which is my own' (MacIntyre 1981: 217) which makes my life intelligible to me and enables me to provide an account of my actions and experiences which makes sense to others.

In general, people are not often called upon to give such accounts in an in-depth way. The question 'Can you explain why you did this?' may be the start of intensive self-examination but is more often than not a minor request for information which enables social action to proceed. Most people spend most of their time 'living out' self-narratives rather reflecting upon them. Never-theless, in the contemporary world, learners need to be encouraged to be more reflective in a general way about their intentions and self-understandings; to be more thoughtful about the immediate whys and wherefores and possible consequences of their actions and, where appropriate, to make such thoughts public, as one would do in a written autobiography. In school contexts, this focus would give rise to a new sensitivity in teacher–pupil relationships. Pupils would come to realize that their personal thoughts about themselves were of interest to the teacher and relevant to the educational process. What should emerge is a *shared understanding* that self-narratives were important refer-ence points for educational action, even if they were not always fully articu-lated. Once teachers and pupils were 'in the know', so to speak, about this, then it would inevitably colour their ongoing relationships. From now on, pupils would be much more aware that their actions would be observed and understood as part of a wider pattern of meaning; and teachers would know that pupils would know this and that their day-to-day reactions to classroom and school events would be interpreted accordingly.

Some objections

Teachers should help learners become more reflexive and see the value of accounting for action in relation to a biographical interpretation of the self, but they also need to be aware of some of the dangers of this approach.

Reflection leading to detachment

First, it might be argued that the self-identity curriculum could easily become part of the problem rather than part of the solution. Stressing the importance of self-reflectiveness could lead to an over-preoccupation with the critical evaluation of all commitments, with students feeling under an obligation to subject all their burgeoning interests to intense scrutiny. Reflec-tiveness itself becomes the overriding priority, so that students are given insufficient space to deepen their involvement in practices and to develop the qualities thus exercised. Unless students are allowed to become immersed in and committed to practices they will have nothing much to reflect on. The self is never given an opportunity to 'lose itself' in its commitments and therefore can never really 'find itself'. The narrative of the self may retain its coherence, but is increasingly impoverished and 'empty' of meaning. Even the activity of reflection itself becomes pointless, since that too involves commitment to a certain kind of practice. What is left is a self that reflects in a kind of criterionless vacuum where one idea is as good as another and where no social commitments are considered of great import for a person's identity. To be at the mercy of whim and fancy as one inevitably is in this socially detached or alienated state is scarcely to be free or autonomous. The self is thus, in Sandel's (1984) terms, 'left to lurch' between detachment and engagement and it is this 'deprivation of self possession and control . . . we associate with the loss of autonomy' (Callan 1994: 38).

The answer to this is not to discourage self-reflection but to make sure that it is not done at the expense of fostering commitment. If alienation and self-impoverishment are not to be the outcome of school activities – as they so frequently are – it is important that curriculum practices are selected which are genuinely involving and meaningful to both staff and pupils, and which build upon pupils' existing qualities and experiences. What needs to be understood is that the quality of individual and social existence depends upon quality of commitment. If commitment is the aim, then it would be preferable to go for cognitive and emotional 'depth' rather than 'breadth', so that pupils could come to a fuller understanding of what it meant to be seriously committed. The self is thus defined not only by its specific commitments but also by the realization of its capacity for commitment as such.

Of course, not all educational activities which foster self-reflection need necessarily involve the intensive kind of self-examination that working on an autobiography entails. Learners can approach the self via consideration of the lived experience of others. As Raphael Samuel (1995) has noted, although the current concern in the study of history with deconstruction and demystification involves a de-emphasis on the contribution of individual agents, 'personification' itself is not necessarily incompatible with this approach. The life of the cultural hero or villain is open to a variety of interpretations. The democratic heroes and heroines of reflexive modernity would recognize themselves as socially constructed and as open to interpretation and reinterpretation. They would exemplify the dilemmas of living in 'new times' and could be found in all walks of life, in all cultural milieux and in the past and present. The authors of novels also construct a social world. The pupil is provided with a highly contextualized and richly textured example of personal qualities at work in a particular narrative context which adds to the repertoire of vantage points from which to view the self. Also, there are many types of writing which are autobiographical without being explicitly labelled as such. In fact, as Porter and Smith (1989) acknowledge, a great deal of writing in school involves writing autobiographically as opposed to writing an autobiography.

Reifying the self

The second objection is that encouraging reflection on something called a self will lead to the wrong kind of objectification of self. Young people in particular, it is alleged, have enough on their plate already without being saddled with what must inevitably be something of a 'heavy', over-personalized philosophical debate about the nature of self. Is it not really too early for them to be doing this? In attempting to cope with the resulting confusion and uncertainty generated by such reflection (on top of all the other confusions they experience) they may opt for the easy way out and accept a version of self which is conventional and manageable. In so doing they are likely to accept an 'off-the-shelf', common-sense view of the self as a fixed entity defined in terms of a number of psychological traits. This is at the opposite end of the spectrum to the alienated, over-reflective self, but it is just as antagonistic to the ideal of autonomy. It is reflective but only in a limited way; a reflective but reified self.

The commitments of this self are regarded as unalterable because they seem to stem from determining factors outside the consciousness and the control of the individual concerned. Such factors may be regarded as 'God-given' or more typically as rooted in the 'facts' of nature revealed by 'reason' and 'science', but, whatever its source, this reified view of the self leads to judgements being made about the self within strict parameters. A person may think they are being open and unconstrained in making choices or deciding upon a course of action but in fact they have not recognized that their intentions and purposes spring from fixed views of their own nature or self-in-the-world. They may even claim to hold a view of the self which is discursive and contingent, but this actually only applies to that part of the self where commitments and attachments are considered to be revisable. In short, although reflectiveness is a feature of the self, it is a reflectiveness which is contained within unacknowledged boundaries. It is not a reflective self through and through. It is a view of the psychology of self which fails to understand what Grumet (1981) describes as the depth of society's penetration of the individual psyche – the 'thorough infiltration' of this psychology with 'those assumptions of the society to which it is supposedly a dialectical alternative'(Grumet 1981: 120).

Since education requires a more open concept of the self, I would argue that trait models and other reified models of the self are antagonistic to educational values. They are a source of concern because often the contingent nature of such models is unacknowledged and the reflecting self appears open to more possibilities than it actually is. As with the first objection, the answer really is to achieve an appropriate balance between two desirable activities. Young people need to experience what it means to become committed and they need to become involved in practices in a way which is not superficial. Yet this is never just about induction into a set of traditions the value of which, in terms of their own development, a young person is not allowed to question until they have become fully inducted. There will always be at every stage of the induction process some scope for encouraging critical reflection on practices and the self and for fostering a sense of agency even in the early years of schooling. What form this takes and how much of it is appropriate will, of course, depend on the particular students concerned, but it should not be thought there is any definitive adolescent or child development research on the matter. By the time they reach secondary school age, one would suggest that students are quite capable of responding to requests for accounts of their actions and linking these to an emerging sense of self. Whether they want to do this or are capable of doing it well is another matter. The purpose of the self-identity curriculum would be to help them to develop their capacities in this area.

Narcissism

A third objection relates to the possibility that a focus on the self could re-inforce the narcissistic tendencies which are a growing feature of the consumer culture we inhabit. Narcissism is characterized in various ways in the psychiatric literature, but in general terms it refers to an exaggerated self-regard which usually precludes an interest in and understanding of the needs of others. As Porter and Smith (1989: 32) put it, the person becomes 'fixated . . . upon the gratifying appearance of things, an idealized picture of the self'. In their search for gratification and fulfilment they have a constant need for the approval of others in the context of intimate relationships, but their obsession with self prevents genuine and lasting engagement with others. They remain unfulfilled and oscillate between despair and exaggerated feelings of self-worth, whilst remaining over-dependent on others whose praise they need like a drug.

We know that narcissism is particularly associated with regard for physical appearance, and it is in this area that young people are especially at risk because of the salience of the biological changes of puberty in interpretations of the self. Thus one could argue that the self-identity curriculum could easily make too much of the often temporary narcissistic tendencies of this body-oriented phase of development. But I would argue that with regard to the dilemmas of 'new times', the body cannot be ignored since it is such an important 'site' in the business of constructing and maintaining a coherent sense of self. Certain aspects of the body are particularly relevant to self-identity – appearance, demeanour and sensuality, for example. Body care and body 'regimes' and projects thus need to be considered and integrated with life plans and lifestyles.

Narcissism is often equated with self-love, but the two need to be distinguished. If we excluded the idea of self-love simply because it was too closely associated with pathologies like narcissism, we would fail to come to terms with what Fromm (1971) perceived as one of the paradoxes of modern society – on the one hand there is a taboo on selfishness, as exemplified in much Christian theology, whilst on the other 'egotism' is considered praiseworthy and the basis of the welfare of all in a competitive society. This contradiction is resolved, however, if whilst condemning 'egotism' we allow for the possibility of self-love. For Fromm (1971: 130) self-love is not to be equated with selfishness:

> my own self, in principle, must be as much an object of my love as another person. The affirmation of one's own life, happiness, growth, freedom is rooted in one's capacity to love . . . If an individual is able to love productively, he loves himself too; if he can only love others, he cannot love at all.

The privacy issue: is trust enough?

A fourth objection relates to the constraints on securing trust relations in modernist institutions like schools. In their study of secondary pupils' writing, Barnes and Barnes (1984) found that personal writing made up 21–45 per cent of topics addressed by pupils in English classes. Pupils were asked 'what writing they liked or disliked' and this was followed up by asking them what they thought 'of writing about themselves, their families and their own experiences'. Most pupils said they preferred writing stories, but the authors were surprised at the large numbers whose attitudes to personal writing were predominantly negative. The authors explored several possibilities, but clearly the privacy issue was significant. Some things were perceived as just too personal and private to write about. Obviously the context was not perceived by them to be appropriate for this kind of self-disclosure. An important aspect of this was undoubtedly the quality of their relationships with the teachers – whether they trusted them sufficiently and felt them to be humane, sympathetic and genuinely interested in them as individuals.

The following quotation from Bishop (1996: 433) neatly summarizes what she describes as the 'there is no trust' argument which seems to get to the heart of the problem here:

> Given the imperfect conditions within most classrooms, the student who discloses personal information in the classroom runs the very real risk of censure, paternalism and the possibility of the unethical abuse of information. . . . In our imperfect world, the liberty and autonomy of the student is threatened by being compulsorily appraised, evaluated and rated. The larger the scope for teacher appraisal, the larger the scope for ill-judged paternalism, for the abuse of personal information, for errors of judgement and the operation of favouritism and bias that may blight a student's prospects.

But although we have to take account of the realities of institutional life, this does not mean we have to abandon our attempts to reform curricula in the ways suggested. In fact, stressing the importance of self-identity and focusing on autobiographical work are part of a strategy for changing institutions. Doing so is unlikely to produce changes overnight but the need for change along these lines will be increasingly recognized, rooted as it is in an understanding of how most people have to live today. Some institutions are more likely than others to take the new ideas on board. Some teachers and learners are more likely than others to resist such ideas. It could well be that introducing a class of 13-year-olds on a Monday morning to autobiographical writing is not the best tactic(!), but there are many other teaching approaches. The hope is that, whatever the structural constraints, there will always be some space in institutions for experimenting with teaching and learning strategies which have the development of self-identity as a major focus.

However, there is another argument against teaching for self-disclosure in the classroom which is made forcefully by Bishop. Even in ideal conditions of trust, she argues, there are still 'threats' to the self-discloser 'albeit of a rather different and more subtle kind' (1996: 435). However sensitive, supportive and sympathetic the teaching, it will always lack one vital dimension, namely 'existential rapport' which involves, as she puts it, 'a sensitivity to, and understanding of, the special personal significance of the objects, values and experiences that these "cared for" selves "care about"' (1996: 435), which can only come from being on the 'inside' of the experience. Thus self-disclosers value the kind of rapport which they receive in support groups – such as Alcoholics Anonymous – where they are disclosing to people who have had the same kinds of experiences as themselves. Such rapport is unlikely to be found in the classroom because there is usually too great a diversity of interests, backgrounds and temperaments. The lack of genuine understanding is a recipe for 'aborted communication', too much of which can be harmful for the discloser because of the self-alienation to which it can so easily give rise.

Clearly, one has to react sensitively when matters are being voiced which are obviously of great personal significance to the speaker. There is a big difference between responses which convey openness and a desire to understand, and ones which reflect a closed mind, unaware of the extent of its own ignorance. Sympathetic enquiry may not involve existential rapport of the kind referred to by Bishop, but it need not necessarily result in aborted communication. A supportive environment is supportive precisely because it provides a setting where people feel that others will take a genuine interest in their experiences, not because they think that others will already know about their experiences. Existential rapport also has its dangers. It can lead to a ghetto mentality, where the desire and ability to communicate with a wide range of people are restricted because of over-involvement with those of like mind.

Concluding comment

And so what can one say about the purpose of the self-identity curriculum in the light of the above? First, it is evident that if we are concerned with personal autonomy we have to focus on the committed as well as the reflective aspects of the self. In so doing, what it means to be committed needs to be fully understood; we are not referring to identities which can be worn like suits of clothes, and which are as readily discardable, but features of the self grounded in the moral and emotional attachments which constitute the character of the person. Second, the *way* commitments are held is important. All commitments are revocable even if they are perceived as constituting the fundamental aspects of the self. A values-led view of a non-reified self-in-the-world (see Coles 1985; Quicke 1988b) involves commitment but also a certain capacity for scepticism, a willingness to tolerate ambiguity and a lack of dogmatic certainty. Third, fostering the reflexive self involves the idea of 'improvement'. We would want to encourage students to evaluate and prioritize their commitments in terms of some conception of a 'good life'.

In this chapter I have assumed that the characteristics and trajectory of the self in reflexive modernity are consonant with the educationalist's concern for personal autonomy as a major goal of education. In so doing I have stressed the nature of the self as socially constituted and committed to joint activities and relations with others in social practices. The self is robust because for most people most of the time 'normalcy' or what phenomenologists call the 'natural attitude' prevails, but it is also peculiarly fragile because of the continuing need to construct and reconstruct self-identity in rapidly changing circumstances. It is precisely because of this that there needs to be a focus on self-identity in the curriculum.

Of course, there is always the danger of becoming *too* introspective and self-regarding. The notion of the self-as-project fits too readily with the selfish, egocentric, narcissistic tendencies which have been fostered in all areas of society in recent years. However, the self-identity curriculum, as I have tried to demonstrate, opposes such tendencies and should do nothing to reinforce them. Unlike communitarian approaches which fail to problematize such notions as the 'common good' (see Mouffe 1993), it grasps the nettle of individualism and addresses questions to do with the dilemmas of the self in reflexive modernity. The creative reflexive self is concerned with 'appearances' but only because it wants to be properly understood by others. It is self-regarding not because it is self-indulgent but because it wants to be autonomous. It seeks intimacy not because it wants a mirror for its fashion-conscious ego but because it wants to be supported as a self- and other-respecting agent.

3 | Becoming a 'good' learner

Introduction

An important aspect of the curriculum for self-identity is the development of students' capacities for acquiring insights into the learning process, and in the light of these to act in ways which foster the development of their own learning. In this chapter I shall examine this curriculum from the perspective of the individual learner, whilst recognizing the essentially social nature of all learning and the importance of learning communities in the construction of learner identities. In Chapter 5 the emphasis will shift to the group and the development of collaborative learning, but here the focus will be on the development of the individual as a 'good' learner.

In thinking about ways to develop this curriculum, we first need to briefly clarify its goals and purposes. In the light of the moral-political perspective on education identified in Chapter 1, these goals would be derived from a view of education which is 'critically valuable' in the sense used by Peters (1966) in that it establishes criteria for differentiating a 'better' form of learning and thus makes possible the identification of an improvement in learning. Becoming a 'good' learner therefore means students constructing themselves and being constructed by others as particular kinds of learners rather than just as learners *per se*. We would want them to be reflexive and think about learning as an activity which should involve them as active rather than passive participants. We would expect them to appreciate that learning should be 'meaningful' by dint of being connected with their existing knowledge, and that it should involve constant change and activity, growing familiarity with a whole network of concepts and an effort to relate learning to a broader context of understanding. The 'good' learner would also be someone who thought *critically* about learning in the sense of developing an understanding of the way features of the social environment – such as power relations – constrained or facilitated 'good' learning.

In schools, this might seem a tall order given what we know about how many pupils currently identify themselves as learners. In a study carried out by Quicke and Winter (1994) secondary school pupils defined learning as an activity in which they themselves were on the receiving end of something being provided for them by the teacher. They assumed a model of teaching very much like that described in the research literature as a transmission model (Barnes and Shemilt 1982). They thought that learning was mostly to do with 'listening to what the teacher said', 'concentrating', 'taking things in', 'remembering things' and so on, and that teaching was 'passing things on'. Yet, we know that pupils can also be insightful in ways which accord with more enlightened approaches to teaching and learning. As countless ethnographic studies have shown – see Woods (1990) for a review of these – pupils' actions in school are guided by rules and principles which in many instances, even in the case of pupils who are anti-school, are clearly grounded in values compatible at some level with educational values (Quicke 1994).

In the current period, there are probably more opportunities for developing something called 'the learning curriculum' because of the obvious link with the notion of the competent learner as effective, flexible and self-regulated, which has been recognized as a significant goal of education and training in several contexts, both in school and post-school. But we need to be wary, I think, of being seduced by ideas and teaching programmes which may have a certain appeal because they appear to involve a radical reconstruction of existing curricula but which are ultimately out of kilter with the kind of understanding of learning identified above. There are many such programmes, but for our purposes here it will suffice to identify those which revolve around the notion of 'thinking skills', particularly as the teaching of such skills has come to the fore recently as an example of a way of 'stretching' and 'challenging' children. In its White Paper, *Excellence in Schools*, the Department for Education and Employment (DfEE 1997: 39) refers to 'the systematic teaching of thinking skills' which, along with target grouping, fast-tracking and accelerated learning, are seen as part of the drive to modernize the comprehensive principle.

In this chapter the ideas behind a 'thinking skills' approach to teaching and learning will be critically reviewed and an alternative pedagogical strategy suggested which builds on the strengths of this approach whilst taking account of its weaknesses. A key feature of the rationale of most thinking skills programmes is the stress on 'process' as opposed to 'content'. It has been argued that the main problem with traditional, subject-based education is precisely its over-emphasis on content, on facts and information which are transmitted to pupils without allowing scope for their active involvement in the learning process. Although most advocates agree that pupils need to be familiar with the content used in such programmes, the main aim is to teach principles, skills and procedures which are applicable to a wide range of problems in different contexts involving different content. It is anticipated that these general skills will 'transfer' when pupils are confronted with a problem in a new situation, in the same way that a craftsperson applies his or her tools of the trade on a new job.

In general, it will be argued, these kinds of programmes have two problems. First, there is an over-emphasis on 'process' at the expense of 'content', mainly because the dialectical nature of the learning process is not fully acknowledged. Second, although students are encouraged to reflect on their own cognitive strategies, there is no injunction for them to take account of the impact of the social environment on the self as learner or to reflect on the social conditions which give rise to 'good' learning or do not as the case may be. I shall explore each of these criticisms in turn.

A systematic approach to thinking skills: problem-solving and transfer

Support for the active learner in many thinking skills programmes is reflected in the emphasis on the development of the cognitive skills required for efficient and creative problem-solving, and on the analysis of such skills into elements for teaching and learning purposes. For example, in one of the most popular programmes of the recent past, the Somerset Thinking Skills Course, the authors claim to have identified these skills and analysed them into teachable sub-components. Whilst rejecting the idea of intelligence as fixed capacity, they support the idea that something called 'cognitive ability' can be enhanced by systematic teaching, with the implication that this will improve approaches to learning in a variety of contexts (Blagg *et al.* 1988). More recently, similar claims have been made about computer-based programmes which have the added advantage of alleviating a number of difficulties in organizing and managing problem-solving in a classroom context (McFarlane 1997).

As Blagg *et al.* (1988) point out, the cognitive skills required for successful problem-solving form a hierarchy with cognitive resources at the lower end, that is, basic skills and knowledge taught in relation to specific tasks (for example, paying close attention to detail, recording information in different modes); and 'higher level general processes concerned with the selection and co-ordination of specific cognitive resources for particular processes' (Blagg *et al.* 1988: 13) at the upper end. It is these high-level strategies that Whitebread (1997) has in mind in his description and analysis of the educational uses of computer-based adventure games. His way of breaking down the skills involved is clearly grounded in the findings of educational and psychological research (see, for example, Nisbet and Shucksmith 1986) but also reflects what many people would in any case regard as a rational approach to problem-solving, one familiar to all teachers who have used enquiry-based methods with or without computers. The skills include 'understanding and representing the problem; gathering and organizing relevant information; constructing and managing a plan of action; reasoning, hypothesis-testing and decision-making; and using various problem-solving tools' such as notes, measurements and diagrams (Blagg *et al.* 1988: 17).

The hope is, of course, that once these skills have been nurtured in a context which is familiar and meaningful to learners they will *transfer* to other contexts which are less familiar and act as a spur to active engagement with a new area, subject or situation. The problem of transfer has always been something of a hardy perennial for educationalists. The nub of it has been expressed succinctly by Brown (1984: 213) who asked why 'a child will display competence in one task but will fail to employ it in another task where it is equally appropriate?'. Difficulties arise whether we are referring to transfer across knowledge domains within the context of the school (Layton 1991; Hennessy *et al.* 1993) or the transfer of school subject knowledge to the practical contexts of everyday life outside school (Lave 1988). The development of generalizable thinking strategies and problem-solving skills, by fostering an active learning approach across the boundaries of knowledge, has been seen as a way of resolving these difficulties. The more learners use such skills the better at it they become and the better learners they become.

The 'process' versus 'content' issue

As indicated above, thinking skills programmes and problem-solving games tend to emphasize 'process' at the expense of 'content'. Although most of them recognize that the context must be meaningful, they do not operate with a sufficiently dialectical model of the learning process – one that recognizes the way different knowledge domains exert their own special influence on learning strategies. 'Good' learning approaches, therefore, in any particular domain cannot 'take off' without some familiarity with the central ideas and 'exemplars', to use Kuhn's (1970) term, of the disciplinary framework involved. As Barrow (1984: 85) remarks, it is a matter of 'simple logic' that the 'disciplined mind' cannot be automatically transposed from one subject area to another 'because all disciplined (and undisciplined) activity of mind has to take place in a context'. No matter how sophisticated one's cognitive strategies and awareness of such strategies, one cannot switch to another subject and 'transfer' cognitive strategies, without some understanding of concepts in that area of knowledge. Writers such as McPeck (1981) would argue that it is only by internalizing the subject-specific norms of a discrete knowledge domain rather than applying 'generalizable skills' that one can develop competence in that subject. Does this mean, then, that knowledge about one's own mental processes and cognitive strategies is of little use from an educational point of view? Would such knowledge really facilitate the transfer of competence from one subject area to another? Does learning how to learn or reflecting on how we learn in, say, maths help us to learn in English?

In the literature on critical thinking and thinking skills (Ennis 1982; Marton 1986; Siegel 1986; Paul 1987; Perkins and Salomon 1989; Brell 1990) there has been much debate about this issue. Adherents of what for the sake of brevity might be called the *context* school have developed a powerful critique of the *process* or *generalizable skills* approach to cognition and learning. Researchers in this school certainly have a point and few would argue that context and content are not important. However, others would take issue with how content is often defined in this debate. Whilst thinking may occur within discrete conceptual frameworks, does this mean that it always has to take place within conventional academic disciplines? Clearly ways of thinking and knowing which we use in everyday life to explore issues and resolve problems are not circumscribed by these disciplines. Many of the criteria we use are governed by norms and procedures derived from cultural understandings which are unconnected or dealt with too generally and often too crudely within school subjects. Consider, for example, the range of knowledge we draw upon when we think about personal relationship problems or when considering which way to vote.

It is also doubtful if the disciplines themselves are what they purport to be – coherent bodies of knowledge or discrete conceptual frameworks. As the philosopher Kleinig (1982) points out in his critique of the 'forms of knowledge' thesis, many school subjects contain diverse perspectives. Thus 'the discipline of mathematics, for example, has to accommodate arithmetic, calculus, Euclidean and Riemannian geometry; the physical sciences have to accommodate geology, astronomy, biology and thermodynamics . . . and so on' (Kleinig 1982: 153) Moreover, new ways of thinking within subjects are continually being developed, so that what at one point appears to be a fixed and bounded body of knowledge, at another is seen to have a multiplicity of cross-references with knowledge from another discipline. Eventually, knowledge from both disciplines may be integrated and a new discipline emerge. This process of what has been described as the 'reconstructive transfer' of discrete concepts and norms is going on all the time and results in the 'construction of new and potentially more integrated ways of understanding and explaining the world' (Brell 1990: 64).

In the context of a discussion about a 'thinking skills' pedagogy the notion of reconstructive transfer is important because it brings together the *generalizable* skills and *subject-specific* approaches. Proponents of both viewpoints should be able to agree that what we think in one domain can make an impact on (can transfer to) what we think in another. Most rational thought is cross-referenced and multicategorical in practice. Take an issue in education like 'truancy'. We can look at it from several different viewpoints – psychological, sociological, moral, legal, economic and so on – but it is highly likely that if we consider it to be morally wrong this will have a different impact on our thinking within other frameworks than if we begin from a position which is ambivalent about its rightness or wrongness. And likewise for other perspectives. In the ongoing process of problem resolution such frames of reference might be said to enter a reconstructive dialogue with each other.

On this view, proponents of 'general skills' are right in assuming that knowledge learned in one domain can transfer to another, but they underplay the extent to which this process is rooted in *specific* knowledge domains and involves the active and deliberate construction of links between different spheres. Such active transfer, of course, requires that the learner possesses an appropriate disposition as well as knowledge and understanding in each domain.

In the light of this, we can agree with Dewey (1910: 39) that 'thinking is the power of following up and linking together the specific suggestions that specific things arouse'. Any subject, from Greek to cooking and from drawing to mathematics, can be used as a resource in this process. The same could be said about any common knowledge or shared discourse with which the pupil is familiar. The teacher's aim is to encourage pupils to make use of existing concepts, knowledge and experience when tackling a new problem and to create a readiness to see connections between apparently discrete frames of reference. In helping pupils to maximize this transfer effect, the 'thinking skills' teacher tries to encourage pupils to become more aware of their own thinking and learning processes. However, it is crucial that this form of heightened self-consciousness should eventually lead to a more implicit use of cognitive strategies and become an integral part of the way pupils go about thinking and working things out in their daily lives. The overriding aim would be to foster a critical disposition rather than merely to teach skills.

Metacognition: the awareness of self as learner in a social context

The second criticism of a conventional 'thinking skills' pedagogy is that the critical disposition it aims to foster is not based on a model of the self which is reflexive or social enough. At this point, it will be helpful to introduce the idea of *metacognition* which I shall use to distinguish an orientation which is at a 'higher' level than the problem-solving skills referred to above. According to Blagg et al. (1988: 18), metacognition refers to an area of self-knowledge involving 'more conscious awareness of cognitive processes' which is at the top of the hierarchy of cognitive strategies and involves self-monitoring, self-testing and self-evaluating at the level of conscious awareness. This is in line with what some other prominent writers in the field emphasize. In the much quoted book by Nisbet and Shucksmith (1986) there is also a stress on metacognition as having an executive function and thus involving the process of 'managing the process of learning', requiring learners to be more aware of what they are doing and to be able to bring their mental processes under scrutiny and thus 'more effectively under control' (1986: 7).

Metacognition therefore involves a process of self-examination and self-regulation of mental processes, whether these involve low- or high-level skills. The question arises, however, as to whether metacognitive knowledge always has to be 'conscious'. Educationalists often make a distinction between 'knowing how' and 'knowing that'. 'Knowing how' requires that a satisfactory performance be demonstrated on a task even if the concepts required to do the task are only implicit. Thus a child may know how to speak grammatically even though they are unable to articulate the rules of grammar. A person may be able to argue logically without knowing the rules of logic. 'Knowing that' involves a more conscious understanding of the conceptual structures which organize experience and in terms of which knowledge claims are explicitly formulated (see Pring 1976). It is evident that 'learning that' is not always necessarily the best way to 'learn how', and that teachers who concentrate on the former may deploy teaching strategies which are inefficient and even counterproductive. This may be particularly true of knowledge and skills which are considered to be more appropriately 'caught' rather than 'taught'.

As Flavell (1979) points out, metacognitive knowledge is not fundamentally different from any other knowledge and can involve 'know how' and 'know that' aspects. It can be activated as a result of a 'deliberate, conscious memory search' or 'activated unintentionally and automatically by retrieval cues in the task situation' (Flavell 1979: 907). Thus when deployed in relation to a cognitive task such knowledge may or may not enter consciousness. Nevertheless, when teaching for transfer, it could well be that conscious awareness of metacognitive processes is what is being aimed for. Although such processes may become automatic and habitual, one assumes that if learners have developed control over their own learning then these processes are also readily available to consciousness rather than deeply implicit, otherwise it is difficult to see what the self being in control of learning means.

Underpinning educational practices which emphasize the role of metacognitive awareness are values to do with the development of individuals as rational, autonomous agents of which their development as efficient cognitive processors is only one aspect. A metacognitive approach to teaching and learning is in fact a step away from a narrow cognitivist view of education to a more holistic view which emphasizes 'total development' and 'development of the self' as agent. On this view the old distinctions between cognition, 'emotion' and 'will' break down, and are viewed 'as abstractions from a single centre of activity, each of which in the experience of persons presupposes the other' (Kleinig 1982: 18–19). Education therefore involves the development of 'whole' persons as self-directed agents and autonomous learners. For the autonomous learner, metacognitive experiences involving metacognitive knowledge entering consciousness are far more common than for the non-autonomous learner. They often portend the development of new metacognitive knowledge. They occur when the 'flow of habit' is disrupted, and indeed are partly responsible for such disruption. For Flavell (1979: 908) these experiences

> are especially likely to occur in situations that stimulate a lot of careful, highly conscious thinking: in a job or school task that expressly demands that kind of thinking; in novel roles or situations, where every major step you take requires planning beforehand and evaluation afterwards; where decisions and actions are at once weighty and risky . . .

Metacognition: a broader perspective

Given that metacognition reflects a concern for placing the self at the heart of the learning process, the question remains as to how the self and its consciousness are constituted in a social context. In the light of the foregoing discussion, it is evident that an emphasis on the cognitive and 'mental' aspects of the process is far too restricting. Self knowledge about such processes would need to include a much broader range of psychological factors (for example, feeling and will) but also knowledge about the way social processes operate in a given context (for example, school) to enable or constrain the development of the self as a 'good' learner.

In exploring these matters further the work of Flavell (1979) is a good starting point. In his seminal article he provides a broader definition of metacognitive knowledge which clearly goes beyond a narrow cognitive skills or strategies approach. For him it refers to all beliefs and knowledge about what factors 'act and interact in what ways to affect the course and outcome of cognitive enterprises' (1979: 907). It would therefore include not only knowledge about strategies but also knowledge of factors relating to *persons*. This latter category 'encompasses everything you could come to believe about the nature of yourself and other people as cognitive processors' (1979: 907).

Clearly, such a definition opens up a wide range of possibilities. There are many ways to describe the nature of people as 'cognitive processors' and as many interpretations as there are theories of learning and teaching. Flavell's own examples seem to draw on a particular brand of psychological knowledge. He refers to beliefs about 'intraindividual differences, interindividual differences and universals of cognition'. An example of the first of these would be the belief of a student that they 'take things in better' when they are listening than when they are reading, and of the second that the reverse is true of their friend. The third would be a belief that it can be difficult to 'work out how well you understand something' and 'whether your understanding is adequate enough for certain purposes' (Flavell 1979: 907).

However, it is evident that there could be other forms of knowledge involved besides those relating to cognitive psychology and the psychology of individual differences. Examples could be given of descriptions of factors which relate to other paradigms in psychology and indeed to the wider field of social psychology and other disciplines such as sociology. If one's concern is with influences on learning processes in an institutional context then there are numerous perspectives that might be relevant and several ways that persons might construct their knowledge and understanding of relevant factors. Borkowski and Muthukrisna (1992), for example, refer to models of the learning situation where competent students position teachers as collaborators in transaction-based instruction and regularly seek to engage teachers in dialogue about the learning process.

But these learners are only free to collaborate and negotiate in a situation which is empowering and facilitative. Our understanding of metacognition needs to be broadened further to include the generation of insights into social processes which can lead to an active and critical engagement with learning contexts. Some of the enquiries that have been carried out into the strategies adults use to manage learning environments are relevant here. The capacity to develop situational understanding is clearly crucial, and some writers have tried to identify the various components of such understanding. In a staff development context, Elliot (1990a), drawing on the work of Klemp (1977), identifies three groups of 'abilities'. First, there are cognitive abilities, such as the ability in organizational settings to discern thematic consistencies, to understand controversial issues and to learn from reflection on experience. These, of course, assume that a person has other cognitive abilities such as the ability to acquire and use information, but crucially they also imply that the individual is aware of their own agency and their capacity to influence their own lives and those of others. A second set of abilities are to do with interpersonal relationships, such as accurate empathy and the capacity for promoting feelings of efficacy in others; and a third set involves certain kinds of motivation in self and others – achievement motivation, risk-taking and micro-political awareness. The view taken here, and one that I shall explicate more fully in the next chapter, is that the crucial element is awareness of how *power* operates in educational institutions to promote or constrain 'good' learning. The discussion in that chapter will focus on adult professionals, but there is no reason why these abilities should not also be fostered in school pupils, particularly as studies of pupil culture have shown that pupils can and often do operate with models of the social context which include political understandings (see Chapters 5 and 6).

Critical metacognition: learning as discourse

In the light of all this, it would seem more appropriate to think of metacognition not as a skill or strategy but as the ability to develop awareness of learning processes through learning the language of a certain kind of *critical discourse* – one characterized by possibilities of talking about learning in a way which demystified the conventional psychological interpretations of the process and took account of the social and political dimensions of school learning. In the current situation we would hope the metacognitively aware pupil would critically engage with a discourse of schooling which positioned him or her as a passive and dependent learner. As Edwards and Mercer (1987: 49) point out, the language of schooling 'is a problematic medium through which pupils and teachers swim with difficulty', and it is because the rules of this discourse are not brought out into the open that pupils become alienated from school learning. The avoidance of explicit communication is not accidental; it is a consequence of the structure of power in the classroom, a particular view of how pupils learn (see also Hargreaves 1972; Hammersley 1977a; Edwards and Furlong 1978) and a particular view of the role of the teacher (see Barnes and Shemilt 1982). The model of learning which underpins much classroom practice is one which restricts rather than enhances the scope for 'handing over' (Bruner 1983) knowledge and control to pupils. The language involved often imposes a perspective that establishes a teacher 'stance' which is 'off-putting and barrenly informative' (Bruner 1986: 26).

Teaching about learning as a discourse of schooling implies a more dialogical and reflexive orientation than the 'bag of tools' approach of most 'thinking skills' programmes. The 'good' learner is one who is 'becoming' a 'better' learner through acquiring a deeper knowledge of what learning means in the school context and what it could and should mean. He or she should develop critical insights derived from a developing understanding of the self-in-context not just in psychological but also in philosophical and sociological terms; that is, the pupil should become a rounded educationalist, not a specialist in cognitive science! He or she should acknowledge that school disciplines have their own discourses which have to be inhabited from the 'inside', so to speak, as a participant in a learning community. The learning curriculum would relate to other disciplines in the curriculum in the same way that those disciplines should do to each other – as open disciplines fostering interdisciplinary conversation and mutual enquiry. At the same time pupils should not be regarded as empty vessels as far as the discourse of learning is concerned, since, as indicated at the beginning of the chapter, their common-sense knowledge is already likely to contain 'folk' conceptions of learning and education, some of which are compatible, others incompatible, with 'good' learning processes.

A worked example: teaching the language of learning

Some of these points are illuminated in the following account of an action research project carried out by the author and his co-worker, Christine

Winter, which involved an attempt to develop reflective and critical discussion on learning with a group of low-achieving boys in a secondary school in the UK. The boys were provided with a stimulus card (called a strategy card) which contained a number of learning points, such as 'get ourselves into a learning mood', 'talk about what we have to do', 'look and listen carefully', 'stop and think – work for several minutes without talking', 'work on the task: have a go', 'ask questions', 'check our work', 'think ahead'. Particular words and phrases on the card were chosen because preliminary discussion with pupils about learning suggested that these phrases would be readily understood by them and recognized as strategies which they in some form or another already acknowledged. Other points were added which were not directly referred to by pupils but which were well within their understanding. Points were also included which clearly represented more of a challenge to pupils' existing way of thinking (see Quicke and Winter 1994).

The researchers found it helpful to keep in mind the idea that the pupils were to be introduced to two discourses – one the formal discourse of the subject (in this case science) and the other the discourse of learning or what I have called the learning curriculum. The strategy card was used as the starting point for enabling pupils to become more aware of the latter whilst actually in the process of engaging with former. The researchers incorporated reflective discussion of the language of learning into their teaching approach and made a point of highlighting and helping the pupils to articulate various learning strategies they had used or were about to use. In this way they were able to engage pupils in a dialogue about learning and develop their understanding of what 'good' learning was.

The research was carried out at a time when the class was doing the topic of 'Materials' in the science curriculum. Most of the research described relates to a period when the pupils planned and carried out experiments about 'dissolving'. The experiments were: to separate the insoluble sand and grit from soluble salt in rock salt using filtration; the separation of salt from salty water using evaporation and condensation; and an investigation to find the effect of increased temperature on the time taken for sugar to dissolve in water. Towards the end of the research period, the pupils designed and carried out an investigation of their own. This was an experiment to find out which of the two solids, salt or sugar, dissolved most quickly.

Highlighting learning strategies was partly a question of seizing opportunities as these presented themselves in the ebb and flow of interacting with pupils. Thus although one might decide beforehand to focus on 'talk about what we have to do', in the event how this particular aspect was interpreted and elaborated depended on what was being taught, how pupils reacted to this and what the researcher judged to be the most appropriate next step. In the following extract from the transcript the researcher felt that it was appropriate to emphasize that talking for learning in this particular context meant talking about the words used in the formal discourse of science:

Researcher: And we had a good conversation yesterday, I can remember it well, 'cos we were talking about words like 'soluble' and 'insoluble'. Now, Martin, can you just recap for us what we were talking about? Start with 'soluble'. That word 'soluble'. Can you tell us what soluble means?

Martin: It means that it can't dissolve.

Kevin: No . . . other way round.

Researcher: Other way round, yeh. Yeh.

Kevin: And insoluble means it doesn't dissolve.

Researcher: . . . it doesn't dissolve. Right. So. Brian.

Brian: Scientists' words.

Researcher: That's right, Brian, scientists' words.

This is illustrative of the kind of dialogue initiated by the researcher around the point 'talk about what we have to do'. A particular use of language is highlighted by describing a previous conversation as 'good' precisely because it was a conversation about such words. This evaluation marks an interesting and essential development in teaching the language of learning. Talking about what you have to do is an important first step, but not just any old talk will do. Some kinds of talk are better than other kinds. In this instance the researcher is suggesting several aspects of this learning-enhancing form of talk. It is talk which involves conversation, recapping and an acknowledgement of a formal discourse of science. The pupil's reference to 'scientists' words' as opposed, say, to describing them as 'science words' is of some significance. It suggests that the pupil might be ready to accept the idea that scientific language is not some abstract, impersonal, unchallengeable way of thinking and talking about events in the natural world but a language which emanates from the work of a particular social group, scientists, and as such reflects the interests and the values of that group. The point, then, is not just that pupils need to use scientific language when they talk but that they are aware that these concepts are part of a social discourse. Of course, it is not being claimed that these pupils have developed an understanding of all these aspects; only that they seem to have made a start.

A further development which occurred when helping pupils to use the learning point 'talk about what we have to do' involved stressing the validity of bringing to the task previous experience, whether this came from previous work in school science or from home or other out-of-school experience. In the following example, the researcher's questioning is typical of the way pupils were encouraged to draw on and value experience:

Researcher: So it was something that you did at home and brought to school. Now I'll give you another example. This morning we were doing grass chromatography, right.

Kevin: Me and Brian didn't do a graphy.

Researcher: No it doesn't matter but you knew what it was all about.

	Did you know that you could separate all the different colours in grass using chromatography?
Pupils:	Yes.
Researcher:	Did anybody hear what Len said to Miss Brown? He said 'You know miss when you fall down on the grass, you get a grass stain on your clothes and it's all different colours?' Can you remember him saying that?
Kevin:	It goes light green, then dark green.
Researcher:	Exactly. What was he doing there? What was he bringing into the lab?
Kevin:	When he plays football it happens.
Researcher:	He's bringing an experience that he's had, he's bringing it into the lab, into school, and using it. He's actually using his experience from out of school in school. You know when we had all these discussions about sea water, and dissolving, about cups of tea and about . . . Michael you told us how your dad uses loads of sand to make cement to make bricks. We had a discussion about house bricks and breeze blocks. Do you remember? Where did that information that you were telling us about come from?
Thomas:	I asked my dad how they made bricks.
Researcher:	That's right and your dad told you.
Thomas:	Miss, at our house I've seen my dad build our pond and our wall. One day I went to work with him as a builder, as a bricklayer. I did a bit of wall.
Researcher:	So you actually found out how to build a wall not just what bricks are made of.
Thomas:	My dad did that line because you needed a piece of string so it's straight. He put some bricks then put the spirit level on.
Researcher:	To see if it's level. So do you think it's important to use what you know from out of school, from home, from round about and bring it in? Is that a good thing to do?
Thomas:	Yes.

This seemed to reflect a necessary part of connecting with the formal language of the discourse to which they were being introduced. It was important for these pupils to recognize that in talking about the task they should be aware of when they had used previous experience and, if they had, that this was a valid thing to do. Such awareness could then feed forward to the next task or next phase in the same task.

The next stage involved critically evaluating the card. The pupils suggested alterations and additions which showed that they had begun to grasp some of the essential features of good learning. The discussion on learning processes was wide-ranging but initially it focused in the various points on the strategy card and the general issue as to whether or not the card had proved useful. At first there was a clear difference of opinion in the group, with some pupils being more in favour of the card than others. Two pupils who were rather anxious and insecure in their learning in class were more supportive of the card and one of them made the following point:

> *Brian*: I think we need a strategy card because if we didn't 'ave 'em we wouldn't look at . . . say if we 'ad that group, we wouldn't know what to do, they'd all be messing about, not in a learning mood and then, if we 'ad that, and they looked at that and it said, 'Number 1 Get into your learning mood', get yourself into a learning mood, they get themselves into a learning mood before they start.

All pupils, however, showed that they were prepared to think about whether or not the card was acceptable as it was or whether it needed some improvements. In this way they demonstrated their critical engagement with ideas about learning and their emerging facility to explore and develop the language of learning. Even pupils who had given a negative response at first when questioned directly about the card came up with some interesting thoughts about how it would be useful to 'make one up' if it did not exist:

> *Researcher*: Do you think you'll use some the ideas from the strategy card in the future?
> *John*: Yeh.
> *Researcher*: Do you think so?
> *John*: I think so.
> *Thomas*: If I were a teacher, I'd make one up.
> *Researcher*: Would you? You'd make a different one up, a second one?
> *Thomas*: Yes.
> *John*: If I didn't have that one what we've got now, I'd make that one up.
> *Researcher*: Oh, would you? You'd make one up very like it, sort of thing, would you?
> *John*: If I could think of ideas.

Another spontaneous and potentially empowering development was the acknowledgement by some pupils of the usefulness of the card in initiating more independent thinking. For one pupil this meant the possibility of working independently of the teacher:

> *Thomas*: Miss, they [the teachers] don't have to tell us it, we just look at that [the strategy card] ourselves . . . Teacher doesn't have to show us about what to do, pupils just look

> at the card and . . . it means we don't have to listen to the
> teacher; we can just look at this and get on with us work.

Even if this pupil did not recognize exactly what was at stake here, his
response, which was spontaneous, suggested that he had grasped one of the
key ideas of the research. Other pupils developed the discussion. They
wanted to design a card for pupils but they thought it would be a good idea
if they also designed a card for the teacher. What seemed to be behind this
was the notion of 'what's good for us is good for them' – implying a desire
for a teacher–pupil relationship characterized by mutual respect, a familiar
aspect of the pupil perspective (see Marsh *et al.* 1980).

> *Martin:*   Teacher comes in right angry . . . why don't 'e get himself
> into a learning mood or some'at . . . ask 'im questions
> instead of 'im asking us.

It was evident that the conversation which took place increasingly
reflected an awareness of social constraints on the development of individuals as 'good' learners. On the strength of this the researcher found it was
relatively easy to extend the discussion further to consider other possible
constraints on 'good' learning in the school context. It was Kevin who was
initially the most forthcoming. He challenges the view of another pupil that
teachers want a relationship of mutual respect with pupils and that their
reason for always keeping him behind is legitimate.

> *Researcher:* Why don't you believe that teachers want you to treat
> them the same as they treat you?
> *Kevin:*   Because every time I do my work, all the teachers just keep
> me behind.
> *Thomas:*   Because you're a slow worker and writer.
> *Kevin:*   That's not my fault.

Conclusion

In general, the study demonstrates the argument of this chapter that teaching pupils to become 'good' learners requires more than just teaching them
a number of 'thinking skills' or cognitive strategies. It means helping them
to become more critically aware of the learning process in a broader sense
and more conscious of themselves as active agents in this process. I have suggested that 'learning about learning' can best be realized through an
approach that develops pupils' language of learning through reflection on
'good' practice in learning within a disciplinary framework, whether this be
an academic subject or some other discipline. A discourse of learning would
be foregrounded but this would be deployed in further learning through
'conversation' with subject discourses – a process promoted by a teaching

intervention involving reflective discussion and dialogue. In so doing, it is evident that pupils' 'spontaneous' concepts derived from their common-sense knowledge would be useful starting points for metacognitive dialogue.

Clearly, although 'learning' has been broadly interpreted in this chapter, there are several questions which require further analysis and discussion. The notion of power as a constraining force in schools has been dealt with rather perfunctorily, and there has been no attempt to examine possibilities and limitations in actual classroom contexts for the development of the kind of intimate reflective dialogue between teachers and pupils demonstrated in Quicke and Winter's research study. Power will be explored in more detail in the next three chapters, and the optimal school organization for dialogical teaching in the final chapter of the book.

4 | Towards a collaborative culture of professionalism

> The difference between industry as it exists today and a profession is, then, simple and unmistakable. The former is organized for the protection of rights, mainly rights to pecuniary gain. The latter is organized, imperfectly indeed, but nonetheless genuinely, for the performance of duties. The essence of the one is that its only criterion is the financial return which it offers to its shareholders. The essence of the other is that, though men enter it for the sake of livelihood, the measure of their success is the service which they perform, not the gains which they amass. They may, as in the case of a successful doctor, grow rich; but the meaning of their profession, both for themselves and for the public, is not that they make money but that they make health, or safety, or knowledge, or good government or good law.
>
> (Tawney 1961: 89–90)

Introduction

Tawney's view of professionalism is clearly of its time. Nowadays, few would accept that there is such a marked moral distinction between industrial employees and employers, of whatever rank, on the one hand, and people who call themselves professionals, on the other. The service ethic has come in for something of a battering both from the Left and the Right, and whether or not professionalism is necessarily 'good' for society has been queried. But in this chapter, I am going to assume that, despite changes in the social and political context and despite the criticisms of professional power, professionalism retains and should retain the same core meaning as it did for Tawney – a meaning which revolves around the notion of 'work' which is not just done for a living but gives meaning to life itself, and is carried out in accordance with standards set by a community of autonomous workers for the benefit of society as a whole.

The purpose of this chapter is not, therefore, to develop a new definition of professionalism, but rather to examine ways in which its essential meaning can be realized in a contemporary context. It will be argued that crucial to the practice of a new professionalism is the emphasis in institutions on democratic *collaboration* as a basis for rational communication in the context of uncertainty which characterizes 'new times'. In suggesting a way forward, the discussion focuses on the bureaucratic constraints on a collaborative model of institutional life and, in particular, on the way these constraints can be exposed by analyses of the way modern power, or what Foucault described as *disciplinary power*, works in institutions. It is argued that reforms which aim to foster collaborative cultures often conceal the extent to which this form of power remains dominant. In relation to schools, even those research-based movements like the school effectiveness/school improvement movement which emphasize the importance of collaboration and reflective practice fail to attend sufficiently to the differentiations of knowledge, as in the National Curriculum in England and Wales, which are an expression of disciplinary power in schools. These problems reinforce the need for a greater sensitivity towards the role of power in the construction of the selves of professionals and their stance towards their own expertise.

The need for a new professionalism

In reflexive modernity, we might conceive of the new professionalism as contributing to the construction of a social and moral order which accommodated the more democratic aspects of 'new times' whilst countering those forces which produced inequality and fragmentation. As we know from the history of modern Western society, this would not be the first time that the professions were linked with the idea of social improvement. One of the great analysts of modern society – Émile Durkheim – was the first to see that the professions could be a positive moral force in society, acting as a bulwark against economic individualism and an authoritarian state. He envisaged the moral communities established by professionals acting as an alternative source of solidarity at a time when the old ties of the traditional moral order had broken down. In England, this theme was taken up by the Fabian Left and social democrats such as Tawney and Marshall, who regarded professionals as a source of stability and democracy in a changing world. Their expertise would be used in the creation of a workable welfare state, with services delivered according to objectively defined needs and in a way that would free citizens from their dependence on state and industrial bureaucracies, and the market.

One of the main differences between then and now is that in the current period the knowledge base of professionals, the source of their previously much valued expertise, has become less secure. From an epistemological viewpoint, there have been changes in the way we typically understand the nature of knowledge and what it means to know. Professionals can no longer claim that their knowledge is a theory-free, unbiased and objective source of expertise; like all knowledge, it is located within a paradigm or 'language game' which has its own discourse rules and truth criteria, and which provides one of a number of possible vantage points from which to describe and explain the 'world'. Thus there can be no knowledge claims which are ungainsayable or uncontestable. However, the problematic nature of professional knowledge is intertwined with another difference in the present context – the *lack of trust* in professionals, which stems in part from the critique of the traditional knowledge base but is also linked to criticisms of how professionals have operated in practice. Professionals are alleged to have engaged in monopolistic practices, and, far from being anti-bureaucratic, are themselves an intrinsic part of bureaucratic mechanisms. Sociologists such as Weber linked professionalization with bureaucratization and saw both as reflecting the rationalization of society. For others such as C. Wright Mills, as Johnson (1972: 16) points out, 'the continued expansion of professional numbers and the professionalization of occupations was seen . . . not as a desired expansion of the learned and liberal profession dedicated to service, stability and democracy, but as an explosion of experts and technocrats – men of narrow specialism and narrower vision'.

The market solution

In education, as we know from recent history, the state took matters into its own hands and attempted to reconstruct the so-called post-war settlement which had involved a partnership between teachers, local education authorities and the state. Since teachers had played a major part in educational policy-making and implementation, it was inevitable that they would be in the firing-line when, in the 1970s, the prevailing values and assumptions underpinning policy began to be questioned. But did the way professionalism was redefined by state policy in the 1980s and 1990s resolve the various problems faced by the state and society? On the face of it, the target for reform seemed to be the correct one. The aim was to debureaucratize schools and colleges, making the professionals who ran them more accountable and the organizations more flexible and dynamic. The mechanism for achieving this was the market. Market discipline was to be used to restore the authority of the state and create an education system which would meet the needs of a changing economy and a changing society.

Have these reforms been successful? Certainly, bureaucratic organizations have been restructured and professionals have become more accountable to the market. But has this empowered professionals to act as a source of solidarity, community and moral leadership in a divided and dividing world? There are at least two reasons for doubting the success of marketization in this respect. First, marketization itself is grounded in values which support the production and reproduction of inequality, and the very conditions – the division of labour, egoistic personalities and instrumental relationships – which produced the kinds of problems for which professionalism was supposed to be a solution in the first instance. For all the talk of restructuring, debureaucratization and the 'freeing up' of relationships, market ideology is grounded in a view of the individual and society which is fundamentalist and reductionist; society is composed of aggregates of self-sufficient competing individuals doing what comes naturally. As we have seen, however, life in reflexively modern societies is dogged by uncertainty and the constant imperative to critically reflect on social structures and the self. This has potential benefits for society in that it enables a flowering of diversity and difference, but there are also the dangers of further inequalities and increased fragmentation. In reintroducing a fundamentalist creed, all that happens is that a set of constraints of the wrong kind is placed on opportunities for self- and community development. Instead of constraints which are drawn up and negotiated with due regard to the 'new conditions of knowing', we have the prejudices of a bygone era imposed, as if no questions could be asked about the model of the economic egoist they take for granted.

Second, professionals could only function as moral leaders if they were allowed to be autonomous and develop their professional knowledge in ways they thought would be helpful to society. Without autonomy, they could not experiment or explore different approaches to the production and reproduction of democratic moral communities in new social conditions, since their own capacities for creativity and moral choice would be restricted. Far from this market form of 'new professionalism' reflecting the emergence of a renewed moral identity, what we are experiencing now is just the most recent manifestation of shifting relationships between the state and the professional. Like other occupations, occupational restructuring has been justified in terms of the need to provide a more flexible workforce, one that can more readily adapt to change but also, from a management view point, one that can be more easily manipulated to meet budgetary targets. Marketization brings with it an enhanced role for managers, in this case headteachers, who become the main instruments through which the 'new order' is implemented and reproduced. Managers are accountable to the state for ensuring that their schools are geared up to the market: flexible enough to be responsive to customer preference in changing market conditions, and more efficient thanks to the 'fine tuning' of costs made possible by the localization of financial decision-making (see Gewirtz *et al.* 1995). The control on teachers is thus not exerted by a distant state but by a local management, namely the headteacher who derives his legitimacy through appeals to the impersonal forces of the market. However, in the context of 'new times', where the 'best' flexible workers are those who are self-motivated, managerial strategies have to be hegemonic; that is to say, they have to capture the 'hearts and minds' of employees rather than ride roughshod over them.

Towards a collaborative culture of professionalism

But if the application and inculcation of market values does not produce the kind of autonomous, morally committed, democratic, flexible professional required in the contemporary context, what are the alternatives? Most non-market-oriented responses envisage an emphasis on the development of a professional culture characterized by a high degree of collaboration and an increased capacity for communication (see, for example, Hargreaves 1994; Nixon *et al.* 1997). For Hargreaves, collaboration is a kind of metapara-digm for what he describes as the 'postmodern age'. It is a strategy for coping with the rapid pace of change and the acceleration of paradigm shifts which are bound to occur in education, and indeed in all areas of social life, in 'new times'. Awareness of the fallibility and provisionality of formal knowledge as well as of the importance of connecting with local knowledge in an increasingly diverse cultural world implies new forms of professional community and new partnership arrangements with clients. Problems can only be resolved by the generation of shared knowledge constructed through dialogue between all parties in a particular context, rather than through the 'top-down' application of a universal, 'objective' professional expertise.

For teachers in institutions such as schools collaboration as 'an articulat-ing and integrating principle' (Hargreaves 1994: 245) has several advan-tages. It provides a mechanism for moral support, it can lead to increased efficiency by eliminating duplication as activities are co-ordinated and shared, and can improve efficiency by encouraging risk-taking and a greater diversity of teaching strategies. But most importantly, it is a mode of relat-ing which is consonant with the 'way of knowing' in the times in which we live. As Hargreaves (1994: 246) acknowledges: 'Collaboration replaces false *scientific* certainties or debilitating occupational uncertainties with the *situ-ated* certainties of collected professional wisdom among particular com-munities of teachers'.

This goes hand in hand with 'an increased capacity for reflection' (Har-greaves 1994: 246) since there is more scope for the kind of feedback that encourages teachers to reflect on their own practice; an increase in the poten-tial of the school itself to become a learning organization, more responsive to but also more proactive in its relations with the external environment; more opportunities for teachers to learn from each other through shared reflection and pooling their knowledge at every level, including learning that takes place as a result of inter-school collaboration; and finally, it is associ-ated with the production of an ethos where change is seen 'not as a task to be completed but as an unending process of continuous improvement' (Har-greaves 1994: 247).

For Nixon *et al.* (1997) the development of these collaborative cultures requires a new kind of professional. Their idea of a 'learning profession' is descriptive of the ideal stance for professionals in an age of pluralism and indeterminacy of outcome. What is required in a diverse and plural society is an emphasis on 'the process of learning about difference and about how difference may be accommodated within integrative modes of decision-making' and the professionalism of the teacher therefore 'focuses on the complex practices of agreement-making, such that collegiality, negotiation, coordination and partnership may be seen as emergent values' (Nixon *et al.* 1997: 16). Agreement is not automatically purposeful but *achieves* purpose through being deliberative and engaging with questions of value that inform 'right' action – a process which is inherently democratic. In Habermasian terms, what 'learning professionals' need to develop is their 'communicative competence', which means their capacity for understanding and mastering the many ways that language can be used to create social relationships characterized by consensus and agreement (see Habermas 1979).

Collaboration in practice

Hargreaves (1994) provides a persuasive account of the promise of collaborative cultures but he is also aware of the dangers. Collaboration can be limited to the safe areas of teachers' work and thus foster complacency and reinforce rather than radically change existing practice. It can suppress individuality and lead to conformity and groupthink. It can be used as an administrative device which paradoxically can produce a situation where teachers do not want to collaborate. It can be used as a mechanism for co-opting teachers and securing their compliance to various reforms of a dubious nature from an educational viewpoint.

Collaboration cannot be democratic or educationally productive if it is merely a vehicle used by management for increasing control over teachers. There is a growing body of evidence that in many schools this is the case (see Smyth 1993; Ball 1994). Some of the most disturbing comes from studies of primary schools. In their research on work and identity in the primary school, Menter *et al.* (1997) show what the rhetoric of collaboration, a participative approach to leadership and monitoring of progress have meant for practices in a number of schools. The evidence suggests that the 'new managerialism' is more correctly regarded as an 'enhanced managerialism' which, as they put it, 'sits uncomfortably on the top of old, established work practices' (Menter *et al.* 1997: 98). Instead of establishing a completely new set of social relations in schools, the 'new' forms merely reinforce many of the 'dysfunctional' tendencies in school work practices. Rather than a policy of delegating responsibility resulting in a genuine decentralization of power and empowerment of the teachers who took on extra responsibilities, the autocracy of the head was in many cases increased rather than reduced. The teachers concerned, also, felt they had less autonomy and less control over teaching and learning processes in their classes. Too much of their time was taken up with administrative jobs to do with managing the budget and implementing centrally directed changes.

As for collaborative work, this took the form of a large number of weekly meetings which, rather than being supportive, were seen more as a threat to the teachers' independence, because they tended to be about implementing decisions which had been taken elsewhere rather than genuine collaboration. In general, much of this increased control could be related to the lack of teaching resources due to under-funding and the direction of existing funding into market-oriented rather than educational activities. It is one of the functions of a market system to make schools more efficient and cost-effective, but it was clear that in these schools the process of marketization and enhanced managerialism had resulted in a reduction in teacher autonomy and an increase in workload, with consequent increases in stress and alienation.

What these authors are describing is the structural base of 'low-trust' situations where the teachers' situated knowledge is not allowed to blossom because of constraints on the collaborative processes which enable such knowledge to be constructed. The only 'new knowledge' is that grounded in a commodified view of persons which is so impoverished that it makes a mockery of any possibility of the 'greater heights' of collaboration ever being achieved. Within this fundamentalist framework, teachers are driven by targets set by others and goals determined by external factors. Lip-service is paid to the value of the teachers' practical knowledge, yet the process of generating this knowledge is severely curtailed by the double bind of the market ideology, which on the one hand encourages teachers to be self-managing whilst on the other determines what the parameters of their knowledge should be.

Prospects in the present context

In England and Wales in the present context, there are signs that an out and out market view of education is beginning to have less of a hold on the consciousness of policy-makers and that educational policy is now seen to be more of a 'mixed economy' with government being more interventionist than in the neo-liberal ideal. Although perhaps there is still too much emphasis on 'effective management systems' (see DfEE 1997: 11), space does seem to be opening up for an approach to school reform involving styles of leadership which are more collaborative and humanistic and which are concerned with fostering a more reflexive and collaborative school culture generally. Much of the thinking here is drawn from the extensive research on school effectiveness and school improvement. Some of this research is associated with a model of change clearly rooted in an anti-bureaucratic and anti-technicist stance on school reform, and one certainly antagonistic to the kind of pseudo-scientific and macho management adopted by those schools which have been overly influenced by business ideology and 'hard-nosed' market approaches.

From a democratic perspective, this paradigm of reform has much to commend. It certainly gives high priority to collaboration and reflection and to the development of schools as 'learning organizations'. And it is precisely because of this, I think, that we need to give it serious consideration. Are we sure, for example, that it takes full account of some of the constraints on the development of collaborative cultures in school contexts? Is the way it conceptualizes collaboration, reflection and the learning school appropriate for the kind of democratic culture we need to foster? *What is its curriculum?* In answering these questions I shall begin with a brief review of some of the features of the paradigm which are most salient for the purposes of this discussion.

The shift from structure to culture

In this area of research there has been a shift in recent years from a preoccupation with school effectiveness to a concern with the practical implications of research on effectiveness for school improvement strategies (Mortimore 1991; Hopkins 1995). This has been accompanied by a shift in emphasis from 'structure' to 'culture'. As Stoll and Fink (1996: 81) point out, whereas school effectiveness research has much to say about structures, strategies for school improvement require a more detailed understanding of the 'processes that a school goes through in its search for effectiveness'. An indispensable part of this understanding involves getting to grips with the culture of the school – with the norms and values and philosophy that guide policy; 'the rules of the game for getting along in the organization; and the feeling and climate conveyed in the organization' (Stoll and Fink 1996: 81); and, at a deeper level, the shared assumptions and beliefs which operate often at an unconscious level and define an organization's taken-for-granted view of itself and its environment.

This emphasis on 'culture' is evident in descriptions of successful practice. In a summary chapter to a book describing how schools in disadvantaged areas became effective Maden and Hillman (1996) identify several principles and practices which are fairly typical of this paradigm:

1 In each school there was a shared vision of success.
2 The vision became consensual through the provision of genuine opportunities for personal participation in a spirit of active commitment rather than passive compliance.
3 Common and agreed approaches to teaching methods, assessment, discipline and behaviour were established.

4 A common philosophy of education was agreed.
5 The vision was dynamic and responsive to change.
6 The vision took effect when it became an integral part of the identity and daily life of the school.
7 An ethos or cultural climate was developed that was orderly.
8 Staff had high expectations but the causal process went in both directions – positive attitudes amongst teachers boosted the pupils' self-esteem, and in turn high pupil achievement enhanced optimism amongst teachers.
9 The importance of understanding the pupils' perspective was recognized as well as the need to foster their self-understanding as learners who took more control over their own work and had a greater sense of responsibility and more autonomy.
10 An ethos of inclusiveness was established in which all stakeholders, including parents and the wider community, were encouraged to participate actively as partners and potential co-educators and co-learners. Staff shared ownership with parents, pupils and the wider community.
11 The headteacher adopted a style that was interactive and responsive, which involved listening to others and building on their expertise, and which was not dominating or authoritarian but nevertheless influential. An autocratic mode of decision-making was avoided and leadership responsibilities were shared wherever possible.
12 Collegiality was developed through a collaborative staff culture where there was genuine dialogue between different groups.

The emphasis on learning and reflection

In school improvement research, it is also generally recognized that schools need to become learning organizations, and if this is to be achieved then teachers as well as pupils have to become learners. Since change in part stems from the thoughts and actions of teachers, the professional development of teachers is a crucial aspect of the process of school improvement. The emerging paradigm of teacher learning has been largely derived from the tradition of action research in which the notion of teacher as reflective practitioner is a key element. For Elliot (1991) teachers develop their practice through reflection in two ways: reflection initiates action, that is, when research on a particular problem results in a new understanding which requires a change in teaching; and action initiates reflection, that is, when a teacher reflects on a change in teaching approach which is a response to a practical problem. Such research provides opportunities for collaboration as teachers get feedback from others on their researches. According to Stoll and Fink (1996), action research of this kind is only one amongst a number of strategies which help teachers to learn; others include the development of mentoring and coaching relationships, appraisal systems, shared decision-making, team-building, conflict resolution skills and interpersonal effectiveness. The school has a role to play in creating a climate of trust in which staff can help each other with their professional development and where ongoing self-initiated learning can flourish.

Teachers reflect on their own classroom practices, but in the most progressive model of the reflective practitioner they also recognize their responsibilities in relation to the school as a whole and their reflections therefore go beyond the confines of their own practice and address issues in the wider community of learning. Fullan and Hargreaves (1991), quoted in Stoll and Fink (1996), provide a number of guidelines for what they describe as 'interactive professionalism', including the suggestion that teachers attempt to redefine their role to extend beyond the classroom. Other guidelines refer to the need to become committed to working with colleagues, to developing trust in the processes of the system as well as in the people with whom they interact and to developing an appreciation of the total person in working with others. At the same time the interactive professional must look inwards as well as outwards – he or she must 'locate, listen to and articulate the inner voice – each teacher is an important individual and needs personal time and solitude to develop their values and ideas' (Stoll and Fink 1996: 160). He or she must be committed to 'continuous improvement and perpetual learning . . . the best teachers never stop learning and they are always looking to improve their practice' (Stoll and Fink 1996: 161).

Critique

Regarding the Maden and Hillman principles, the first point to note here is that the very idea of a single vision imposed by anyone on an organization as complex as a school is problematical. Educational institutions as structures are 'accomplished' by the many culturally constituted interactions which reflect everyday life in the institution. Structure draws attention to the relatively fixed and routine aspects of interactions; culture to the dynamics, the role of interpretation and potential for change. It is a characteristic of educational institutions as we know them that they will be constituted by many varied and differing interpretations of the priorities and purposes of action within them. Sometimes these features can be identified as conflicts between cultures which relate to the broader structures of society – class, gender, race and so on. But they also refer to more localized practices – for example, pupil culture, the culture of science teachers – and thus to a range of micro-political contexts. The social context of the school, therefore, like all institutional contexts, is not a fixed and singular totality but the site for a number of cultural practices which articulate in various ways and where 'structure' cannot readily be separated from 'culture'.

The crucial failing of the school improvement/school effectiveness paradigm is precisely its inadequate appreciation of the cultural diversity and cultural politics of the school. Its analyses for the most part are not grounded in an understanding of the range of pupil and teacher cultural practices which constitute school life at the formal and informal level or any insight into the way power systems are constructed through these practices. The emphasis on culture seems to preclude a proper examination of structure and thus the hidden politics of routine interactions. Although there is an emphasis on reflection, collaboration, 'voice', learning, staff development and so on, there is very little concern with 'deep reflection' on the curriculum of schooling and the way it structures identities and reproduces inequalities. In particular, it tends to under-emphasize two aspects of the curriculum which are of crucial importance: first, the culture of the *formal curriculum*; and second, the way teachers are constructed as *collaborative* and *reflexive* learning professionals. In both these areas the role of power is underexamined. We shall return to these points later, but first the notion of *power* in this context needs further explication.

Disciplinary power

In exploring the way power works in schools, the work of analysts such as Foucault would appear to be particularly useful. For Foucault (1977), power in the modern age does not stem from one political centre but is exercised in institutions at innumerable points, resulting in the much closer control of individual behaviour required by the economy and society in general. In order to understand how power works, therefore, we have to look closely at local networks of power relations in institutions such as schools, universities, hospitals, prisons and factories rather than (or perhaps in addition to) interpreting social processes in terms of the 'grand narratives' of confrontations between capital and labour or the state and the people. As a strategy of control, modern power is not manifested globally but locally as 'micro-powers'. It operates through 'discipline' which involves the replacement of legal principles with the principles of physical, psychological and moral normality. The operation of *disciplinary power* gives rise to a new kind of bureaucracy, albeit one rooted in the same form of rationality – instrumental rationality. Power is wielded through 'normalization'. It is concerned with the bringing about of a certain kind of individual with certain kinds of characteristics. This new moral technology of bureaucratic control does not arise because people in modern societies are seen as individual agents, but rather individual identity itself is a product of this new form of control. Some of the 'truths' about ourselves which we take to be fundamental, such as our sexual natures, are also produced by this new regime of power. The fact that we accept that we have such a nature makes us objects of control.

Foucault's interpretation of modern power as having a particular kind of association with knowledge is in marked contrast to the conventional definitions of power and knowledge. According to the latter, there is a negative articulation between power and knowledge – the former can disguise the way it operates to repress the individual, whereas knowledge or truth can expose this process and challenge it. For Foucault the intellectual disciplines and institutional control are dialectically related. Schools and school cultures, for example, are made possible and validated by knowledge from various disciplines which are taught in schools and inform school practices; whilst institutional processes produce the kinds of individuals that can be 'known' by studying the disciplines. The word 'discipline' is used in two senses: on the one hand as a branch of knowledge and on the other as a system of correction or control. In the same way as it does with the child, the school constructs teacher identities, giving them certain kinds of selves which can be readily managed by the school, and then proceeds to minister to the selves it has constructed. In this way, Foucault makes us sceptical of all claims to have transformed relations in institutions in a direction which is more democratic and power-free. All differentiations (such as ways of categorizing children or organizing knowledge) are suspect, however benign they may appear at first sight. They will always involve the exercise of power. Even the differentiations teachers make in understanding their own natures will potentially reflect the operations of power.

The formal curriculum

The omission of any serious consideration of the formal curriculum in the school improvement paradigm is symptomatic of its neglect of any critical engagement with power structures which maintain the bureaucratic organization of schools. Within the discourse, there are plenty of references to 'achievement' and 'success' and 'high expectations' but the meaning of achievement is usually unproblematized. Why is there no radical critique of the National Curriculum, for example, in school improvement research? From a Foucauldian perspective it is precisely this curriculum which we should be examining. The subject disciplines function as disciplinary power in a Foucauldian sense – they determine the structure of the school which produces the kinds of individuals that can be identified in terms of the disciplines (for example, students described as of above average, average or below average 'ability' in maths or students who are or who are not 'motivated' in science or have 'special needs' in English). The school timetable has to include 'slots' for the various subject disciplines. Learners are required to receive a 'dose' of each discipline each week, partly because of the amount of ground which subject specialists think needs to be covered and partly because of the model of the learner assumed – one who needs to develop good learning habits and routines.

The subject disciplines are power-coercive systems in that, in the final analysis, they act as a strait-jacket on curriculum development and impede change. They can be updated and reinterpreted, but it is always the case that the content will largely be circumscribed by boundary maintenance activities which are the inevitable accompaniment of curricular practice in a bureaucratized system. These barriers have been further buttressed by the way each subject has been broken down into 'level descriptions' arranged in progressive order of difficulty up to ten levels, and an assessment system which aims to establish clear targets for achievement at every level. This attention to detail in the name of rigour fixes the curriculum in a way which makes cross-discipline 'conversation' and thus the development of collaborative teacher cultures almost impossible. Conversations, such as they are, are confined to technical discussions about 'levels', the organization of teaching and assessment, rather than content. Of course, some statements of attainment are broader than others and open to a wider range of interpretations, and some of the targets themselves – for example, the first attainment target in each of science, maths and English – seem to offer possibilities for progressive development, but the new hierarchical structure of the curriculum and the emphasis in assessment on targets set limits to what can be achieved by working for radical curriculum reform from a subject base. Hierarchies assume a rigid mode of induction where the sequence of learning is invariant for all students – a perspective on learning which in itself fails to recognize diversity and difference in relation to both the content of what is studied and the process of learning. Target-oriented assessment fosters a culture of simplisticism where ambiguity and uncertainty, if not exactly outlawed, are too readily 'bracketed' by various procedural devices. Taken together, they act as a constraint on open forms of learning and convey the message to students that learning a school subject is ultimately about keeping within boundaries rather than moving beyond them.

The collaborative self and the reflective practitioner

Another important aspect of the school improvement paradigm relates to the familiar idea of the reflective practitioner. This can give rise to a rather individualistic view of professional development, but it is typically associated with collaboration rather than individual reflection and decision-making. The reflective practitioner is one who is open to suggestions from colleagues, welcomes participation in learning communities and regularly draws on shared professional knowledge in his or her own practice. Again, however, it is easy to underestimate the extent to which these processes might be an expression of power-constrained relations and a power-induced construction of the reflective self.

The process of learning from reflection on experience implies that space is provided for such reflection in the professional community and that the individual retains a sense of agency in a collaborative context. The reflective practitioner is a team player who is highly sensitive to the factors in the situation which make for constraints or enablements on his or her own agency. He or she needs to have a capacity for the kind of *reflexivity* which I have discussed in previous chapters, where the self of the reflexive agent is of a particular type. In this context we can highlight the following features of the genuinely reflexive reflective practitioner – lack of dogmatic certainty; a willingness to tolerate ambiguity; 'healthy' scepticism; ability to use abstract concepts; a values-led view of self-in-the-world; awareness of dilemmas, tensions, ambiguities and contradictions; a sense of the self 'becoming'; and a sense of history continuing. The latter would entail the acceptance of a non-reified view of the self – one, for example, which did not rely on concepts of a 'natural' self or on a trait model of personality or on a role theory model of the individual in a social context (see Quicke, 1988b).

Thus we need to go beyond the idea of the reflective practitioner as merely a teacher who thinks about and deliberates upon his or her practice. This generic concept of reflection has no heuristic value because it has no substance; it is a catch-all term which can be linked to any educational ideology. Rather we need to think of him or her as more 'deeply' reflective and much more aware of constraints on agency. As John Elliott (1990b: 23) puts it,

> such awareness brings with it insights into the ways in which the self in action is shared and constrained by institutional structures. Self awareness and the awareness of the institutional context of one's work as a teacher are not developed by separate cognitive processes, reflexive and objective analysis. They are qualities of the same reflexive process. Reflexive practice necessarily implies both self critique and institutional critique. One cannot have one without the other.

This, of course, also applies to cultural processes as well as to structures. It is crucial for the development of genuine collaborative cultures that collaborative policies do not just 'capture' the commitment of the individual but do so in ways which allow the individual thus captured to remain an agent. Unfortunately it is too often the case that managements aiming to establish collaborative cultures do not take individual agency seriously; they want individuals to identify voluntarily with the organization but the means they use convey a different message. These features are not always transparent to those on the receiving end of managerial power, not just because of the subtleties of management strategies but also because of how teachers themselves conceive of the 'voluntary participation of the self'. Their understandings of self as agent have already been constructed within certain parameters, the power elements of which may be unacknowledged. This point is crucial to our understanding of how power works in schools. It is the aspect of self-construction which is frequently omitted from analyses of the 'learning professional' within the school improvement paradigm.

We need to bear these points in mind when considering policies allegedly aimed at promoting 'interactive professionalism' in a school context. Stephen Ball's (1990) critique of appraisal schemes is instructive in this respect. The process of appraisal involves certain techniques which make the individual visible and accountable in his or her own 'particularity', and accumulates detailed information in documents which subject the individual to description and comparison; but, as Ball points out, above all it involves a process of co-optation. 'The teacher is encouraged to view the procedures of appraisal as a part of the process of self-understanding and self-betterment – professional development – which Foucault calls "subjectification": the active engagement of the subject in self-formation' (Ball 1990: 161).The appraisal encounter seems to bear all the hallmarks of a Foucauldian 'technology of the self'. It is strikingly similar to the confessional or the psychoanalytic interview in its emphasis on self-revelation and self-judgement but with reference to the norms of the organization, and in the extent to which it therefore 'brings the personal and organizational into intimate relation' (Ball 1990: 161).

Critique of Foucault

The value of Foucauldian perspective is that it continually encourages us to take a close look at how power works in relation to the lived experience of groups and individuals in local contexts. It has been a valuable resource in developing the notion of the reflective practitioner, first elaborated by Schon (1983), because it has helped us to tease out the hidden agendas of power that limit the scope of reflective practice. We now more readily acknowledge that a Schonian professional would have difficulty in becoming genuinely collaborative if he or she failed to take account of power realities – in all their shapes and guises – in the school context and did not fully appreciate the plural and conflictual nature of school culture.

In concluding this discussion, however, it is important to stress that, although the school improvement paradigm has been criticized for its short-comings, the possibility of improvement itself has not been renounced, nor has the central aim, which should continue to be the establishment of 'better' cultures for learning – ones which were more open and genuinely collaborative and which would lead to 'better' forms of schooling. Foucault's own position is notoriously ambiguous in this respect. On certain interpretations, his analysis appears to offer no possibility of progress towards a better state of affairs. The only prospect is the transformation of one 'regime of truth' into another. There is a certain incoherence here in Foucault's position, which revolves around the relationship between power and domination. As he explains:

> Power is not an evil . . . Let us . . . take something that has been the object of criticism, often justified: the pedagogical institution. I don't

see where evil is in the practice of someone who, in a given name of truth, knowing more than another, teaches him [*sic*] . . . The problem is rather to know how you are to avoid in these practices – where power cannot not play and where it is not evil in itself – the effects of domination . . .

(Foucault 1988: 18)

This seems to suggest that practices, though they must involve power, need not involve domination. But what does the exercise of power mean if there is no one on the receiving end of it? The deployment of power must involve imposing something on someone. Presumably what Foucault means is that the exercise of power need not necessarily result in one individual or group being permanently subjected to the diktat of another individual or group, but that there is always the possibility of the 'circulation of power', as he puts it. People as participants in the discourse of a practice are never completely without power and therefore never without agency and thus the potential to initiate change.

In view of this, at the level of the self, it seems to me that we can speak of some practices or technologies of the self as being 'better' than others in the sense of having greater possibilities for the 'circulation of power' and for self making. Reflections on the self are constrained within disciplinary frameworks, but some of these frameworks are preferable from a democratic perspective than others. Indeed, there is some suggestion in Foucault that he himself deploys ethical criteria in his notion of 'care for the self', where he is concerned, as Gore (1993: 29) points out, 'with the models proposed for setting up and developing relationships with the self, for self reflection, self knowledge, self examination, for the decipherment of the self by oneself, for the transformations one seeks to accomplish with oneself as object'. This is not just about self-fascination or about being interested in the self for its own sake, but suggests an ethic of self-invention, of reassembling the 'already said' and attempting to reveal the hidden. Collaborative cultures, if they are genuine, would be able to foster this kind of approach to the self – one that involved theories of the self and frameworks for self-interpretation which maximized the scope for making moral choices and for developing insights into how power operates in an institutional context.

Concluding comment

The new professionalism should have a similar social and moral purpose to the traditional professionalism as envisaged by Tawney, but it would have to be more self-conscious about the need to create and re-create collaborative culture and reflexive selves. These aspects are interrelated. Thus, the focus on self-knowledge and the awareness of internalized constraints is integral to the development of a collaborative mode of relating both to colleagues and clients. The aim of self-analysis is, so to speak, to pull down the barriers which restrict imaginative engagement with the unique perspective of the other and hold back the development of genuine dialogue and mutual understanding. The activity called self-analysis is not a self-contained activity, carried out away from the scene of the action. It may sometimes involve temporal or spatial separation but it is still essentially embedded in social action. The self of the professional is always salient but it will not always be the object of reflection. Other objects such as the selves of others or the structures of institutions will also figure. Indeed, were they never to be foregrounded, then it is difficult to see how the self could be understood as an agent or as a product in a dialectical relation.

Like John Berger's 'fortunate man', the new professional will attempt to move beyond the understanding of self, colleagues and clients in one-dimensional terms, as institutionalized identities or technically constructed types, towards a broader understanding of the whole personality in context. He or she will first attempt to recognize the other as a person, and then convey that recognition to the other – a process which involves the constant return of 'disquieting questions' rather than the resolution of problems through the mechanical application of expertise. As Berger (1967: 135) writes of John Sassall, the country doctor :

> the harder he works, the more insistently they [the disquieting questions] are posed. Whenever he makes an effort to recognize a patient, he is forced to recognize his or her undeveloped potentiality. . . . If as a doctor he is concerned with the total personality of his patients and if he realizes, as he must, that a personality is never an entirely fixed entity, then he is bound to take note of what inhibits, drives or diminishes it.

Yet Sassall reads medical journals and keeps himself up to date, even though he knows that, in relation to any individual patient, 'no previous explanation will exactly fit, because they depend on the history of a patient's particular personality' (Berger 1967: 62). His professional knowledge, including the Freudian psychology he uses in self-exploration, is a resource which he deploys in attempting to go beyond conservative and unreflective common sense (see Berger 1967: 102) but he clearly does not think medical expertise is enough. He creates 'new knowledge' by challenging orthodoxies and opening up new avenues of enquiry through the care he takes to recognize his patients as persons. Sassall cares for the self in a Foucauldian sense, and he would recognize the kinds of 'danger' to which Foucault alludes. Thus his starting point in the self – the way he accepts 'his innermost feelings and intuitions as clues' (Berger 1967: 102) – is literally that – a starting point – which may eventually involve a re-evaluation of the significance of those feelings and intuitions.

The new professional, therefore, is not one who regards expertise as nothing but 'disciplinary power' but rather one who sees the need to make judicious use of expertise without being dominated by one knowledge form or another; and who recognizes that central to professional activity is the quest to understand the other as person, in the full knowledge that people's personalities are not fixed but ever changing, and in 'new times' are constantly being 'made' and reinvented. As for institutions, she or he has to be wary of being seduced by the appeal of technical-rational 'restructuring', particularly when it is market-driven, whilst at the same time recognizing that institutions are not all of a piece ideologically and that institutionalization itself is not anti-professional. This is the challenge for the 'new professionalism'. Is it possible for professionals to think and act in an open and creative way in institutions in which the language of collaboration is pervasive but where the reality is often rather different? Can they avoid being trapped in bureaucracies of a new kind? Can professional knowledge become a form of knowledge which genuinely prompts the enquiries of practitioners? Or will it always tend to close down more than it opens up? Can professionals avoid reductionism? Can they recognize improvement when they see it? Will professionals become 'fortunate' men and women – that is, will they be able to unite work, life and the search for knowledge; will they be able to believe in the meaning of what they are doing and in the moral worth of their projects?

5 | Pupils' cultural practices and collaborative group work

Introduction

It would be an odd thing if collaborative group work were not seen as fundamental to the process of education since it is only through participating in communicative social action that human beings learn anything at all. And from the earliest years, these acts of communication are always two-way. This is particularly true of that form of communication called 'talk'. Endemic to all forms of talk between human beings is a principle of co-operation, however minimalist this may be. As Pinker (1994: 228) points out, the very act of communication 'relies on a mutual expectation of cooperation between speaker and listener'. These features are intrinsic to language acquisition and inhere in our linguistic or, to use Habermas's term, communicative competence. For Habermas (1979), every speech act, and in fact all language, however distorted, oppressive and debased, reflects a basic consensus about the purpose of and the need for speech, such that the ideal communicative situation or ideal speech situation of dialogue, reciprocity and collaboration is prefigured.

Thus all learning in classrooms relies on the already existing communicative capacities of pupils and teachers to relate to each other in ways which foster their own and others' learning. The teacher is as much a participant in this as the pupil; he or she is inevitably a learner as well as a teacher, just as the pupils are teachers as well as learners. However, when Habermas refers to every speech act prefiguring the ideal speech situation, he means precisely that. The ideal is there to be glimpsed, but we are acknowledging potential rather than realization. Take a look at relationships in any particular classroom – although there are always hopeful signs, actual practices in the here and now leave much to be desired.

As we have seen, in the learning society of reflexive modernity, it is particularly important to foster a collaborative approach to the way teaching and learning are organized in schools. We can examine the collaborative curriculum in a number of different spheres in schools, but in this chapter I shall be concerned with *collaborative group work* as a teaching and learning strategy, with particular reference to the relationship between the official discourse of learning and the unofficial learning of pupils' cultural practices. The main argument of the chapter is that, when it comes to the development of collaborative competence, social insight and reflexivity in school contexts, pupil culture is a most important 'natural' resource. This is not to say that all aspects of such cultures are compatible with educational goals – indeed, they are as full of contradictions as any other school-based culture – but the point will be stressed that an appreciation of such cultures, warts and all, is indispensable if the aim is to foster collaborative group work as a practice which will take root in the school curriculum. Without this sensitivity to the ongoing cultural 'work' of pupils, not only will teaching interventions fail to use the existing communicative competences of pupils, but they might well be undermined by failing to acknowledge that pupils' first allegiance is often to an alternative cultural agenda.

Fostering conversation

To begin with, we need to clarify in more detail just what is 'good' about collaborative group work in its ideal form from an educational and democratic perspective. Genuine collaboration reflects a mode of relating which is highly desirable in a democracy, one that has an intrinsic value and is highly functional for learning. It involves dialogue and conversation. The goal of 'pure' dialogue expresses equality and community in its recognition of perfect mutuality and recognition of the other as an equal partner. A genuine dialogue is one that involves 'turn-taking' and sharing feelings, which are typical features of what linguistic analysts call 'conversation'. Conversation is a form of communication which involves 'talk between equals'. It is an open kind of talk which is organized as it goes along because none of the participants has the right to take unilateral decisions about how ordered action is to be achieved. It is a form which promotes an interplay between different frames of reference which different speakers bring to the encounter; a creative kind of talk, enjoyed for its own sake, which at its best is spontaneous and exploratory as participants bounce ideas off each other. It should be unconstrained by the intervention of any powerful other to disrupt the flow of thought and reflection (see Hadley 1980). For conversation is not only 'talk between equals' in the way turns are organized or topics chosen but also 'talk without a predetermined expert, and without constraints to reach authoritatively defined conclusions' (Edwards and Westgate 1987: 45).

In a school context, collaborative work requires pupils to decide for themselves how they are going to construct orderly talk. In small groups the

purposes and rules of communication have to be negotiated and unacceptable forms of domination resisted or avoided. This process of negotiation
helps *meaningful learning* because all pupils are encouraged to make a
contribution and to enter into dialogue with others on an equal basis; this
usually involves taking note of others' ideas, comparing them with their
own, negotiating differences and shaping meanings for themselves and
others. The ideal group is one where individuals feel they can take risks and
try things out. Traditional forms of teaching may be dysfunctional for intellectual development because they do not allow a wide enough range of
opinions and idiosyncratic experience to be expressed and taken into
account.

At a deeper level, individuals are encouraged or 'provoked' by the group
(see Greenhalgh 1994: 192) to articulate thoughts and feelings which they
may not have given expression to before. Relating in a group can bring
pupils out of themselves but at the same time help them to become more self-
aware. And, of course, in the contemporary context this awareness would
involve recognizing the multiplicity of potential or quasi-selves which
inhabit the peculiarly open and differentiated self of the modern world. As
Greenhalgh (1994: 197) acknowledges, the group, since it is itself pluralist,
can help the individual 'get in touch with, and tap the potential of, inner
resources' of the pluralist psyche; 'we seek and find our potential through
pluralistic experience, and often look for this in groups'.

In general, in facilitating the development of collaborative groups, we
would need to foster participants' commitment to common beliefs and
values grounded in the basic core values of democracy and education. This
would entail an understanding that 'the activity itself should promote certain values, such as sensitivity to others, a willingness to listen, supportive-
ness, the freedom to take risks, tolerance for all contributions, no matter
how tentatively expressed; it should also involve frequent opportunities to
reflect on and evaluate shared experiences' (Cowie and Rudduck 1995: 5).
All participants, in other words, should be regarded as agents who choose
to interact with others on an equal basis.

Contextualization and the need for reflexivity

Teaching approaches which aim to foster collaborative group work have to
be considered in context. In the school situation there are forces at work
which both facilitate and constrain developments in this area. Teachers
clearly need to be aware of these, but in this chapter I shall be particularly
concerned with pupil awareness. An important characteristic of the genuinely collaborative group is its capacity to promote personal and social
reflexivity. Reflexivity in this context implies becoming more aware of how
the group worked – how it involved a process of negotiating meaning and

constructing shared understandings – but also how it was constrained or enabled by the social, cultural and political context in which it was located. Thus a group that was working well would be one that reflected upon pragmatic issues – what it needed to do to survive in a particular context and to cope with dysfunctional factors, such as the intrusion of powerful others in the group process. It would also need to be reflexive about its own dynamic nature – the fact that it was never completely static and that this was a 'positive' rather than a 'negative' feature, as was the capacity for openness so that others could be admitted to the group and conversations could take place with other groups.

At the level of talk it is important to bear in mind that the putative collaborative group does not exist *in* a social environment but already contains the environment within itself, so to speak. The 'presses' of various social and cultural practices are already evident via their contribution to the construction of 'speech acts' – in the way speakers speak to each other and understand what has been spoken in the group. But what exactly is involved here? In answering this it will be useful to consider Barnes and Todd's (1981) view that speech acts involve two 'frames' – the 'content' and the 'interactional'. The former refers to talk which is about thoughts a speaker wants to communicate about the topic being discussed, whereas talk relating to the interaction frame conveys a view of the relationship between the speaker and the listener. The authors identify ways in which pupils' contributions are constrained by the competitive nature of the communication system of the groups they are in. They also observe how pupils terminate discussion too soon and reach a contrived consensus too quickly because of the possible consequences of disagreeing with friends.

However, though Barnes and Todd's concept of frames is useful, it requires further elaboration. Interactional frames are far more complex than suggested in the examples provided. They are usually not coherent 'wholes' but can be broken down into a number of different perspectives and practices. A better approach might be to examine interaction sequences in terms of the conflicting and competing discourses which are drawn upon by individuals as they position themselves in relation to others. In so doing one would need to look at far bigger 'chunks' of interaction across a number of sites and in relations between a number of groups and individuals. It is here, I think, that the notion of pupil culture is important. Cultures might include a number of interactional frames, all of which are at least potentially invocable in an interaction sequence but, as we know from studies of pupil cultures, may convey contradictory messages. The question is: given that we have some idea of what we are aiming for in terms of collaborative goals, to what extent do the informal cultures of pupils facilitate or impede the realization of such goals? To think positively, in what ways are their purposes and processes to be regarded as strengths on which a good educator can build?

Pupil cultures

In what follows I shall make a few general points about pupil cultures before going on to provide specific illustrations of their connections with educational processes. What sociologists describe as pupil culture has often been regarded with suspicion by teachers. It has been seen as a vehicle for the introduction of commercial and anti-educational elements into the curriculum, as a threat to the disciplinary structure of the school and as a divisive rather than an integrative force in the school community. But, on the other hand, pupil cultures can be viewed more benignly. They seem to represent the first steps towards personal autonomy for the pupils concerned. They seem to be about pupils acting as agents, about them taking initiatives and taking control of their own lives and acting on their own without reference to adults. They often appear to involve 'spontaneity' and 'creativity'. They are also often an attempt by pupils to establish a form of social order characterized by mutual respect and the absence of power relations, although because the social circumstances as a whole are oppressive these aspects are not always easy to discern.

This optimistic view of pupil culture is derived from assumptions about the nature and origins of this form of life which need to be clarified. Pupil cultures are seen as versions of child or adolescent cultures, which are themselves a function of the way childhood is constituted in modern societies. The social, cultural, political and economic processes which precipitated the 'invention' of childhood are complex and there is not sufficient space to explore them at length here. In passing, we can mention the need for a new kind of labour force at the end of the nineteenth century which required different forms of socialization resulting in a longer period of dependency than in pre-industrial traditional societies, where children were allegedly given much more independence (Pollard 1985: 38). But whilst undoubtedly economic factors played a part, at another level an important contributing factor at this time was the fundamental reconstitution of the relationship between the individual and society which, amongst other things, led to the need for a preparatory phase in individual development. Thus a period of dependence called childhood (and thus later childhood and adolescence) was paradoxically a function of the value given to independence. If it was a time when the young were defined as more dependent, it was also a time when the independence of the individual became possible. In a sense children, although they may have been given 'little adult' status in traditional societies, were not independent in the modern meaning of the term since such independence was not possible.

As far as schools are concerned, recognition of the potential of children to become autonomous adults should lead to an authority structure which is ideally liberal paternalistic rather than authoritarian (see Aviram 1991). In the former the use of a certain amount of coercion is justified in the context of an overall aim to foster the development of pupils as autonomous persons and of a view of childhood as an exceptional period when the principle of equal relations does not apply. In this situation pupil culture may be regarded as an attempt by pupils to become more genuinely self-determining by setting up their own communities in a way which for the most part should be supportive of and supported by the democratic teacher. In fact, it might be argued that the development of pupil culture should be celebrated as an indication of how a school was becoming more rather than less of an educational community. Such cultures might be seen as inevitable developments in a society which purports to be open and democratic, because there is the expectation in such societies that the next generation will want to change things and act creatively rather than just repeat traditional ways of behaving and reproduce the status quo. It suggests that young people are exercising their rights to inherit and alter the cultural legacy as they see fit. The hope of the older generation is that they will do so in a way that builds on the best of the past.

Some conflict in pupil–teacher relations is almost inevitable, since there will always be a tension between freedom and paternalism even in relation to practices which are genuinely educational. On the one hand the young have to be inducted into the cultural traditions which will equip them to live a full life and enable them to self-improve, whilst at the same time they are expected to experiment and try things out for themselves without any interference from adults. It is a commonplace that teachers and indeed parents, in their treatment of the young, have to tread a fine line between these two facets of growing up.

That said, however, there are enormous differences between pupils' cultural actions with respect to their educational value. Some cultures, for example, are enabling in the sense that they operate in a way which is consonant with educational goals; others build upon their members' initial resistance towards teachers and schools to produce cultural identities which are not only anti-school but also anti-educational. In order to understand pupils' adaptations, however, we need to look at the pressures they experience in the school context as well as what they hope to obtain from the educational encounter. Pupils' cultural values may not be ideal but nor is the official culture of the school ideal from an educational viewpoint. Not only are the formal practices in which pupils are supposed to participate compulsory, but their status as educationally valuable activities is questionable.

So what are we to make of pupil cultures? Clearly, in the light of the foregoing, our initial response might be one of optimism. However anti-school and anti-educational or 'deviant' or 'conformist' they may seem, at least pupils are represented as active agents rather than passive objects; at least they are seen to be making some attempt to control their own lives and to act in solidarity with others. There is some potential for autonomy and a sense of community here which, as educators, we can recognize and work with. But although the ideas, values and beliefs which inform pupils' cultural actions would have to be appreciated and understood by teachers, they would also have to be critically engaged with. It is a question of establishing dialogues with pupil cultures rather than accepting them at face value, rejecting them out of hand or ignoring them altogether. Of course, teachers and adults generally may be reluctant to relate to pupil cultures because they would see it as involving an illegitimate intervention in what is, after all, in part at least, an expression of pupils' desire to escape from adult surveillance. But I am assuming here that all educational practice worthy of the name cannot but take into account the 'views of the world' of both the teachers and the learners. The very idea of establishing a dialogue implies a conception of pupil cultures as 'ongoing', relatively autonomous systems situated in a context where they inevitably interact at some level with other cultures, including the official culture of the school.

A democratic society, therefore, allows space for the development of pupil culture within the benign constraints of liberal paternalism. Since it is fired in the same furnace, so to speak, as democracy and education, we would expect to find elements within it which would be consonant with the aims of liberal democratic education. At the same time, however, because present social arrangements are not ideal from a democratic viewpoint we would also expect the various imperfections and contradictions of society to be reflected in pupils' cultural practices.

Pupils in action: an evaluative framework

Establishing dialogues with pupil cultures involves making judgements based on an understanding of conflicts of value within those cultures. In what follows, I shall explicate and illustrate an evaluative framework which might act as a guide when making such judgements. It has two major aspects. The first is the reflexive aspect which involves the use of a modified version of Willis's (1977) distinction between *penetrations* and *limitations*. That author coined the term 'penetration' to describe the insights of the group of working-class 'lads' in his study into their social position in relation to the education system and society as a whole. But the lads held ideas and had concerns which were self-defeating and counterproductive. He referred to these as 'limitations'. If penetrations were useful insights into their social existence, limitations were those conceptions which prevented those insights being developed in a way which enabled the lads to break with their occupational destinies. My use of the terms is similar to this but refers specifically to educational principles. Thus, the term 'penetrations' refers to insights into teaching and learning processes derived from and consonant with democratic educational principles, whilst the term 'limitations' refers to pupils' conceptions which are self-restricting and incompatible with such principles.

The second feature of the evaluative framework involves reference to the typical themes of pupil culture which, according to Woods (1983), revolve around three elements – *relationships, status* and *competence.* In an ideal situation one might suggest that relationships would be developed in a way that was supportive and 'open', status would be defined as dignity for all individuals in the group and competence would be defined as the ability to behave democratically in groups. However, in practice we know that these themes can be enacted in ways which are anti-educational and undemocratic. Relationships might involve friendships with peers and attitudes to teachers which are dysfunctional for learning. Status can be expressed in terms of a status hierarchy with all the negative features that accompany this, such as labelling and stereotyping. Competence might refer to conformity to class, race or gender roles in a manner which is restricting rather then liberating.

The cultural practices of pupils in schools are likely to involve a number of contradictory elements rather than be purely of one orientation or another. Following Pollard (1985), it is useful to conceive of pupils having a range of immediate interests stemming from cultural themes. In relation to classroom events, pupils often 'juggle' their interests in the ebb and flow of interaction. They do this, according to Pollard (1985: 155), 'to seek an overall level of satisfaction of the self' and purposive activity is thus focused on primary concerns to do with several facets of the self.

'Best friends': a case study of an intervention designed to foster collaborative group work

An example of the deployment of this framework in an action research context can be found in a study carried out by Quicke and Winter (1995). The study involved a fully contextualized account of how two high-achieving 13-year-old girls, Joanne and Karen, reacted to a teaching intervention designed to foster collaborative group work. The girls resisted the official practice of collaborative work, but their resistance was not all of a piece. At times they were co-operative, seemed to recognize the value of collaboration and did make attempts to communicate with other pupils in a collaborative way. The tensions and contradictions in their relationships with each other and with other pupils often reflected the conflicting imperatives of their cultural practices. However, in general their dominant interest was in retaining their identity as high achievers relative to other pupils and the main strategy they used to accomplish this was derived from a perspective grounded in a fairly coherent world view which is illuminated in the account.

The teaching intervention involved working with small groups of pupils in ways which encouraged them to communicate dialogically and reflexively. The girls were part of a group which was carrying out a collaborative enquiry in science. The members of the group were required to follow a strategy which they were then asked to reflect upon, discuss and alter as they saw fit. In evaluating the responses of the two girls to collaborative activity, it was important to understand the friendship patterns and social relationships in which the girls were enmeshed and how these were accomplished. The girls were 'best friends' and therefore had the mutually supportive, *alter ego* type of relationship said to be more typical of girls than boys at this age, where pupils 'appear to feed and feed off each other's desired identities, and hence seem to grow together' (Measor and Woods 1984: 105). But what was this relationship based on? Whose interests were served? Was it too exclusive and too much of a 'closed shop'? Did it in fact facilitate the 'growth' of the girls in an educational sense? In what follows we begin by looking at what this friendship seemed to mean to the two girls.

Karen and Joanne's perception of their relationship seemed to be guided by similar values to those which Davies (1979) found amongst friendship groups in her study. They clearly wanted *their* relationship to be collaborative and mutually beneficial, and felt they had achieved this kind of relationship in their day-to-day interaction. If the rest of the pupils in the class had pursued these values in all their relationships then the class would have become a democratic community of pupils, and this would undoubtedly have facilitated the implementation of collaborative teaching and learning strategies. However, if one examined the two girls' behaviour in general, there was evidence of an ambivalent attitude towards collaborative friendships. On the one hand when describing the micro-culture of their own relationship and, at the level of rhetoric, when they were describing ideal *relationships* with others, they saw these through the prism of a democratic perspective, but on the other hand in many of their descriptions of actual relationships and in their day-to-day practices other values were evident. Thus it was clear that they did view friendship groups as more exclusive and 'closed' than they publicly admitted, that *status* for them was often a hierarchical affair and that *competence* was defined in relation to narrowly conceived academic criteria.

The girls attended an 11–16 comprehensive school on the outskirts of a northern city. They both came from what might be described as upper working-class backgrounds. Their economic awareness and sense of social structure may well have been influenced by the favourable material conditions in which both lived relative to other pupils. It is a sociological commonplace that people who live in predominantly working-class neighbourhoods use the terms 'rough' and 'respectable' to distinguish various persons and locations in their own neighbourhood, whilst at the same time still recognizing the neighbourhood as a whole as in some sense a community – see, for example, Hall and Jefferson (1976). In recent years this sense of community has broken down in many areas due to the ravages of unemployment and the under-resourcing of public amenities.

Relations with other girls

The tension between the democratic and hierarchical principle was nowhere more evident than in Joanne and Karen's relationship with other girls in the class. Neither of them would make explicit the view that they did not want to work collaboratively in a group with other girls, with whom on the whole they had reasonably good relations. They could easily be recruited to a common cause based on the gender divide. They were just as angry and annoyed about the boys' disruptive behaviour and they could be just as supportive of a girl in trouble as could any of the other girls. Nevertheless, it was clear from their behaviour and from their interpretations of the nature of group work that they preferred to work in a collaborative way as an exclusive pair with their own standards of work and their own code of conduct. If another girl wanted to join them, and several made an attempt to do so, then this 'outsider' would have to conform to the rules that Joanne and Karen laid down.

Acting in concert as 'best friends' was a survival strategy which realized several immediate interests; there were those to do with maintaining their position at the top of the academic hierarchy and those which were more focused on securing support for the emerging self. In a sense, in so far as Joanne's own aspirations as a high achiever were bound up in her relationship with Karen she had an interest in making sure that her *alter ego* was functioning as an ontologically secure, 'together' person. The nature of this friendship was reflected in and also constitutive of the duo's orientation to other pupils. Thus any pupil who was perceived as a threat to this relationship was likely, at some point, to be socially distanced, whatever their perceived academic *status*, and, of course, if they were perceived as a lower achiever they would be distanced for more than one reason.

One of the ambivalences in the two girls' view of the world was reflected in their social class attitudes. Whilst on the one hand they distinguished between the 'rough' and the 'respectable' in their own area they were also aware of the difference between the class to which they and all their classmates belonged and the class of 'posh' people to which teachers belonged. Their evaluations of teachers were *penetrative* in the sense of the term used above; they objected to teachers who were arrogant and distant, who did not treat them like people, who lectured at them, who did not talk things over with them and who did not know the names of individual pupils. They would act in solidarity with pupils against teachers when they judged that an injustice had been perpetrated by the latter on the former. In this respect they could be extremely supportive, and indeed open, democratic and collaborative in their relations with peers, both boys and girls.

Relations with boys

Like other first-year classes in this school, Joanne and Karen's class had an imbalance of boys and girls, there being 18 boys and only 11 girls. In the year as a whole two-thirds of the pupils were boys. The boys were perceived by the teachers as more disruptive than the girls, and the girls complained bitterly about the boys' misbehaviour in lessons. The boys' informal relations were influenced by an emergent male macho culture as they progressed through the year, even though this culture was not the force it was, perhaps due to economic changes. For their part, Karen and Joanne used a variety of constructs when referring to boys. Boys were one of their main topics of conversations. One of the other girls thought that Joanne was 'always talking about boys'. They both said they had boyfriends in other classes. In common with most other girls in the class, they liked boys who were 'sexy', who were 'jokers' and who 'got on with their work'. They disliked boys who were 'silly' or who went 'giddy' or who, in Joanne's words, 'treated girls like toys'. On the whole, the boys in the class were perceived by both sexes as less academically competent – less 'brainy' – than the girls. Even the most able boys in the class tended to hold this view of themselves in relation to the 'top' girls. At this stage the link between 'braininess', femininity and dull conformity did not appear to have been made.

But their view of most boys as 'immature' was by far the most salient construct in relation to collaborative work. The researchers witnessed several events where this view was reinforced by the teachers. On one occasion, when the boys had been particularly disruptive in lessons, the girls were taken aside and received explanations as to why boys were silly at that age and informed of what disciplinary action was to be taken against them. Incidents like this merely confirmed what Joanne and Karen felt they already knew about boys in their peer group. 'Immaturity' could be interpreted in a number of ways, but what all shades of meaning had in common was reference to 'facts' about child and adolescent development which put boys on a lower rung than girls on the maturity ladder.

Examples like this seem to reflect the predicament that most girls are in – one which has a direct bearing on the idea of collaboration. On the one hand boys' behaviour and attitudes are clearly disruptive of collaborative activity across the sex divide, but on the other the explanations that are available to girls, couched as they are in psycho-biological terms, seem likely to lead to further constraints on collaborative activity. The development of boys' self-regulatory and collaborative behaviour is further constrained by using reductionist concepts to legitimize their continued infantilization; whilst the girls are being encouraged to counter themselves being treated as 'objects' by treating boys as 'objects', and moreover 'objects' which they as females may eventually have maternal responsibility for. The paradox is that being encouraged to see boys as more childlike than themselves, in a sexist world where 'care for children' is primarily associated with the female role, could well be interpreted to mean that allowances should be made for boys in the same way as allowances are made for children, and that one-way collaboration, with girls always helping the boys, is seen as part of a girl's duty. Such explanations may be 'good' neither for boys nor girls from an educational viewpoint; they exemplify a *limitation* of their capacity for developing genuine insight into each other's behaviour.

However, although both Joanne and Karen, along with other girls, used these reductionist constructs to explain away boys' behaviour, it was also evident in their actions that these constructs were jostling with others with which they were in contradiction. Although they used words like 'thick' to describe other pupils, particularly boys, they were aware of labelling processes and did not want to be thought of as 'boffs' of the class. 'Boffs' were not just clever or 'brainy' people but were those who tried to separate themselves off from everyone else, who were 'stuck up' and who liked to show they were cleverer than other people. In relation to pupils who were called 'thick' the girls agreed that you could not always 'judge a book by its cover' and, if you did, you might unfairly label someone. They clearly understood the notion of labelling but recognized that the label did not have to determine a person's behaviour.

Summary

For these two aspiring working-class girls, the power systems of rank, class and gender were in constant interaction such that it was difficult to pinpoint which of them had the greatest weight in any one instance, let alone over a period of time. In all areas the girls' responses reflected both their capacities for *penetrative* social insight and their *limitations*. Examples of the former would be their appreciation of the effects of labelling, their view that they did not want to be identified as 'posh' or as 'boffs', their support for girls who were the targets of sexist comments from boys and their solidarity with pupils against the 'improper' behaviour of teachers. These seemed to reflect attitudes which were about redressing the balance in power relations and were derived from the assumption that all pupils were of equal value. However, on the negative side, the girls in their day-to-day practices did in fact discriminate against pupils they perceived as inferior to themselves in terms of academic competence and rejected those they saw as a threat to their survival as high achievers. In the final analysis it is arguable whether or not these girls' achievements were at the level they could have been had their collaborative action been less discriminatory and had they been less competitive. Their typical mode of learning was only minimally reflective as they went about the daily task of 'getting things done' in an effort to keep ahead of others. The micro-culture of their 'best friends' relationship certainly did not help in this respect. It made them far too inward-looking and resistant to 'outside' influences, so much so that on occasion they often failed to recognize the value of other pupils' positive contributions to the learning process.

Concluding comment

Teaching interventions which had the aim of fostering collaborative group work would have to take into account the pupils' sophisticated use of social strategies, their awareness of group dynamics, their capacities for 'political' action in their everyday relationships (see Quicke 1995) and their intuitive cultural understandings of democracy and hierarchy. They would have to be based on an appreciative rather than deficit view of these pupils as social actors, building on the strengths of pupils' cultural practices rather than focusing on their weaknesses from a democratic and educational viewpoint. The aim would be to make their understanding of the nature of democratic discourse more explicit and thus provide them with the reflective skills and qualities to refine and develop their existing democratic practices and to be more critical of undemocratic elements within their own cultures and in the social environment of the school.

There is usually a balance to be struck here. On the one hand, pupils need space for the development of their own cultural forms – how they want to construct their relationships, how they want to define friendship, how they want to conduct their lives as persons free of adult surveillance. On the other, the forms of life they create may need to be challenged if not perceived by teachers to be in the pupils' best educational interests in the short or long term. In general, fostering collaborative group work and becoming appreciative of pupil culture are dialectically related. A teacher who creates an open classroom where there are plenty of opportunities for collaboration and dialogue is likely to create the conditions in which pupils are more willing to give voice to their own preoccupations and concerns which can then be taken account of by the teacher in his or her attempts to extend and deepen the collaborative process.

6 | Teaching for cultural pluralism

Introduction

Societies have always had to accommodate cultural differences, but in reflexive modernity the situation has become more dynamic. Cultural identities have become less fixed and more open to revision and development. Moreover, as the scope for cultural interaction increases in a multiplicity of contexts via new communication systems, so the opportunities for experimentation and negotiation give rise to an increasing diversity of new cultural forms, each wanting 'space' and resources for its own expression and development. These new forms draw selectively on existing cultures and through a process of creative dialogue generate new syntheses. Thus elements of one culture – its artistic expression, its lifestyles, its religious beliefs and so on – become taken up by another in a way which enriches and also changes the host form. These mutual borrowings and reciprocities are potentially enriching to cultural life in society as a whole.

In a democratic society this 'flowering' of cultural communities would be seen as a healthy sign, since it would be an expression of the central values of democracy – the freedom of individuals and groups to develop their idiosyncratic identities and live according to their own beliefs and values unconstrained by external forces. Clearly, problems would arise over resource allocation but in general one would expect these to be resolved amicably, since it would be in no one's interests to undermine democracy by imposing their own will. Schools in such a society would represent the social and political framework in microcosm. Thus they would establish the conditions for cultures to emerge and flourish by providing opportunities for cultural expression and intra-cultural and inter-cultural dialogue. Such conditions would require all pupils to be citizens with an allegiance to democratic rules and practices in addition to their specific allegiances to the cultures which constituted their identities.

Schools and other institutions which subscribed to what Mouffe (1993:

83) describes as the 'articulating principle of democracy' would provide a dynamic framework in which cultures could develop and function in the reflexive, open and self-critical way appropriate to community life in a plural and global society. In effect, this would mean developing a multicultural curriculum based on a notion of culture which had certain key characteristics: a capacity for providing a 'home' and a sense of belonging for its members which was enriching and self-fulfilling for the individuals concerned and which empowered them as agents; a capacity for self-recognition as a social form in the process of 'becoming' rather than as a fixed entity; and a capacity for self-evaluation through critical 'conversation' both between elements within its own conceptual framework or, to use Foucault's term, 'regime of truth', and between itself and other cultures.

The purpose of the multicultural curriculum would be to encourage cultures to develop along these lines. And, of course, there would be many constraints on this process, some of which, as we know from past experience, are derived from anti-democratic forces which run deep in society even when it has ostensibly become more progressive. Thus, in developing a multicultural curriculum, schools would have to be aware of the many ways in which the project could be undermined and the many different forms that a counter-activity could take, from the promulgation of questionable beliefs about the nature of culture itself to overtly oppressive approaches towards particular cultures. In what follows I shall examine some of the ways we need to think about culture and inter-cultural interaction if we are to develop the curriculum in a manner which reflects a sensitivity to the many adverse factors we are likely to encounter. To begin with, I shall take a critical look at a particular view of culture which has been influential in recent years because of its association with the dominant New Right ideology.

The 'normality' of prejudice thesis

There is a certain view of culture which, correctly in my view, highlights the tension between the 'belonging' aspect on the one hand and the self-reflexive and conversational potentialities on the other. Liberal educational programmes often focus on the latter. The 'belonging' aspect of culture is associated with pre-judgements, which are regarded as phenomena to be clarified and critically reflected upon. Such reflective activity need not result in the elimination of pre-judgements. This may be the fate of some, but others will be further elaborated and refined by educational processes. The idea is that once articulated and made visible through critical reflection, pre-judgements can be assessed in rational terms, enabling a person to become more fully conscious of their significance for his or her identity and sense of purpose. If 'good education' involves encouraging students to provide reasons in support of a point of view and to show respect for evidence then clearly education has inherent within it an antagonism to unreflective action in accordance with pre-judgements.

However, this formulation of the relationship between education and cultural pre-judgement seems to place the 'belonging' aspect of culture in a negative light. The inevitable tension between this and the reflective aspect is resolved in favour of the latter; it is the latter which is pro-educational and rational and the former which is anti-educational and irrational. But is this downgrading of the non-reflective component of culture justified? In addressing this issue, we need to consider an important objection to the rationalistic view – an objection which involves taking a different stance from the latter on the value of pre-judgements and the 'normality' of the prejudice of the members of a culture in favour of those pre-judgements. According to Jones (1988), far from being 'negative', the shared prejudices one has in favour of certain pre-judgements and foundational beliefs make for community and social stability via attachment to a 'home form of life'. These basic beliefs are grounded in the way we have acquired our basic understanding of the social world – a world we are born into and which is not of our own making. We are thus immersed in a particular culture which provides us with a ready made scheme – a system of basic meanings or 'foundational pre-judgements' (Jones 1988: 40) – for acting in and inter-preting the world. Often, then, our prejudice is not to question our pre-judgements, or at least not all of them, because to do so is to question an identity to which we feel emotionally and morally attached and to which, for the sake of the survival of our community, we indeed should feel so attached. We may not deliberate on this too much, but we sense the import-ance for our well-being as ontologically secure selves of our continuing allegiance. To force upon ourselves, as a result of too much critical reflec-tion, a state of alienation and also, via the same process, a destruction of community, far from being rational, is arguably itself irrational. Allegiance to pre-judgements is 'natural' in the sense that it reflects the way human beings go about the business of producing and reproducing themselves and their society. We all live with meanings embedded in our personalities and in our actions as tacit knowledge. This is the way culture works, and gen-uine critical awareness takes this into account. We should have sense enough to know that we cannot articulate, nor would we necessarily want to articulate, all the tacit knowledge which guides our actions from moment to moment in daily life.

One of the strengths of this view is precisely that it challenges the notion that prejudice is 'caused' by defective thought processes – as with the rigid, inflexible, distorted and over-simplified processes involved in stereotyping. This assumes that all would be well if the prejudiced person received some form of instruction in cognitive skills which enabled them to start thinking in a more open-minded, more 'fluid' and undistorted way. But, as Billig (1985) has pointed out in relation to racial prejudice, although racially prejudiced and non-racially prejudiced persons clearly have different values and weigh things differently in moral terms, the cognitive strategies they use may not be dissimilar. Both, for example, are likely to use the two key strategies of 'normal' thought – categorization and particularization.

Categorization is fundamental to cognition because without it incoming information would not be cognitively manageable. Simplification, intolerance of ambiguity and distortion serve the requirement that differences between phenomena often need to be minimized or de-emphasized and similarities highlighted. Thus some stereotypic thinking is an unavoidable outgrowth of normal cognitive processes within cultural forms. Particularization is also fundamental; it is the process where the main focus of cognitive endeavour is differentiation.

It is often said that a prejudiced person is over-categorical in their thinking, but rigid categorization can only be maintained by subtle particularization. For example, when a racist needs to believe that all whites are different from all blacks, then they can get round the problem of blacks and whites having common attributes (for example, both being Christians) by proposing that being black or white affects all other characteristics. Thus being a Christian is different if you are white than if you are black. In order to explain this away, the racist would have to split the category of Christian and therefore need to find a criterion for the distinction. They might suggest, for example, that, although there are some superficial similarities, black Christianity is basically different from white Christianity in that it is derived from superstition whereas white Christianity involves consideration of doctrine. Thus, the emphasis is on the use of particularistic strategies – on making fine distinctions in subsidiary categories in order to defend the main category and involving flexible, creative and imaginative thought, albeit from a non-racist viewpoint, also involving a somewhat bizarre (if not to say sinister) exercise. None of this is to say that it is never appropriate to criticize racist views on the grounds of their using rigid, inflexible and over-categorical thinking. Such views would be open to this criticism, for example, if they involved the assertion that black people could never be Christians with no evidence to the contrary being acknowledged.

Critique

The 'normality of prejudice' thesis is certainly an antidote to the over-reflexive approach to culture, and as such provides a much welcome contribution to our understanding of the nature of culture. But its appeal to the New Right should perhaps make us as wary, particularly in view of the latter's flawed response to the imperatives of reflexive modernity (see Chapter 1). We can see some of the problems which may arise by taking a closer look at

Jones's view. For Jones (1988) people's experience of the culture in which they have been reared is dominated by feelings of 'at homeness', and this is normal and 'natural' because it meets certain basic needs of the individual and society. The meaning of the word 'natural', however, needs to be probed. Jones opines that these shared prejudices are 'natural' in the sense that they meet a basic biological need in social animals like human beings. Our 'ideological' support for the ritual repetition of received views serves the role of signalling group membership and creating 'group cohesion in feelings of trust, comfort and at homeness' (Jones 1988: 228). It seems that Jones is attempting to bolster his model of culture by claiming it to be grounded in biological 'facts' about how human and animal societies work. But these 'facts' are clearly disputable. One could argue that the capacity to reflect critically upon one's culture is just as much a 'basic biological need' as feeling at home within it. This does not necessarily imply alienation from the nurturing culture. A person may relish the conflict which participation in the internal debates of the home culture entails and enjoy living through periods of upheaval and radical social change.

There is a tendency within the 'normality of prejudice' perspective as outlined by Jones for this intra-cultural conflict to be played down and the internal cohesion of culture to be exaggerated. The implications of this for educational practice can be seen in the conversational method advocated by the same author. The method proposes that the aim of 'conversation' between people from different cultures is to arrive at an understanding of what another's person's culture means to them. These conversations would not involve suppressing fundamental differences of perspective between members from different cultures. On the contrary, an effort would be made to make explicit precisely those understandings that may be contradicted in the other culture. The aim of making explicit the values underpinning commitment to a culture would not be to enable people to 'come to believe in' (Jones 1988: 51) these values but rather to manage their prejudices in the light of a full understanding of each other's commitment. Thus compromises would inevitably be involved because, at first, views to which people were basically opposed would have to be tolerated for the sake of social stability. Of course, once successful working compromises had been established people might come to adopt 'agreed principles at a deeper level of belief' (Jones 1988: 51). This process would inevitably be slow and almost certainly take more than a generation to complete.

However, important as it is to encourage conversation between cultures, I would argue that it is just as necessary to encourage it between members of the same culture. Indeed, in relation to phenomena such as racial prejudice and racism, it may be more important to have such a focus. Most conflicts or clashes are not at the level of foundational pre-judgements. In some ways, it would be easier if they were, because differences would be visible and the need for compromise for the sake of social survival more obvious. Rather, most of them are between people, often 'black' as well as 'white', who claim to have similar commitments at this level and claim to share a common culture, but who nevertheless hold profoundly different views on questions to do with race. Other 'conversations' take place 'within' the individual, reflecting tensions and contradictions within the 'home culture' and the ambivalence and confusion experienced by many participants.

But whether conversations are intra-individual or between individuals from the same culture, it is clear that in our society both racially prejudiced and racially tolerant options are available as cultural reference points for self-definition. If we acknowledge this, then Jones's view of the nature of prejudice and the aims of inter-cultural conversation raises certain problems when applied to intra-cultural conversation.

If the starting point is the 'normality of prejudice', do we begin by accepting racial prejudice as well as racial tolerance as a 'natural' feature of our culture? Jones would argue that racial prejudice is neither natural nor valuable because it is dysfunctional, but it is just as easy to argue, from a racist or anti-racist position, that racism has been and still is an intrinsic, authentic and even in a sense a legitimate part of the British tradition, and therefore is part of the 'home form of life', with which some or even most people identify and are prejudiced in favour of.

Clearly, then, from an anti-racist viewpoint (and presumably, in a different way, also from a racist viewpoint) the 'conversational' approach poses a dilemma. On the one hand racism in our culture must be recognized and engaged with, but on the other engagement in the form of conversation leading to compromise is totally unacceptable. If the aim is to eliminate racism, one would be more inclined to think in terms of 'critical dialogue' rather than 'prejudice management' in Jones's sense. Underpinning Jones's approach is a view of culture as an essentially harmonious, functional whole in tune with the 'facts' of human biology rather than as a changing pattern of conflicting perspectives and developing traditions. At the level of action, this view can lead to smugness and complacency and an unwillingness to examine 'comforting' pre-judgements which may in fact be more closely associated with racial prejudice than many members would like to think. Awareness of the historical contingency of cultural pre-judgements and reflection on pre-judgements through education act as a counter to this, but an initial reluctance to subject such cherished beliefs to scrutiny has to be overcome before these can make an impact.

From an educational point of view, a more appealing perspective is one which, whilst recognizing the significance of historically determined pre-judgements for cultural production and reproduction, also acknowledged the conflictual aspects of life within cultural traditions. Living within a culture can often be a contradictory experience and our 'common sense' may contain contrary elements which are widespread throughout the culture.

Thus we are not only aware of points 'for and against' but often ourselves use contradictory arguments on different occasions. Billig (1985: 98) gives the example of attitudes towards poverty and quotes research which suggests that people can and do switch readily between 'deploring' explanations referring to the social circumstances and 'blaming' explanations which are concerned with personal defects. In a study carried out by the author (Quicke 1993) it was found that sixth-formers oscillated between an 'elitist' and a 'nostalgic' attitudes to their working-class roots. Studies of working-class adolescents have revealed the complexities of racially prejudiced and tolerant arguments used. In discussion groups it was observed that most participants were likely to use arguments based on both racist and tolerant themes, with the discussion going full circle, so that some people ended up expressing views which directly contradicted those used at the start of the discussion (see Billig 1985: 98).

Critical reflection on one's own culture does not just involve acknowledging contradictions, it also means trying to resolve them; and this means understanding how they arose in the first place. Contradictions do not just arise willy-nilly but are usually related to tensions within cultural action conceived as a whole in the context of its operation. Any particular attitude, judgement or action of a group or an individual has to be considered as part of a complex of cultural beliefs and strategies which reflect perceived needs and interests in a particular social and political context. We should remember that for most of the time people go about their everyday lives in what might be described as a pragmatic mode, where their main concern is whether their knowledge 'works' for them and they are not particularly interested in the clarity of their knowledge or the consistency of their views. In this mode, their 'thinking as usual', to use Alfred Schutz's phrase, will be maintained as long as the same problems require the same solutions and 'our former experiences will suffice to master future situations' (Schutz 1971b: 28). Such thinking will be changed when it proves to be inadequate in the face of the various challenges to it prompted by changing circumstances which require a more reflective mode. These circumstances will include developments in the material conditions of existence but also all those radical and innovative influences encountered through interaction with other cultures and thus other ways of thinking and being.

Teaching approaches: the case of racism and working-class culture

In order to clarify these ideas further, let us take a look at a specific example. How should teachers in state schools go about teaching pupils from white working-class backgrounds who express racist views?

Becoming appreciative

The term 'working class' is used here as a convenient shorthand to describe cultures associated with communities which are mainly, although not necessarily solely, composed of people who are employed in unskilled or skilled manual occupations or non-managerial service occupations. Such communities may include a number of people who do not work or some who work in other kinds of occupations, but by and large the dominant culture of the community, usually defined geographically, is associated with the kinds of jobs which most people in the community do. Individuals and sub-groups identified and identifying themselves with this community will usually be positioned unfavourably in terms of material circumstances and cultural resources with respect to a 'better-off' middle class.

In relation to any specific teaching intervention, understanding such cultures would require exploring the particularities of the context in some detail. This would mean acknowledging the history of the school's relations with the local working-class community, which itself would have to be identified in all its specificity and complexity. Are we justified in speaking of one community and one culture? How do we identify it as a working-class culture? What kind of working-class culture is it? Are we talking about a section of the community (for instance, youth) or the whole of the community? How are race and gender taken up in class culture? In answering these questions, teachers would begin to be appreciative of the culture and its role in giving members a sense of belonging. The focus would be on a non-deficit model which looked at the positive connections between the moral beliefs and practices of this culture and the values of democratic culture. Teaching for the development of *all* cultures – including those of majority groups – is an aspect often underplayed in multicultural/anti-racist strategies which focus exclusively on ethnic minority cultures or the 'negative' aspects of working-class culture.

In 'conversation' with working-class culture a democratic educationalist would look for value in the creative activities of that culture, a process which would clearly involve examining his or her own values as well as those of the 'other'. If we take the youthful version of this culture, we might identify manifestations which are local and particular but which, as products of a creative process, are not qualitatively different from those of other groups in society. Our starting point would be essentially the same as that of Willis in his book *Moving Culture* (1990). We would not assume that the forms of creative expression supported by the official institution, in this case the school, would necessarily play any part in working-class pupils' lives, but that nevertheless, like the young people in Willis's studies, their lives would be full of art – 'full of expressions, signs and symbols through which [they] . . . creatively establish their very presence as well as important elements of their identity, purpose and meaning' (Willis 1990: 10).

Nor in 'new times' would we assume that the use of material from the mass media or commercial establishments as a cultural resource was necessarily exploitative or productive only of commodified selves, although clearly there are dangers here. Far from being passive consumers, young people often creatively engage with the latest offerings in the world of, say, fashion, pop music or television, and use them in the production of new and highly personalized cultural forms. Such activities are about 'fun' and enjoyment – aspects of the celebration of culture often forgotten about in the 'drive for achievement' in schools but also under-emphasized or even completely ignored by well-meaning anti-racist teachers who sometimes appear more concerned with condemnation than celebration. They are also activities which, even when they are clearly suspect from a democratic perspective, are rarely entirely devoid of value. As Willis demonstrates in what he describes as a 'limit case' for his argument – one that attempts to make the argument more effective by demonstrating the presence of 'coherent human meaning and feeling' even in 'brutalized conditions' (Willis 1990: 42) – even the 'drinking and fighting' activities of white, heterosexual, working-class males, despite their violent and often sexist and racist nature, can be viewed as a reflection of a certain kind of dignity, 'a desperate kind of honour' and 'a mad courage which confronts banality with really live drama' (Willis 1990: 51). Rather than outright condemnation without understanding, educationalists should be thinking about engaging with such cultures in ways which seek common ground and enable genuine dialogue about opportunities and possibilities for positive development.

Understanding racist subjectivities

Teaching approaches will therefore involve becoming more appreciative of value in the particular form of working-class culture represented by a particular group of pupils, but of course racist elements cannot be ignored. The hope is that such approaches will have created a climate where the pupils concerned feel more trustful and less alienated to such a degree that they will accept criticism from the teacher and accept the need for self-criticism. But in making these criticisms and tackling the question of racism it is important for teachers to understand the role that racism plays in working-class community life, if it plays any role at all.

The problem here as far as working-class pupils' cultural development is concerned is that racist views can, in certain circumstances, be an intrinsic part of the culture, and difficult to avoid in any celebration of it. How this racism is perceived and dealt with is clearly crucial, since such ideologies act as a corrosive and constraining force within any culture and are as 'bad' for the self- and community development of the perpetrators as they are for those on the receiving end. However, this is not say that racist ideology has no 'logic' to it or that it somehow derives from defective thought processes, since it reflects an attempt to make sense of the world on the basis of certain assumptions about the 'other' – assumptions grounded, as they are for all of us, in pre-judgements, even if they are not in their particulars ones that we would support. But despite its 'logic', I would argue that racism is always ultimately irrational if rationality is defined in terms of that which realizes the genuine cultural interests of members, since how could it be rational to support an ideology which corrodes one's own culture?

To explicate this further, let us look at a critique of the notion of 'false consciousness' as an explanation for racism, a critique which is typical of much of the so-called postmodern writing in this field. In his review of studies of white working-class racism, Rattansi (1992) criticizes the work of Phizacklea and Miles (1980) who argue that white racism in the particular inner-city context that they researched was part of the process whereby white people tried to make sense of the housing shortage, unemployment and other features of urban decline. For Rattansi, although racism must be interpreted as part of a broader picture of the conditions of working-class people in this area, one could not assume that if they were provided with the 'truth' about the cause of unemployment and so on they would no longer rely on racist explanations. This caveat is often squeezed out by those who seek to educate the working class by providing them with these 'superior' explanations. Racism is clearly anti-democratic but it is not 'inferior' in the sense implied by the false consciousness model.

But this critique involves a confusion between two issues – one is to do with whether we can talk at all of superior explanations, and the other whether explanations, whatever their epistemological status, will be accepted if they are provided by well-meaning 'outsiders', particularly if these 'outsiders' are middle-class teachers or middle-class political radicals. Now, provided the context is clearly identified and understood, it is self-evident that one explanation for action can be judged superior to another. Racist ideology will not necessarily wither away once the 'truth' is known about the 'real' causes, but an embrace of this ideology can reasonably be described as false consciousness if there are grounds for thinking that continued adherence to it would not be in the long-term interests of the working-class community. It is not a question of the truth will out; but more a question of working-class people becoming self-critical and probing their own assumptions about the 'causes' of their condition.

But – and this relates to the second issue referred to above – how this call for self-criticism and dialogue is mediated is crucial. In so far as an intervention is associated with the middle-class-ness of teachers then it may well be interpreted as just another form of class domination and surveillance, and consequently resisted. This class resistance itself, of course, is often ambivalent – does it stem from an alternative discourse of democracy or is it merely a manoeuvre within the existing discourse of economic power relations? But such is the contradictory nature of human cultures that racism often goes hand in hand with more laudable motives, such as opposition to an oppressive authority or resistance to class domination, as well as less laudable ones such as economic self-interest.

Conversations between cultures

Pupils need to feel that their own culture is appreciated, but they also need to experience the value of conversing with the 'other'. From an educational perspective, the question is how best to represent the culture of the 'other'. The 'positive images' model reflects a natural reaction to racism. If people from that culture have been on the receiving end of demeaning and derogatory remarks evoking historical stereotypes, then it seems reasonable to counter this by emphasizing positive aspects. But such 'positive images' are themselves problematical if they merely counter one stereotype with another, or if they reflect what teachers and others in authority consider to be 'positive' rather than how members of the culture themselves want to be represented. Cultures are diverse and forever changing; teachers cannot presume to know the many different ways that black or white people see themselves and interpret their lives.

Once expressed, cultural 'voices' have to be critically engaged with. All kinds of tensions and ambiguities are involved here. If racism is endemic to a culture, how can such a culture be conversed with in a way which enables members to retain their dignity? But one person's or one culture's dignity may be achieved at the expense of the dignity of the 'other'. The purpose of dialogue between cultures is to deconstruct unacceptable bases of dignity and to create alternative forms which are more acceptable to both parties. Racism could not be tolerated but other fundamental differences – ones which had no negative implications for the other – could be acknowledged. The purpose of making deeply held values and beliefs explicit would not be to convert others but rather, as Jones suggests, to help cultural members accomplish social relations in the light of a full understanding of each other's commitments. The cultural pre-judgements of both parties, once unearthed and examined in the light of day, might eventually be recognized as being more consonant than was initially supposed. Such intercultural conversation might also generate insights into whole areas of one's own culture which one had no reason to examine previously. Thus, such conversations might help both parties to a greater degree of self-understanding.

The question of nationalism

The racism of working-class youth often includes an element which expresses a nationalistic sentiment and thus a desire to go beyond parochialism and see oneself as part of a wider whole. If this need to identify with a larger community is valid, might it not be appropriate for educators to foster an alternative version of nationalism? It could be argued that in a period where opportunities are opening up for individuals and cultural groups to reconceptualize and redefine themselves, nationalism could be reinvented as a focus for the creation of a new citizenship – one that reflected a morally justified form of life in keeping with the imperatives of the age in which we lived. This is certainly the view of John White (1996) who, from a liberal perspective, argues for the importance of reinventing a form of nationalism which redefines 'British' in more acceptable terms than those deployed by conservatives and other reactionaries. This for him means getting away from ethnocentrism and chauvinism and some of the more unsavoury aspects of the heritage, such as racism, and retaining the more liberal and democratic parts. There is evidence in history of other values such as benevolence, tolerance and concern for social justice which could form the basis for unity and a sense of common purpose under the banner of a more liberal nationalism.

It is not as if this reinvention therefore involves starting from scratch. It really means invoking those already existing sentiments of which, from a liberal democratic perspective, we can be proud, and playing down those which are more suspect. But why national sentiment in particular? White cites Miller's (1988: 648) belief that national identity has value because historically it relies on

> the belief that each belongs together with the rest; that this association is neither transitory nor merely instrumental but stems from a long history of living together which (it is hoped and expected) will continue into the future; that the community is marked off from other communities by its distinctive characteristics; and that each member recognizes a loyalty to the community, expressed in a willingness to sacrifice personal gain to advance its interests.

Such sentiments already exist below the surface, as it were, and despite the alleged demise of the nation-state in the current period, most of us readily accept that the national community is one of the most important social and cultural frameworks for constituting identity. Nationality is important for personal identity because 'for many of us the work that we do, our attachments to other people, our values would lose much of their point if this national framework were removed. We need it to make sense of our lives, to help us towards a sense of who we are' (White 1996: 331).

In evaluating these ideas, let us begin with the important distinction White makes between a community based on civic friendship and one based on national sentiment – two forms of commitment which are often conflated. Civic friendship involves a widespread feeling of fraternity fostered by the construction of attachments to the democratic polity itself and typically involves emotions which relate to universal moral-political principles. However, White does not think much of a community bound together by attachment to principles only. Just as one would not like to live in a family where parents did things for children out of duty rather than affection, so it is preferable to live in a wider community where 'people felt a more immediate sympathy for each other' (White 1996: 332). For him, it is the national community which can provide 'this more spontaneous, less intellectualized form of attachment, thus strengthening bonds at the civic level' (White 1996: 332).

But it seems to me that there are at least two problems here. First, the distinction he makes between civic friendship and national community allows for certain forms of exclusion which are suspect, to say the least. For instance, as he points out, it allows minorities to be treated as citizens in the civic sense but not as full members of the national community, particularly if, as is sometimes the case, they do not choose to identify with this community. But this suggests a rather old-fashioned and inaccurate view of the cultural make-up of British society. To be sure, there are minority cultures and majority cultures and everyone is a member of at least one of these cultures, and may even be a member of more than one, but none of these cultures by itself represents the national community in White's sense. In all cultures in Britain, there are those who identify with their counterparts in other nations, but this has always been so, particularly when religion is involved, and it is in any case often a transitory phenomenon reflecting a reaction against the attitudes of dominant groups who make similar distinctions to those made by White.

The second problem with White's argument is that he assumes that the kind of bonding that takes place between individuals in families and between friends can also occur at national level, and that this is desirable. But is bonding at this level either necessary or desirable? Most of us recognize an allegiance to the national community but do not assume that our relationships with other members of that community are of a similar order to those we have with 'close' friends and relatives. Of course, there are links between these two modes of relating. It is undoubtedly true that without the experience of what one might call primary bonding an individual would have enough appreciation of the 'other' to see why the principles of civic friendship should be as they are or why he or she should have allegiance to them in the first instance. Valuing social justice stems from the experience of 'love' and 'being loved' in families; the principles would be meaningless if one had no knowledge of the kind of mutual respect and reciprocity of which human beings were capable. But nevertheless, social justice is an abstraction from this experience – we assume that everyone in the nation to which we belong has the same need for dignity and, although we do not know them personally, we support their rights in this respect. To do this all we need to know is that they are human beings like us; we do not need to know that we share certain national characteristics with them. Nations do not have to be bonded in the same way as families.

However, White argues that, even if it is not absolutely necessary, it would make for a far nicer world if this sense of common national community could be established. But would it? All knowing of peoples beyond the particular and the intimate involves abstraction, whether these peoples are defined in terms of an ethnic group, a class, a nation or as citizens of the world. They are not particulars or 'locals' and their 'needs' can only be defined in universalistic terms. Thus what White describes as civic friendship is all that can be hoped for – but this is in fact quite a lot. In this way of thinking about the 'other' there seems to be a natural progression towards widening the community to include all peoples. In fact, trying to pretend that a nation is like a family, by demanding the impossible, militates, if anything, against this imaginative leap towards an all-inclusive civic friendship. A strong sense of the national community is, in fact, not much good either way. It can restrict the expansion of our universal concerns, whilst at the same time doing nothing for our close relationships. Actions in intimate life should only rarely, if ever, be done for 'king and country' or 'for Britain'; and the process of loving someone can only perversely be called 'doing' one's British identity.

Summary and conclusion

A progressive multicultural education will stress the importance of establishing conditions in schools which enable 'conversations' to take place between different cultures (however cultures are defined, be it local or national; pupil school-based cultures or out-of-school cultures). Such conversations are dialogical and can include critical comments, but they give a 'voice' to each party and are open-ended. One would hope for the development of mutual understanding and reciprocity, even if this meant agreeing to differ. There are a number of features in the school context and in society generally which prevent this happening, but one of the most important is racism.

Racism implies that one culture sees another in pejorative terms and that the representations deployed are grounded in certain essentialist assumptions. In situations where one culture is dominant, racism implies an intention to maintain social arrangements which disadvantage the 'other', and a greater interest in retaining and exercising power than in having a 'conversation'. Where groups have equal power it implies stand-offs, with the possibility of conflict at any time. Racism is often covert and part of the hidden curriculum of schooling. A strategy which fostered inter-cultural conversation would have to take this into account, but in doing so it would have to be informed by an understanding of how racism functioned in a particular context.

One of the problems here is how racism has been conceived in an educational context. It has been viewed as irrational, and the racist individual has been pathologized. In the circumstances in which many people find themselves, the embrace of racist ideas is part of a survival strategy which has its own logic and self-validating mechanisms. Racist ideology can be argued against but it is not necessarily any more or any less intellectually sophisticated or cognitively complex than, say, a liberal world view. It is grounded in experience and constituted in knowledge developed in the same way as all knowledge of the social world – things need explaining, 'theories' are proposed and understanding develops. The only difference between racist explanations and other types of explanations is that they are racist and not that they do not qualify as explanations.

Finally, it is important to remember that racism, like other forms of domination and discrimination, plays on insecurities and uncertainties endemic to life in contemporary society. Feelings of 'homelessness', of belonging nowhere, of being excluded, of having no identity are a possibility for anyone at any stage of life. Teaching approaches must therefore be grounded first and foremost in the assumption that people want to 'belong' and that cultures are an expression of this. But in reflexively modern society they will want to belong in certain ways – ones which involve a sense of moving from the familiar to the unfamiliar; of exploring possibilities for cultural development from a known starting point; of retaining a sense of the future being open; of relishing similarities and differences between cultures and the 'worlds' they represent; and of enjoying the process of intra- and inter-cultural conversation and critique, and the wisdom it brings forth.

7 | Gender politics and school achievement

Introduction

From the outset it is important to clarify the link between gender, politics, school achievement and policy which frames the discussion in this chapter. Gender will refer to socially constructed differences where the male–female dualism is still dominant, despite the changes that have taken place in the way sexuality and gender are construed in 'new times'. Politics is involved because these differences are not 'innocent' but reflect asymmetrical power relations where men historically have been in the ascendancy, and it behoves democrats and putative democratic states to redress the balance with policies which afford social justice to women. In education this has meant the introduction of policies designed to give boys and girls equal access to the curriculum and equal opportunities to achieve.

In the light of recent developments, these policies clearly need to be reassessed, and in this chapter I shall do this by examining reactions to differences between boys and girls in terms of school achievement. Of particular interest at present is the gender gap in favour of girls in results gained in the General Certificate of Secondary Education (GCSE), and the explanation of this in terms of boys' underachievement. I shall critically examine the conclusion that equal opportunities policies now need to be reviewed and even 'reversed' so that positive action is now directed at boys' learning problems. I shall then go on to consider issues which go beyond equal opportunities policies as we presently understand them. It will be argued that the main emphasis of policy should be curriculum reform which is not gender-blind but is nevertheless guided by an understanding of what *all* pupils need to learn in the contemporary context.

The main focus of the discussion will be gender, but many of the arguments deployed here apply equally to class, ethnicity and disability, and clearly in any particular situation gender will interact with other forms and structures in complex ways. However, there are features of the experiences of learners and teachers which are specifically gender-related and can be identified as a common pattern across structures. It is these which are foregrounded in this chapter.

Before exploring these issues further in an educational context, we need to look at the the broader societal context and take stock of the situation regarding gender relations. Most people are familiar with the notion of a patriarchal society, but they are also aware that attitudes towards sex, marriage and the family as well as relations between men and women have changed. The question arises as to what is the current state of play, so to speak, between the sexes; to what extent has male power been neutralized and the patriarchal ideology which underpinned it become a spent force? In addressing these issues, in what is a notoriously confused and confusing area, we need to begin by identifying the main contours of patriarchy and assessing the influence of this ideology in the current period.

Patriarchy: the state of play

Patriarchy is a complex concept but its main defining characteristics would be familiar enough to most educationalists. For the sake of clarity, we might construe it as grounded in three main assumptions: first, that the separate spheres of men and women are 'natural' divisions based on biological differences; second, that women are defined in relation to men and children rather than as individual beings; and third, that women are inferior to men (Purvis 1981). The different spheres involve a number of interrelated aspects – psychological, social and economic – which give rise to separate identities and a division of labour based on the alleged inherent and irreducible essences of masculinity and femininity. Thus women are 'emotional', irrational, caring and sensitive and men rational and assertive, for example, because that is the way the traits are constituted in 'nature'. These psychological attributes are thought to be functional and necessary for the different roles men and women play in society. The former will have a dominant role in the rationally organized political, commercial and other institutions of modern society, whereas women's role is essentially subsidiary and confined to certain types of low-status work, 'women's work', even when they *are* involved in activities outside the home. In the family, the father has autonomy and authority and is the 'natural' breadwinner, whilst the mother is a home-based, financially dependent caregiver for whose self-fulfilment being a mother is thought to be sufficient.

Historically women's supposed inferiority has taken different forms depending on the social and cultural context. For example, in traditional middle-class culture, 'high' intelligence and 'genius' have been seen mostly as male attributes, but in manual working-class culture manual work has often been associated with the social superiority of masculinity and mental work with the social inferiority of femininity. In fact, even in the latter culture, men have associated their skills with 'real' intelligence and female academic accomplishments have been interpreted as more to do with conformity than ability. As far as sexuality was concerned, in both cultures, the dominant ideas about women's 'desires' were consonant with their perceived inferiority and lack of agency. They were generally regarded as passive sex objects, or, the counterpart of this, as unnaturally sexually active. 'Bodily relations of intimacy' between men and women were often about domination and misogyny. Conforming to the patriarchal definition of masculinity involved men in dominance behaviour, with women being on the receiving end of teasing, abuse and general harassment. In schools, such behaviour was part and parcel of boys learning to be 'masculine' (Wood 1982). The denigration of girls' bodies, according to Lees (1987: 181–2), exerted 'a form of control which steered girls into "acceptable" forms of sexual and social behaviour'. Girls were routinely put down as a daily part of classroom life. They were categorized as 'slags', 'drags' or 'lezzies', placing them in a no-win situation as far as sexual activity was concerned – if they showed no interest they were abused as much as if they showed interest. Girls capitulated to stereotypes because they saw no alternative to doing so and in this way traditional gender identities were reproduced.

Some would argue, however, that this ideology has been undermined in recent years by social and cultural changes, in particular those associated with the increased participation of women in the labour force, improved educational opportunities for girls, the transformation of family forms and changes in sexual attitudes and practices. Economic changes, restructuring, the increasing importance of formal qualifications and the break-up of traditional, male-dominated labour markets have meant improved job opportunities for women, particularly in the areas of part-time work and access to high-status jobs. The progress of girls in school achievement, as measured by improvements in GCSE exam results and access to higher education, has provided them with more independence and more scope for meaningful choice in terms of life goals. The nuclear family is now only one amongst a number of family forms and is itself changing its nature with more scope for mothers, fathers and children to relate in ways which differ significantly from their previous roles. Women now expect and achieve a greater degree of equality in the home and at work, and as traditional stereotypes of male and female are deconstructed so new gender identities are emerging.

The various links in the chain of patriarchal ideology have allegedly been broken. Sexuality, marriage and the family, which were compounded in the minds, 'bodies' and moral career practices of both men and women, have been separated as forms of social action. Changes in sexual practices and the 'liberalization' of sexuality have led to a more open view about sex in society generally (Lees 1993). Individuals see themselves as having a 'sex life' which may taken several forms according to preference – it may be monogomous or involve several partners, heterosexual or homosexual, auto or with another and can involve high or low activity, even periods of celibacy, and different physical practices – but in all cases presuming an active agent for whom sex is viewed in lifestyle terms. Sexuality is a malleable feature of the self which has to be 'reflexively grasped, interrogated and developed' (Giddens 1992: 14) and it has to be 'worked into' a personal life where there are many other, often competing, desires and needs. But there is no automatic connection between sexual life and destiny as marriage partner or parent, as in the patriarchal tryptych of sex, marriage and children bonded by romantic love and the idealization of motherhood and fatherhood. Sex may or may not be involved in close relationships between men and women or between people of the same sex; parenthood may not involve 'natural' mothers and fathers; and 'destiny' may or may not involve having children.

However, whilst there is no denying the quite dramatic changes that have taken place in the last thirty years or so, it is important to bear in mind that these emerging cultural arrangements are still contested and progress is not inevitable. In relation to the economic sphere, as MacEwen Scott (1994) concludes in her summary of a number of research studies carried out in the 1980s and 1990s in a range of sectors, despite the profound economic and social changes of recent years men and women still remain highly segregated at work, and this segregation is still strongly related to inequalities in pay, career prospects and employment protection. Moreover, the influence of the traditional division of labour in families is still much in evidence :

> Despite the economic changes . . . , women's increased labour market participation, and changes in family structure, such as increases in divorce and single parenthood, there appears to be enormous stability in women's and men's domestic roles and the value system that underpins them.
>
> (MacEwen Scott 1994: 35)

The research provides evidence that women's long-term career development is disrupted by their continuing role as primary childcarers and that the primacy of the male breadwinner role continues to result in structures of employment and payment which are an expression of gender segregation based on primary or secondary earner status. In addition, the research shows

> that naturalistic beliefs about gender, embodied in notions of strength, dexterity, sensitivity and so on, play a fundamental role in the sex-typing of jobs . . . [the lack of desegregation] is mainly due to enduring inequalities in the domestic division of labour and deeply held beliefs about the nature of gender itself.
>
> (MacEwen Scott 1994: 35)

As for boy–girl relations in schools, it is evident, as Cockburn (1987), quoted in Mac an Ghaill (1994: 111), points out, that girls still live their lives in ways which are complementary to boys, not as separate and equal but on the 'dark side of a gendered youth subculture, male-dominated and male advantaging'. The main route to manhood for many boys is still through a process of 'distancing women and femininity from themselves and maintaining the hierarchy of social superiority of masculinity by devaluing the female world' (Arnot 1984: 145). In his own study, Mac an Ghaill (1994: 92) found that this superiority was achieved in many ways but particularly in relation to 'sex talk' and 'sexual narratives' which involved 'misogynous boasting and exaggeration of past heterosexual conquests and male heroic fantasies, in which women were represented as passive objects of male sexual urges, needs and desires'. These fictions were part of the way male students established the framework of rule conformity which was required of someone claiming to be a 'man' and were the way sexual boundaries were 'policed'.

Another significant component of this boundary maintenance activity was homophobia, which differed in form amongst class and ethnic groups but in all cases involved the construction of homosexuality as a disability or an 'unnatural' practice. In recent times the 'coming out' of homosexuality has played a major role in the sexual revolution and the anti-gay practices of heterosexual males are, together with misogyny, part of a strategy which 'holds the line' for the traditional order. They act as cultural markers and reference points for self-definition, as a way of avowing publicly that this identity of the 'poofter', the man who acts like a woman, is the very opposite of what one takes oneself to be. It is evident that oppression in this area is still a continuing feature of life in schools. A recent report quoted in the *Times Educational Supplement* (13 March 1998: 1) 'found that more than 80 percent of schools admitted some homophobic verbal bullying while just over a quarter reported assaults on pupils believed to be gay'.

Intervention

What does all this imply for action in educational contexts? Clearly, teachers need to sensitize themselves to the oppressive features of the schools in which they work. As indicated in previous chapters, a useful starting point is the social insight generated by pupils in pursuit of their own cultural practices and within these cultures the perceptions of those mostly on the receiving end in relations of sexual dominance, girls and gay pupils. Not that the views of the most oppressed should always be privileged or taken at face value, but they certainly need to be taken seriously because, as history shows, whether the main focus is gender, race, class, disability or some other form of oppression, it is the voice of these groups, rather than the powerful and the privileged, which are often the most discerning of micro-political processes. As Mac an Ghaill (1994: 112) observes, the views of the young women interviewed in his study helped the researcher to understand the specificity of the production of masculine identities at the local level of the school [because] . . . like young male gays, these heterosexual female students occupy a critical social position from which to speak of masculinities and their cultural and political impact on their lives and future socio-sexual destinies.

In general, since gender bias has been a pervasive phenomenon in schools, the best strategy is for teachers to examine all school practices for evidence of it. We know that such bias works in subtle ways and that it operates at a tacit as well as explicit level. This is not to say that it will always be a salient factor in the construction of academic or any other kind of school identity, and we should certainly avoid the kind of over-interpretation which sees gender as always the most significant relation. In other words, we have to try to keep an open mind, whilst of course recognizing the impossibility of complete detachment. But an intellectually rigorous and critical approach always requires us to go beyond appearances and to examine official and unofficial accounts for assumptions and interpretations which reflect hidden agendas of power. In developing the discussion here it will be useful to take a detailed look an area of contestation which is particularly pertinent at present, namely the differential achievement of boys and girls in terms of measured academic outcomes.

The case of boys' underachievement

For several decades now, the main focus of liberal equal opportunities policies has been 'access for girls', but recently there has been a distinct shift of emphasis. 'Equal opportunities' is now just as likely to be associated with boys' as with girls' achievement. The talk is of making the curriculum more 'boy-friendly' and of encouraging boys to be better organized and motivated as 'learners'. Although girls have for years outperformed boys on so-called language-based subjects (English, English literature and modern languages) it is now evident that they have also caught up in the traditionally male-dominated subjects of science and maths and are even edging ahead (although, as we shall see below, the situation is more complex than this). The differences have been evident even at younger ages, with girls doing better on reading tests and being generally more competent in language and communication skills in all areas of the curriculum (Swann 1992; Office for Standards in Education (Ofsted) 1993). It has always been the case that more boys than girls have been labelled as having learning difficulties and more of them have been allocated extra help in designated special needs groups or classes (Ford et al. 1982).

But what does all this mean in terms of gender relations? In exploring this question, we might begin by examining how this 'gap' between boys and girls is being explained away. In the past the typical explanation for differences in achievement has been 'immaturity'. Thus, boys were usually said to need 'support', but no other measures were thought to be necessary because boys would eventually 'catch up'. However, it is clear from GCSE results that boys do not now 'catch up' in the way they did in the past. In the current period, there has been a shift of emphasis towards interpreting the 'gap' in terms of boys' 'underachievement'. In a study carried out by the author of a sample of secondary schools across two local education authorities, teachers explained differences in various ways but most of these were based on assumptions about boys' unfulfilled potential (Quicke 1995). There are reports of schools adopting strategies for identifying underachievers and providing such pupils with extra help of one kind or another. Some have used standardized tests as predictors of GCSE results and defined underachievement as failure to realize 'potential' as measured by such tests. Gold (1995) reports on a school in Suffolk which used scores on a reading test at 12+ to ascertain which pupils were doing worse or better than expected in the run-up to GCSE. The majority of underachievers were boys, who were then invited to work with a teacher 'mentor' once a week on study skills and examination preparation.

Explaining the 'problem' as 'boys' underachievement' carries with it a number of interrelated meanings which are often ignored in policies involving the development of remedial strategies which target boys. To begin with, it is typically associated with the assumption that girls may be 'overachieving', which itself is often related to the more general point that GCSE has become easier, particularly in the areas of maths and science (Harris *et al.* 1993). It is alleged that the content is easier but also the method of assessment has favoured girls. Thus, for example, the 'hardworking but not too bright' girl does better because course work now counts for more. Despite the numerous research studies which have challenged the common-sense view (see, for example, Baker and Jones 1992), the general belief persists that gender differences in cognitive skills are innate and that girls' achievements are often the result of 'hard work' rather than 'innate intelligence'. Thus the notion of boys' underachievement and its counterpart in girls' overachievement brings with it sexist assumptions about intellectual differences between the sexes which have a long history. It is not so much that girls overachieve in language-based subjects but that their achievements are in these 'easy', non-cognitive subjects and therefore are of less significance in the long term.

But there is no justification for discriminating between boys and girls in this way. Girls' better performance on literacy and language tests does not in itself mean that there is not as much underachievement amongst girls as boys. Girls come to school with a 'flying start' on the language and literacy front, which constitutes the 'baseline' of their achievement. On average girls have more cultural and linguistic resources to draw on at the start of their education, and their future achievements must be related to these differences;

that is, in current jargon, they must be seen in a value-added way. Even if we assume there is no gap between the sexes to begin with but that this emerges during the early years of schooling (for whatever reason) then for all practical purposes we are still looking at a different starting point for boys and girls (Gorman *et al.* 1988).

We can also look at the notion of underachievement in another way. Given the position of women in society, girls need, in a sense, to achieve more than boys whilst they are in school. What constitutes achievement and underachievement therefore will be different for them. We can tease out some further issues here by taking a closer look at the so-called gender gap in performance in public examinations. Although, as indicated above, girls are now achieving 'better' GCSE results than boys, the picture is more complex than implied by simple comparisons of overall results. Girls are achieving success in traditional 'male' subjects (design and technology, computer studies, mathematics, chemistry and combined science) but still do relatively less well in these subjects than in others (Equal Opportunities Commission (EOC) and Ofsted 1996). In choosing options at Key Stage 4, there is still a tendency for boys and girls to make choices which reflect traditional stereotypes, with scientific and technical subjects attracting more boys, and language and arts more girls. There is also evidence that subject choice in the sixth form is heavily influenced by gender. As the EOC and Ofsted (1996: 13) point out, 'despite their success in these subjects at GCSE, relatively few young women are taking A-level courses which are wholly mathematical, scientific or technological, thereby denying themselves some career opportunities in science, engineering and technology'. As far as results at A level are concerned, the pattern of performance of the sexes at GCSE level does not appear to be continued. For example, of those with GCSE scores of 60 points or more in 1992, 32 per cent of male candidates and 22 per cent of female candidates achieved A-level or AS-level scores of 30 points or more in 1994 (Department for Education 1994).

Further support for these trends comes from analyses of gender differences in patterns of subject choice, standards obtained in the Scottish Certificate of Education and post-school intentions in Scotland, where Darling and Glendinning (1996) found evidence of 'gender tracks'. In their study of third- and fourth-year pupils in seven local authority schools they identified three groups: 'male-academic' orientation (group A); 'female-academic' orientation (group B); and 'non-academic' orientation (group C). The findings suggested a distinct set of interrelationships between choice and structure, like class and gender, and also between choice and career trajectories. The first two groups were divided along gender lines both in terms of character and in the actual composition of the groups (although the study also showed there was a substantial minority of girls who chose 'male subjects' and boys who chose 'female subjects'). The authors noted that group A aspired to higher-status occupations than group B, thus reflecting traditional stereotyped constructions of career development. Group C appeared to be less gendered at first sight, but further analysis of educational and career aspirations revealed significant differences between boys and girls, with boys much more likely to consider leaving at the minimum age.

Additional support for the notion of 'gender tracks' comes from studies of pupils' own assessments of their academic abilities. The achievement of self-confidence and a positive approach to learning in the long term may not always go hand in hand with high achievement in the 'here and now' as reflected in school tests and exam results. Several researchers have found that high-achieving girls do not always have a corresponding belief in their academic abilities. Teachers may unwittingly reinforce this by the way they respond to pupils in the classroom. Thus Licht and Dweck (1983) observed that teachers in the primary school had high expectations of girls but still managed to contribute to the girls' lack of confidence in their academic abilities. Girls receive fewer criticisms of their work than boys but those they receive refer to the intellectual quality of the work. Girls tend to attribute failure in academic subjects to lack of ability and to equate success with 'luck'. They tend to be more easily put off by failure on new tasks and to underestimate their degree of success on all tasks. Thus they tend to prefer language-related work because this is perceived as easier and there is less chance of failure. Moreover, it has been suggested that school literacy may actually be harmful for girls. For example, the reason why girls' success in school writing is not translated into career success may be related to the fact that too many of the books that girls read anticipate futures where women are subservient to men. Girls are also often given the impression that creative writing is the 'best' writing; and this reinforces their disinclination to write in the non-literary genres required in science and other subjects (Millard 1997; Janet White 1990).

Recent evidence of girls' success in GCSE maths and science may still not dispel notions which are deeply embedded in cultural understandings of gender identity (Department of Education and Science (DES) 1989). The relatively low level of take-up of science at A level by girls may well reflect their belief that the subject is too hard for them (Ofsted 1994). In their study Darling and Glendinning (1996) found that the 'male-academic' group rated their abilities more highly than the other groups. Interestingly, pupils in their sample tended to regard their own views about their abilities as more significant than those of teachers and parents, suggesting that although pupils claimed ownership and responsibility for their choices, the latter were in fact heavily influenced by structural factors. The following quotation from EOC and Ofsted (1996: 2) neatly summarizes most of these concerns about gender differences in school achievement:

> While girls are now achieving better academic results than boys at age 16, there is little evidence that this is leading to improved post-school

opportunities in the form of training, employment, career development and economic independence for the majority of young women. Are schools focusing on the academic achievement of girls, and neglecting the important and complementary skills of individual development and decision-making which enable young people to maximize their opportunities later on? How can schools challenge traditional expectations and roles in order to improve pupils' aspirations and strengthen their life choices and chances?

In the light of the above, therefore, it seems that the emphasis on boys' underachievement is misplaced if the latter is defined in a way which means resources for the realization of opportunities are directed away from girls towards boys. It is by no means certain that girls' life chances have improved so dramatically relative to boys' that teachers now need to take positive action in relation to the latter rather than the former. Moreover, the way underachievement and achievement are explained may reinforce assumptions about gender differences which are not in the best long-term interests of girls in that they serve to reproduce the traditional division of labour, albeit in a different form than previously.

Beyond equal opportunities

However, we need to recognize the limitations of equal opportunities policies. Whilst we should be wary of policies derived from the notion of boys' underachievement and recognize that girls, too, may still be underachieving both in the short and long term, we should not forget that the overall purpose of equal opportunities policies is to even things up in terms of opportunities to compete in the education system and subsequently in the labour market. But a critical perspective on schooling would take us beyond this position. The instrumentalism of an approach to learning where success is measured in terms of performance in competitive public exams puts paid to the development of a curriculum which would be genuinely educational for all pupils. Girls achieve equality of opportunity and this certainly provides them with more options, but it may do so at the expense of a good education.

We can explore this further by looking at an example. As indicated above, girls now perform better in science subjects than previously, but have some way to go if they are really to catch up with boys. It is still the case that many more boys than girls study the prestigious science subjects of chemistry and physics, and more go on to do A level and seek careers in science. There is a continuing picture of inequality here, but does it tell the whole story? From a conventional equal opportunities perspective, we should be advocating policies which closed this gap, but in whose interests would this be in the medium or long term? If society wants citizens who are more aware of scientific and environmental issues, are we sure that making girls more competitive in science in the current system will produce this outcome? It could be argued that the kind of science that is girl-friendly is in fact a 'better' form of science; and rather than encouraging girls to develop their interests so that they are more like those of boys, it would be preferable to question whether the specialist science curriculum is any good for boys or girls. We should remember that girls' recent successes in science were achieved not just by altering teaching methods but also by reforming the content of science so that it was more related to girls' interests. But if this means 'better' science then it is a reform which is surely in everyone's interests?

In developing the argument here, it does not help, I feel, to talk about replacing masculinist science by feminist science. This seems calculated to alienate male pupils and teachers for no good reason. Writers such as Kelly (1988) have criticized proponents of feminist science for exaggerating differences between males and females, and the extent to which feminist science can be said to have a distinctive epistemology is contested. Feminist science is said to be an approach to science which is more holistic and where 'feelings, reactions, values and intuitions become important starting points for the development of principles and theories . . . [and where] evidence can be unique, anecdotal, partial and partisan' (Bentley and Watts 1987: 214 cited in Riddell 1992). But all 'good' science, as pointed out in the discussion of Kuhn in Chapter 10, is a very social and human activity, where values are always involved, where there is a concern for 'connectivity', where emotional and aesthetic aspects do play a part and where 'subjectivity' and 'objectivity' are not separate entities but dialectically related and intrinsic to the process. The proponents of a feminist science are at best merely part of the chorus critiquing positivism and at worst the advocates of an epistemology which is of questionable value from a democratic and educational perspective. An example of the latter is the eco-systemic approach favoured by many green feminists. Watts and Bentley (1994) argue for a pedagogy in constructivist science which acknowledges anthropomorphic and animistic thinking, since in their view this would help to foster a more humanized science. These opinions are supported by Kincheloe and Steinberg (1993) in their account of approaches which lead us across the boundary dividing 'living' and 'not living'. In some postmodern versions of science, it has been argued 'that the best definition of life is the entire Earth' and that 'postformal teachers can design lessons that illustrate the physical and spiritual connection between self and ecosystem' (Kincheloe and Steinberg 1993: 310).

The problem with this line of reasoning is that although the interconnectivity between the human and the non-human, the living and the non-living, is obvious at one level, it can easily lead to a denial of the very human agency which is so crucial to the dialectic of the scientific enterprise. Rather than humanizing science, this approach seems to dehumanize it. It fails to recognize that the living and the non-living are only contingently defined and connected; human consciousness can intervene to make or break any connection. The ecosystem is not conscious and there is no 'implicate order of the universe' (Kincheloe and Steinberg 1993: 310) or, for that matter, any implicate disorder. A humanistic perspective would surely stress that humans, if not completely in control, should at least have some say in the construction of a 'natural' order rather than being completely enthralled to God or nature? The interconnectivity which should be strived for is that which connects scientific thought and action with other human practices. Good scientists, like those who are 'good' in any other practice, are those who understand their science as an 'open' body of knowledge in search of dialogue with other forms (see Chapter 10).

The link between masculinity and science

However, whilst 'good' science is not gender-based, there is no denying the historic link between positivism and conventional forms of masculinity as a gender–power complex. Certain socially constructed characteristics of males – assertiveness, individualism, cognitivism, objectivism, the need for dominance and so on – might be said to predispose them to a positivist world view, even though we have to bear in mind that these links are historically contingent and that there is no essence of maleness or, for that matter, of science which is 'naturally' given. Likewise, historically constituted femininity – with its mirror-image characteristics of passivity, subjectivism and the like – is out of kilter with positivism. Each complements the role of the other in the division of labour and in their positioning in the patriarchal discourse.

Our approach to developing the science curriculum, therefore, should not be gender-blind because this historical legacy still has some resonance, despite the changes that have occurred in recent years. The way forward perhaps is to acknowledge boy–girl differences but to treat them critically; so that it is a question of accepting difference not just as a 'fact of life' but as a socially constituted form which, though originating in the 'sin' of patriarchy, may be regarded as potentially enabling and empowering in a Foucauldian sense. Put simply, we might think in terms of the strengths of both groups, whilst recognizing that these very strengths can easily become weaknesses. In practice,we clearly have to tread carefully here. Even the supposed appeal of 'good' science for girls is often grounded in assumptions about difference which relate to a division of labour infused with asymmetries of power.

However, it is possible that these boy–girl differences in attributes might be turned to good effect in a new science curriculum. Each will approach learning science from a different angle with different interests, concerns and capabilities. The object of the exercise is not to devise curricula which reinforce these differences, but rather to use such differences as starting points for curriculum development in relation to not only the science *but also the gender curriculum*. This is an important point which needs further explication.

The hope is that capabilities can be extracted from their location in patriarchal discourse and recontextualized in the science curriculum in a way that promotes genuine learning within the enabling discourse of good science – science which does not carry with it the vestiges of past inequalities. Once constructed, the new identity in science can react back on gender relations and become a source for re-evaluation and emancipation. In a school context, there is a great deal that can go wrong here, since gender oppression is ubiquitous and can derive from a multiplicity of sources – from the way a classroom is organized to the content of a textbook, from the way pupils are defined and define themselves as learners to the way teachers define themselves as teachers. All differentiations, as Foucault reminded us, are suspect because each carries with it a promise as well as a possible threat – the promise of being empowered and the threat of being subjugated.

In exploring this further, it will be helpful to look at an empirical study of gender differences in learning styles carried out by Tolmie and Howe (1993). The authors found that on a computer-based task in secondary school physics, both boy and girl pairs made equal progress in understanding but employed markedly different styles. Males tended to take more account of the implications of 'feedback', whilst girls tended to explore what the problems they were investigating had in common. The authors interpreted this as reflecting how the different pairs coped with conflict. Their study supports previous findings which show that males are more inclined to assert and elaborate when faced with a conflict of opinion, whereas girls typically avoid conflict and focus on what has already been agreed. Both these styles have positive and negative features from an educational viewpoint. If boys' assertiveness becomes too extreme this can then lead to outright argument which is too confrontational to be productive for learning. On the other hand, the evaluation of different ideas and rival explanations, via attention to input and feedback, is potentially a useful way to explore what should, after further consideration of the evidence, be held in common. Similarly, girls' tendency to avoid conflict could lead to their ignoring discrepant feedback and 'unsettling' ideas which, again if taken to extremes, would be dysfunctional. But their focus on commonalities provides a useful basis for seeing connections between problems.

Clearly, this study gives grounds for hope that a *modus operandi* can be constructed based on mutual respect between boys and girls and an understanding of difference, which can only be of benefit to both parties. But there are questions which need to be asked. Is it implied that these differences in interactional styles between boys and girls are fundamental and 'neutral', one of the facts of life that teachers have to take account of? Or is there some recognition of the possible hazards? If we do not take this matter seriously then the differentiation of interaction styles might well function as part of, in Madeleine Arnot's (1994) words, the 'symbolic separation of the sexes' that gives the oppression of girls 'the seal of approval'. Associating girls' strengths with seeking commonalities and boys' with assertive and conflictual behaviours seems to define them in a way which is remarkably close to those gender characteristics which supposedly are a function of the asymmetrical power relations between men and women. Girls and women grow up to be more co-operative, sensitive and caring because of the kind of role women have traditionally played in families. Boys are more assertive because they have to maintain their dominance.

We can see some of the possible consequences of failing to take account of gender power relations by considering the alleged female capacity for 'care' and 'nurturance'. Like the capacity for seeking commonalities, this might be seen as a strength which complements the male capacity for independence and 'standing on your own two feet'. There is clearly scope for dialogue here, but, unless wider democratic change occurs, it is doubtful if retaining these gendered constructions of psychological traits is in the interests of girls – or, for that matter, of boys or of society as a whole – in the long term.The 'nurturing' or 'caring' behaviour of girls is potentially just as problematic as the 'aggressive' and 'assertive' behaviour of boys. Thus, whilst girls may need to be encouraged to become more assertive, they also need to examine their approaches to 'care'. If these are derived from assumptions about an emotional division of labour supposedly founded in 'natural' characteristics, then they merely complement and legitimate uncaring behaviour in boys. Thus the notion of care has to be reviewed for girls and fostered in boys in ways which recontextualize it in democratic models of social and personal relationships.

What really needs to occur, therefore, is an interaction between boys and girls which enables each first to acknowledge and then to appropriate the strengths of the other. Both interactional styles represent a valid approach to learning in science and becoming adept at both can only enrich the learning experience for all pupils. It is here that action on gender needs to begin. Tolmie and Howe acknowledge that mixed group work is a way to facilitate this mutual appropriation but this is precisely the mode which is resisted by pupils in the school context. The teacher is faced with choices which relate to long-standing debates about co-education. Is it best for girls to be taught in single-sex groups away from the constant intrusion and disruptiveness of the male 'gaze'? They could still be taught assertiveness and how to make productive use of conflict, but this would be done by teachers in an enabling context rather than through what might be picked up in the always potentially disturbing association with male pupils. Or is it better to engineer mixed-sex teaching on the grounds that the advantages would usually outweigh the disadvantages? In view of the progress that has been made on the gender front in recent years, it would seem as a general rule more appropriate to opt for the latter than the former, although it would clearly all depend on the circumstances.

Circumstances will also determine the significance of boy/girl differences and dictate whether certain differences are more salient than others. Identifying girls as 'carers' is always likely to have important social consequences because of the association of care with the kinds of jobs people do and the kinds of role they play in society. In our culture, it is also perceived as a key element in people's moral ideals and their political orientation. But clearly this is not necessarily true of all differences between boys and girls and men and women in all situations. More men than women may be interested in chess, squash and cars, and clearly these activities are gendered and might in certain circumstances be the site for political struggles around gender, but it is just as likely that pursuing them will have no dire consequences for gender relations. What really has to be constantly considered is whether socially constituted differences reinforce inequality, are just harmless expressions of group or individual identities or, more positively, are signs of a healthy and culturally enriching diversity.

Sexuality and intimacy

All this applies, of course, to practices which relate directly to pupils' consciousness of the other as a gendered and sexualized subject and object in personal relationships. As we have seen, the reflexive self has a particular interest in 'close' relationships which act as a main source of support in these uncertain times, yet at the same time because of present-day attitudes towards sex, sexual intimacy with the other can be 'purely physical' rather than psychologically 'close'. These matters constitute an important part of the curriculum for life and in one way or another preoccupy all of us, but they are particularly germane to the life activities and identity work of young people.

Recognition and explanation of difference are a crucial component of pupils' practices in this area. The theme of 'liking' – who is liked and who is not liked or 'fancied' or 'lovable' – is heavily influenced by gendered assumptions about what kind of other should be desired by boys or girls. Of all aspects of a person's make-up, desires are the most difficult to reflect upon critically because, once felt, they are experienced as so compelling both physically and psychologically that they seem to be 'natural'. Thus, it is not difficult to understand why sexual relations can involve misplaced or misdirected desires, that sex can be 'good' or 'bad' and that in 'wanting' someone it is not whether motives are ulterior that is the problem but whether they are corrupted by power. Sexual acts cannot be divorced from the social, cultural and political context of their enactment and in seeking 'good' sex pupils should be helped to become more aware of the possible impact of gender power (R. Jones 1989). The message of sex education should not be 'no sex without love' but 'no sex with domination'.

Yet if we recognize the changing nature of the times, and, along with Giddens (1992), we accept there has been progress, then schools as we find them will not be so deeply oppressive that no scope for 'purer' and more democratic relationships can be envisaged. Not only do pupils resist stereotyped identities and contest sexual conventions but they also develop their own sexual curricula as part of an ongoing celebration and enjoyment of life as young people in 'new times'. To say that one of the main interests of youth is sex and relationships is perhaps to state the obvious, but it is still an area which finds little space in the formal curriculum, and when it does it is mostly associated with supposed problems of 'growing up' or with moral panics about promiscuity, schoolgirl pregnancies and HIV/AIDS rather than, say, with the 'joys of sex' or what it means to have 'good' sex or the healthy diversity of sexual practices.

A reformed curriculum which dealt with sex in this way, as well as with other topics directly related to relations between the sexes such as love, close friendships and marriage, would clearly be a development which would have some chance of connecting with young people's interests and concerns, and thus facilitating a dialogue between the informal culture of pupils and the formal culture of the school. Like 'true love', the course of close relationships and 'good' sex never will run smooth, but it is precisely the messiness, the strains and stresses of these important human attachments with which good schools should be able to cope; and more than this, because there is no reason why these experiences and how to handle and evaluate them could not be seen as a central part of the school curriculum. Moreover, the development of desire for forms of intimacy free of the baggage of patriarchy is bound to contribute to changes in the way young people relate to each other which are *beneficial for learning*.

Concluding comment

To sum up: schools should certainly examine their curricula and pedagogies with a view to ascertaining any patterns of discrimination which are gender-based. In view of present trends in achievement, particularly as reflected in GCSE results, there is probably no longer any need for positive action in favour of girls, although there is a need for some form of radical action; and likewise for boys, further action is required but not at the expense of girls in terms of resource allocation. Schools also have to be aware of any other patterns of discrimination, such as those stemming from race or class or disability oppression, which might be interacting with gender or which, in a particular instance, might even have more significance than gender for anti-discrimination policies.

The discussion in this chapter gives an indication of a possible way forward for schools in constructing a gender curriculum. In the first place, it is apparent that gender issues are still salient and should be addressed specifically. Second, rather than just developing anti-sexist policies, schools should actively promote democratic gender identities throughout the curriculum. At the moment gender differences are usually associated with inequalities but this may not be true of all differences either in the present or the future. In conditions closer to the democratic ideal, it could be that gender ceases to be a significant category in the construction of identity in educational contexts. What gender differences continued to exist might have little social significance or, if they did, this would no longer be symptomatic of oppression.

8 | On learning and democracy in families

Introduction

On 17 October 1997 it was reported in *The Guardian* that in Ireland teachers in Catholic schools were being encouraged to use terms like 'the people who look after you' rather than age-old terms like 'mummy and daddy' on the grounds that the latter had become too 'exclusive' and failed to recognize the changing structure of the family in present-day society. Nothing could be more indicative of 'new times' than this remarkable development in a country which, as far as the family is concerned, has always been a bastion of conservatism. It reflects the uncertainties, possibilities and forebodings of a new reality. With such a fundamental institution of society on the move, the threats to social order are obvious, but the opportunities that flow from 'liberating' the family from its traditional form are immense, in terms of the possibilities both for individual freedom and for the development of democratic communities.

Because tradition can no longer be relied upon, it is likely that present and future citizens will need to develop a critical awareness of those aspects of family life which many parents previously took for granted. They will need to develop a capacity for reflecting upon family relationships in a way which fosters openness and experimentation but does not undermine the capacity for commitment in 'close relationships'; and they will need to be able to evaluate family forms and make judgements about the appropriateness of this or that form in terms of their own future lives as 'good' parents and/or citizens. Since change occurs so frequently and such a great deal is at stake, the family and parenthood should clearly have a central place in the curriculum for lifelong learning.

The discussion in this chapter will focus on the way 'good parenting' and the values associated with family life are mediated in schools. The chapter begins with a discussion of education for parenthood and a way of looking at this through an analysis of the operation of the informal curriculum. It is suggested that it would be helpful to consider home and school as involving two distinct discursive practices – each with its own strengths and weaknesses from a learning perspective – and that an appropriate way forward would involve fostering a dialogue between these two practices. The prospects for the family are reviewed in the light of its historic role as an institution of modernity and its problematical role as a force for education and democracy.

Parenting skills: origins of the direct approach

In recent years in the UK there has been an increase in direct attempts to teach parenting skills through government-sponsored agencies. The curriculum content of this intervention is a function of the form of the programme and the motivation of its proponents. Some programmes are focused on improving parenting skills in 'problem' families, whilst others target the wider audience of all those who are parents now or might be parents in the future. In the early 1990s the interest generated by the launch of a new pamphlet by Lord Joseph (Joseph 1991) and a major debate in the House of Lords echoed concerns in a number of government departments about the relationship between quality of parenting and certain undesirable consequences for children and young people. The link between criminality and the quality of parenting, supposedly demonstrated by research, gave rise to a number of programmes funded by the Home Office, and likewise the Department of Health and the Department for Education and Employment took initiatives in relation to the problems in their areas which also seemed to be associated with poor parenting – for example, schoolgirl mothers and school exclusions.

This focus is also evident in the first White Paper of the new Labour government on *Excellence in Schools* (DfEE 1997). In a section on 'Skills for Life' in Chapter 6, three areas are singled out: work-related learning, citizenship and parenting. Parenting is considered to need urgent attention.

> Few factors have a more profound effect on individuals and the nature of society than the contribution of parents to their children's development. But young people often leave school without ever having given any serious thought to whether they will have children, or how they would cope if they did. We want all secondary schools to help teach young people the skills of good parenting, both formally and through contact with good adult role models.
>
> (DfEE 1997: 63)

In addition, schools are to be encouraged to build on this experience of teaching pupils by developing 'educational programmes in partnership with local education authorities, further education colleges, adult education institutions, voluntary and family groups and family nurturing schemes to support parents who are bringing up children' (DfEE 1997: 63).

Much of this is derivative of a neo-conservative analysis (see Chapter 1 and below) which interprets social ills as resulting from family breakdown due to the moral deficiencies of parents. Thus the White Paper emphasizes the deficit view of the parenting skills of young people and parents in much the same way as the restorationist rhetoric of the previous Conservative government. On the other hand, the bland nature of the statement – which contrasts with the apocalyptic, 'doom and gloom' language of most Conservative tracts – and its lack of reference to 'tradition' suggest perhaps that there is more scope for alternative readings (see Smith 1997).

Education for parenthood and the school curriculum

In examining how education for parenthood and family life is actually accomplished in schools, we need to consider both the formal and informal curriculum. The teacher may convey to the pupil covert messages about good parenting which either support or contradict the explicit messages of the formal curriculum on 'parenting skills' or whatever they are called in the syllabus. Thus, in formal lessons the teacher may recognize a diversity of family forms but in practice go along with the school's support for a traditional idea of the family, as expressed, say, in letters home which are addressed to both parents even in the case of one-parent families, or in home–school contracts which tacitly assume that the rhythms of family life are the same for all and reflect traditional behaviour patterns.

These contradictions can occur between the way the family is constructed in different subjects of the formal curriculum, as when one view of the family is expressed in religious education and another in English. There are also differences between teachers as well as differences between pupils and between pupils and teachers about what is understood to be the nature of particular families and the nature of the typical family of the catchment area. In some cases, the homes of pupils in general are viewed by teachers in terms of deficit models, and thus as homes where there is 'bad' parenting and an unwholesome family life; or in terms of other stereotypes where it is assumed that parenting in pupils' families is not necessarily deficient but is incompatible with what the school expects. Of course, although teachers may have more power to impose their definition of the situation, the teaching is not all one-way. Pupils may teach teachers things about their own family life and family life in general. We can illustrate some of the ways in which the informal curriculum of the family is negotiated in school by looking at an example from case-study research carried out in an American context (see Hansen 1993).

Kimberley, the latchkey kid

The researchers wanted to find out why Kimberley's relationship with her teacher deteriorated in the sixth grade. They had followed her through the fifth grade in a quiet suburban elementary school and into the sixth grade and the more robust atmosphere of the middle school. Kimberley was described as 'unusually oriented towards adults, never failing to acknowledge the entry of any adult' (Hansen 1993: 71) and frequently had after-school chats with the teacher, but recently she had stopped this and had become more defiant and questioned the authority of the teacher, Mrs Thorncliff. The teacher was annoyed and angry at this turn of events but it did not confuse her because she put it down to 'incompetence in attitudes' and 'lack of self control', which required a teaching approach characterized by 'strong and consistent demands, close monitoring and tight control from the teacher' (Hansen 1993: 72). The trouble, Mrs Thorncliff believed, was located in Kimberley herself, but its source was in the home background. She was aware that the mother was divorced and living as a single parent, and she assumed that the whole family 'lacked control', allowing Kimberley to do more or less whatever she wanted, even to the point of ignoring her mother's inconsistent demands.

The way Mrs Thorncliff located Kimberley's problem 'within' the child and as a function of her home life is typical of a particular way of looking at the family. First, the child-in-the-family is viewed as a passive recipient of adult socialization rather than as an active constructor of meaning in family life. Second, Mrs Thorncliff's view of Kimberley as a product of faulty socialization in the family seems to have been 'read off' from her beliefs about the nature of family life in single-parent families. There is no evidence that she has arrived at this view through a careful examination of this particular family.

Kimberley however, resists this interpretation of herself and her family life. Although she knows she has a problem, she also recognizes that the situation is more complex than the teacher imagines. The teacher is not herself prepared to learn what Kimberley tries to teach her. Kimberley resents not being treated as an agent, and resents the implication that her family life is in some way deficient. The following 'letter incident' illustrates the difference of perspective between child and teacher. Kimberley was very embarrassed one day when, in front of the whole class, the teacher read out a phone message from Kimberley's mother, asking her to pick up her younger brother and sister after school and to take care of them for the whole evening. For Mrs Thorncliff reading notes from home to the entire class was 'only routine' and she could not understand why it bothered Kimberley so much, but from the latter's point of view it was a threat to her self-image, particularly in relation to peers. Reading the note conveyed a certain meaning about herself and her family to the rest of the group which she rejected. As the researchers point out:

Her private problems at home have been publically revealed, in a way that is surely being distorted by the other kids . . . The notes tell them that her home life is somehow different from theirs, more limited in time, money and other resources. Her parents are divorced, her mother has a demanding job and K is expected to do things which demean her age and status. While her peers can enjoy their independence and maturity after school, she is forced to remain in the role of mother's little helper.

(Hansen 1993: 83)

In another incident, the teacher interpreted Kimberley's attitude as 'open defiance'. Walking up to the teacher's desk, Kimberley explained that the assignment Mrs Thorncliff had given the class had 'confused everyone' because she had not explained it correctly. When the teacher asked the class who was confused, no one responded, which confirmed her belief that Kimberley was just being defiant. Kimberley said they were too scared to answer: 'I have to do this, because they are too scared of you. I'm the one who has to stand up for people in this room, because they are afraid of you' (Hansen 1993: 90). But she was clearly hurt by their lack of support for her. The teacher was surprised but, as the researchers note, she should not have been because Kimberley was clearly using her as foil in her project to gain acceptance by peers.

In her day-to-day interactions Kimberley is engaged in continuous identity work in countering or reinforcing or representing versions of her self-in-the-family and her self-in-the-school, which are in line with who she thinks she is and how she would like to be seen. From what she says and how she reacts we know that both she and her mother are aware of certain ways in which their life is structured and how their position might be viewed by others. They both call Kimberley 'the latchkey kid'. But equally Kimberley seems to know that the problems they face at home are largely to do with her mother's vulnerability – constant money worries, the fear of losing her job and the stress of long hours. In other words, she interprets family life in socio-economic rather than psycho-pathological terms. If she could express it in this way, she might recognize that to describe her as 'lacking in control' was to misrecognize her. In fact, she is no more or no less in control of her life projects than any other child of her age. Her so-called defiance could be interpreted as act of control – she was trying to control the way she was seen by peers and she was trying to control the teacher by using her for her own purposes. She does not really mind defining herself as a 'latchkey kid', but she wants to reconstruct this version of self-in-the-family so that it does not entail a view of the family as being in some way deficient. Kimberley and her mother recognize that the future is open and think that life will be easier for her than it has been for her mother, but there is the constant threat of the school, via teacher and peer attitudes, constructing a different and less optimistic way of looking at her family and herself, one that closes the future down.

Discursive practices: the differences and similarities between home and school learning

Kimberley resists the teacher definitions of her self-in-the-family and thus in a sense is teaching the teacher about family life, whilst Mrs Thorncliff is attempting to impose on Kimberley an alternative construction based on her version of the ideal family. The characterization of the process in terms of resistance and imposition implies a lack of mutual understanding, but this is not to say that no communication is taking place and one can imagine a situation where the teacher responds in a more positive way to Kimberley's actions. She would clearly learn more about Kimberley and Kimberley's interpretation of the family through critically engaging with her rather than by trying to impose her views through strategic action. We might think of this as a productive conversation between two individuals, but, at a different level, as a conversation or dialogue about family ideology between two institutions – home and school. Such a conversation could, of course, be around many themes. In this instance, it is around the theme of life in single-parent families, but the focus could be, say, on the differences between school and home interpretations of 'learning'. 'Good' parenting – as practised by parents and learned by pupils – could be defined in terms of what kind of learning it makes possible in the home and what it recognizes as 'good' teaching in school. One of its defining characteristics would be that it promoted a positive approach to learning and enabled offspring to benefit from their educational experiences in home and school.

We can explore these issues further by thinking about home and school as two distinct discursive practices. If constructive dialogue is to be fostered, we need to identify the differences as well as the similarities between the two discourses. A useful starting point – mainly because it challenges many teachers' common-sense assumptions, particularly those which stem from a deficit model of their pupils' home backgrounds – is to examine ways in which 'home learning' might be superior to 'school learning'. Hannon (1995), for example, having identified the possible characteristics of children's learning at home and in school, remarks on the plausibility of the idea that home learning might be more powerful than school learning. 'For example, the scope for children satisfying their needs and interests, the relationships with adults and the comparative lack of time constraints seem to point to the superiority of the home as a learning environment' (Hannon 1995: 39). The home is a more person-centred and flexible environment where there is the possibility of closer and more continuous relationships between children and adults, and this contrasts with the school environment where learning is of necessity driven by curricular objectives and where adults in the form of teachers are more distant and do not have the time to cater for the individual needs of their pupils.

It is important to note that this view of home learning as superior does not rely on a definition of achievement which is necessarily different from that of the school, certainly not of 'good practice' in school. There is no distinction necessarily being made, for example, between 'affective' and 'cognitive' learning. Home learning may be emotionally more powerful, but one could argue that it is also potentially intellectually more powerful, since it provides opportunities for children to become creatively and actively involved in real-life problems rather than contrived problems. Even what Hannon considers a strength of school learning – the possibilities of planned curricular progression – may be a weakness from a cognitive point of view, since the opportunities provided in the home environment for a non-linear approach to concept learning may be an advantage. Concepts learned in the home may be richer and more multi-faceted than those learned in school because of the different dimensions of knowledge that are typically deployed and integrated in home practices. The following analysis of parent–child conversations by Walkerdine (1990) will serve to illustrate this.

Money in home and school

In her review of the Tizard corpus of conversations between mothers and their pre-school children relating to 'money', Walkerdine found the focus of attention tended to be the domestic economy. In several conversations a connection was made between the cost of goods, the value of labour and the receipt of wages. It was quite clear from the transcripts that the children were learning that small amounts of money did not have much purchasing power because of the high cost of goods, and were being encouraged not to be wasteful because of the high costs and the labour involved in earning sufficient money for purchases – if he doesn't work dad 'won't get lots of money and then you won't get new slippers' (Walkerdine 1990: 141). As Walkerdine (1990: 140) points out, 'although, in one sense, the arguments about exchange value and the money economy are highly abstract and complex, the elements of the argument are presented to the children in such a way that they have actual material consequences in their day-to day lives'. Thus, the hierarchical sequence of young children operating at a concrete level before they can move on to an abstract level, which is often assumed in pedagogical strategies in mathematics, does not reflect the more sophisticated understandings that young children deploy in their everyday lives.

Walkerdine also cites the 'shopping game' as an example of how the school discourse of mathematics fails to acknowledge the meanings with which the children are already familiar and thus how a teacher deploying this discourse would fail to understand how the game might be interpreted.

In the game, items can be bought using a price in pence. The children in an infant class are provided with ten plastic 1p coins which they can spend in the shop on various items. They work out a subtraction operation with the coins and then record change from 10p in the form of a subtraction sum on paper. The contrived nature of the exercise is immediately apparent to these 6- and 7-year-olds. It is certainly not like real shopping. Such small amounts buy practically nothing in the real world, certainly not the goods that they have been asked to purchase, such as an aeroplane. In the transcript the children show that they have a realistic assessment of real prices and that they can talk about large sums of money.

The shopping game is supposed to provide a meaningful context which will facilitate the process of learning mathematical rules, in this instance subtraction. One important aspect of the home context is that conversations take place which involve reference to more than one knowledge dimension at a time. Thus in relation to conversations about money there are mathematical aspects but one might say there are also economic and, in so far as family members have different interests, even political aspects. Walkerdine also gives examples of conversations between mothers and children about gardening which involve mathematical and natural scientific terms such as size, speed, time and growth. When the focus is mathematics, specific aspects can be abstracted, like the time taken by plants to grow to certain heights.

In the light of all this we can with some confidence assert that the school has much to learn from the home. In fact, what we often regard as 'good' practice in school learning involves an awareness of the typical limitations of school learning and of the need to counter them. First, good teachers appreciate the importance of ascertaining whether or not a practical example is a 'real-life' situation and if not they try to make sure that it is a situation which the pupils can easily conjure up in their imagination (as in imagining there was a shop where everything could be bought for a few pence). Second, they are aware of the significance of the integrative potential of the home discourse, and of the way it reflects how mathematical knowledge is actually deployed in multi-faceted practical contexts. Thus they try to alter school discourses in ways which foster integration and the practical application of subject knowledge. Third, good teachers are aware of the importance of bringing the 'personal' back into mathematics as well as into other so-called impersonal subjects such as science (see also Chapter 10).

So what are the differences between home and school learning?

So far, we have been concerned with the strengths of the home discourse from a learning point of view. Not only are there many possibilities in the home for 'good' learning and teaching, but learning may even be superior. Children are socialized into the 'ways of knowing' of the family; this is where the first learning takes place and where their sense of self and what it means to be committed to a social practice is nurtured. If this process is successful, then the learning which occurs must by its very nature be morally, emotionally and cognitively engaging. Families are good, therefore, at giving children a sense that learning is a serious business; that it is a process which requires the development of a sense of belonging to a learning community and that what we learn is what we are. Usually in family learning all this is at the tacit level, with the curriculum – for a curriculum there is – being constituted largely through identification with the parents as role models.

The role of school learning

These are the undoubted strengths of home learning, strengths which have certainly been grossly underestimated in the past by schools, but what are some of the potential drawbacks? Home learning may be more powerful but it also potentially more threatening to the children's basic understanding of themselves as individuals. What the parents help to create, they can also destroy. Individual identities are associated with positions in a 'totalizing' family discourse, which are in one sense 'strong' – in that they involve strong feelings and genuine commitment – but in another sense are 'fragile' because if validation of this position is withdrawn the self could be completely annihilated. The dread of this – felt more acutely in some families than others – makes the distancing required for a radical appraisal of the values of one's own family an extremely risky business.

So what about the role of school learning? Children 'emerge' from the home into the 'outside' world as individuals in their own right, but then have to develop a more self-determining mode of being than was possible in the 'totalizing' environment of the home. An important part of this outside world is the school. In school, the idea of disengagement from any particular practice for the sake of reflection may be easier to achieve because the school environment is potentially more pluralistic and diverse, providing more opportunities for taking alternative standpoints. Pupils may compare and contrast the nature of their involvement in one practice with that in another and begin to see that there are different 'ways of knowing' in different learning communities; or they may compare one teacher's approach to a subject with another's, or one style of learning with another. The downside of this is that they may become too reflexive, and thus fail to develop that capacity for attachment required for genuine participation in a learning community. Of course, the existing state of affairs in schools is not of this ilk. The problem is not that there is too much reflexivity but too little. However, we can see how there may be more scope for the development of reflexivity in school than home, the latter usually being a more monocultural environment; which is not to say that home always compares unfavourable with school in this respect, since it is always possible that in a particular family the parents may be liberal-minded enough to provide a pluralistic educational environment in a way that a particular school does not.

The 'dark side' of the family

School and home, therefore, may have much to learn from each other. At the level of teacher–child interaction this means that teachers and pupils are both teachers and learners in an ongoing process of appropriating each other's knowledge about learning. It is a process which involves critical engagement. Although the strengths of home learning should be recognized and understood in all their particularities in individual families, teachers cannot assume that all learning that takes place in the home is educationally functional. Education for parenthood should involve interacting with pupils in ways which reinforce those aspects of the home discourse which are educational and democratic and discourage those which are negative and dysfunctional. It means helping pupils to become more aware of what it means to be 'good' learners and 'good' teachers in the home.

However, just as things can go wrong in schools, so they can also go wrong in families which also have their 'dark sides'. Indeed, it could be argued that just as society needs to be deschooled so the equivalent process has to take place in relation to the family as an institution. The idea of involving families more intensely in education might be considered to be naive. Teaching children to appreciate the strengths of learning in the family so that they will become aware of how parents can be good teachers might be even more naive. It could be that the family itself is too riven by contradictions to provide an environment where the kind of learning that children need for survival in reflexive modernity can be sustained. The in-built constraints against the development of reflexive learning may be tied in with an inherent tendency for families in our society to work against rather than for the production of democratic learning communities. Even with respect to the strengths of the family in fostering a committed approach to learning there are a number of anti-democratic features which, despite all the changes that have taken place in recent years, might be so endemic to family life that they are always likely to resurface.

As many critics of the neo-conservative perspective have pointed out (see Abbott and Wallace 1992) the historical role of the family as a progressive force was always a middle-class dream rather than a reality. Assumptions about the Victorian period as the 'golden age' of the family ignored the appalling conditions under which most working-class families lived, the physical abuse of women and children in families, the economic dependence of women and other aspects of the 'dark side' of the family stemming from Victorian hypocrisy and male double standards. With political democratization and the growing affluence of Western society there have been some changes, but the family is still not the symmetrical structure desired by democrats and continues to be a basically patriarchal and authoritarian institution.

However, whilst one can sympathize with some of these criticisms, the view taken here is that there is still a moral consensus about the core values of family life and that these can be identified in the multiplicity of family forms which exist in the contemporary world. Perhaps one positive outcome of the rise of neo-conservatism in the 1980s was that, unlike the neo-liberal wing of the 'New Right' or the current libertarian strain, it did put the moral dimension of family matters firmly on the policy agenda. In seeking a way forward both for policy reform and for education for parenting, therefore, rather than simply deconstructing restorationism, it might be worth trying to tease out those aspects of what in an earlier period would have been described as the *bourgeois* family that may have acted as an impetus to the progressive reforms which occurred later. It has too often been the case that those who have opposed the neo-conservative version of the family have not said much about what kind of family they are for. In what follows I shall attempt to identify those features of the bourgeois family which seem to me to characterize it as a modern as opposed to a traditional form. In attempting to highlight what is at issue here, I shall critically examine Berger and Berger's (1983) analysis of the family, which has been described as based on a neo-conservative perspective (see Roche 1992), although the authors themselves have denied this.

Berger and Berger's argument

For these authors, the bourgeois family developed historically in tandem with those social forces which created modern democracies. The family nurtured the capacity to participate in social life – the capacity to develop shared understandings, to love and to trust others – which was an essential prerequisite for participating in wider communities. Taking an interest in and taking on responsibilities for others are capacities which are first nurtured in families. A child who developed no social and emotional bonds in the family would have difficulty in developing allegiances to larger social groupings in later life. The leap of imagination required to empathize with the unknown other is only possible if one has experienced feelings for the other in close relationships – otherwise there would be nothing for the imagination to leap from! This has been true in all societies, but it is particularly important in a society where autonomy is a valued goal that the socializing agency is one which can provide a balanced upbringing, with self- and social interest nurtured in equal measure and as compatible elements in an individual's motivational structure. Without the development of individual moral responsibility, society would have to be coercive in a way which would be unacceptable in a democracy. If social cohesion is to be achieved in modern societies with their 'organic' as opposed to 'mechanical' solidarity – to use Durkheim's (1933) terms – then it is essential that individuals are produced who are capable of creating a social consensus, and are willing to do so.

It seems to me that there is much here with which a democrat would agree, but in exploring the issues further, we ought to note the limitations of the Bergers' argument. The family is, at every turn, caught up in contradictions stemming from the anti-democratic aspects of its own structure and those of other modernist institutions. The Bergers have some appreciation of these contradictions, but the way they engage with them is clearly more conservative than liberal. Although they think that the bourgeois family ethos may have had within it the seeds of its own destruction and that the husband/father's role as a 'figure of power and authority within the household . . . was undermined by the emancipated bourgeois wife/mother' (Berger and Berger 1983: 102), this emancipated woman is still fundamentally a 'homemaker' – 'companion and helper to her husband, supervisor and "facilitator" of her children's development and education, arbiter of taste, culture and all the "finer things of life" ' (Berger and Berger 1983: 102). Perhaps this could be read as a statement about the way things might develop in bourgeois families *which were in the process of change*. The wife would become more of a 'companion', and later this companionship might evolve still further when mother/wife and father/husband began to share the breadwinner role and the nurturing role.

Hyper-individualism

But this is not the Bergers' view. Instead, they see many recent developments, particularly those prompted by the rise of feminism, as a reflection of a form of individualism which they describe as 'hyper-individualism', where 'the individual woman is now emphasised over and against every communal context in which she may find herself – a redefinition of her situation that breaks not only the community between the spouses but (more fundamentally) the mother–child dyad' (Berger and Berger 1983: 120). They regard the 'life planning of individuals' and 'the search for individual identity in isolation from all community definitions' as symptoms of this distorted form of individualism which legitimates 'what quite frequently are brutal assertions of self against the claims of others (such as : notably, children and spouses)' (Berger and Berger 1983: 120).

But what the Bergers would interpret as evidence of 'hyper-individualism' (for example, a mother wanting a career and being concerned with self projects) others would regard as evidence of a woman's self-actualization and self-fulfilment, a highly valued state of the self in a democratic society. The Bergers fail to distinguish the positive developments of the period from the so-called permissive society of the 1960s to the feminist ideologies of the 1980s – the stress on authenticity, on being in touch with feelings, on the development of self and the capacity for productive love (see the next section) – from the negative aspects such as narcissism, anti-intellectualism, mysticism and self-absorption which also occurred but were clearly a distortion of the main progressive theme.

Indeed, the Bergers would associate some of these positive developments with what they call counter-modernism – that antagonism to modernist institutions which derives from anti-rationalism and anti-individualism, as exemplified by the romantic yearning for traditional collectivism found in certain species of Marxism, the counter-culture and many other radical ideologies of the 1960s. But there is another interpretation. It was not so much an allegiance to past 'forms of life' that was the main motivation of groups who embraced such ideologies – although undoubtedly there were some who in seeking alternatives drew inspiration from the past – but rather a desire for democratic revolution motivated by modernist, not counter-modernist, urges. In the cultural revolution of the 1960s and 1970s, the critique of the bourgeois family was not anti-individualist *per se* but sought to expose the pseudo-individualism of the family and other structures implicated in the reproduction of a patriarchal and class-dominated society. It was in that period that an impetus was given to the development of a reflexive and democratic society, a development that was therefore forward- not backward-looking.

Hope for families and democracy

For the most part what these modernists aimed for was the renewal of the family along democratic lines rather than its total deconstruction and reconstruction. The ideal form of 'love' in this new family has been described in many ways and taken many forms, but in essence it is what Fromm (1971) described as 'productive love' – the kind of love which involved 'union with somebody . . . outside oneself, under the condition of retaining the separateness and integrity of one's own self' (Fromm 1971: 37). Such love is not unconditional; it is not 'edgeless' or without boundaries. For if it were, as Rose (1995: 98) has suggested, it would be a 'counsel of despair' where 'existence is robbed of its weight, its gravity'. 'Unconditional love' takes the risk out of a relationship, but at the cost of denying scope for self-development, including the development of the capacity for love. 'To grow in loveability is to accept the boundaries of oneself and others, while remaining vulnerable, woundable, around the bounds' (Rose 1995: 98).

The lack of symmetry in family relationships is directly attributable to 'ways of knowing' the other which give rise to a definition of his or her needs and capacities that is limiting and reductive. In the social conditions of an imperfect democracy this reductive view is associated with patriarchy and class, but it is also linked with the 'distorted' adult–child relation of oppressive child-rearing practices which illegitimately subject the children to the will of parents. The mistake the Bergers and other conservatives make is to assume that statements like this can be quite simply dismissed as anarchist and anti-authority, a clear example of the hyper-individualism of the permissive society. But there is a world of difference between parental authority which is based on justified as opposed to unjustified paternalism, an important distinction which liberals have always resorted to when coming to terms with some of the apparent contradictions in their position (see Aviram 1991).

These constraints on the development of democratic families (and thus the role of families in the production of democracy) are familiar, but they do not provide sufficient evidence for the complete abolition of the family. For Fromm the possibility for self-fulfilling intimacy and family democracy could be 'glimpsed' in the here and now. For the production of democratic character, it is difficult to see what could replace the family or some family-like institution. In the period of reflexive modernity where the counter-modern tendencies of class and patriarchy are increasingly challenged, space is opened up for experimentation with a variety of family forms (single-parent, same-sex parents and so on) but I would argue that what all these should have in common are relations that allowed for regular interaction of a 'loving' kind between the infant and one or two others acting in parental roles over an adequate period of time.

One is, however, left with certain doubts. Even in the most democratic of families, where good parenting involves teaching children about other forms of life and where relationships between partners are companionate, there is still a possible contradiction because of the role that family decision-making plays in the wider context. The family can never be seen in isolation from the rest of society. At the level of rhetoric parents may be democratic and practice productive love, but they are still caught up in a system where their choices provide advantages for their own children at the expense of those in other families. Liberal families may worry about this more than non-liberal families, but there is not much either can do about it.

The problem is evident in the bourgeois family even at its so-called 'best'. A study by Jordan et al. (1994) of 36 higher-income British couples with children is of interest here. The authors examined the 'interpretative repertoires' used by the couples in day-to-day decision-making and concluded that they were operating with an individualist perspective which did not enable them to make appropriate links between two key terms in their dominant model of citizenship – 'property' and 'democracy'. The upshot of this was that without actively endorsing selfishness or greed, the couples used the advantages which flowed from property (in this case, defined as the possession of at least one secure job) to ensure that their children gained 'every competitive edge' (Jordan et al. 1994: 181) in their own future attempts to secure such a job.

The focus was thus on getting them the best possible education. Private education was only chosen if it was seen as the best way to achieve this.

This emphasis on 'putting the family first' sprang directly from a democratic morality, however, where concern for the individual was the dominant perspective. Thus strong commitment to choice and 'making something of oneself' (Jordan *et al.* 1994: 89) was linked to respect for the dignity of the individual and their entitlement to consideration, support, consultation and empathy. Accounts of family crises were always careful and reflective, focusing on the different needs of individuals in the situation, and in particular the needs of members of the nuclear family rather than those of the extended family or friends.

In fact, as the authors demonstrate, this strategy does not always work out as intended and there are structural impediments to it being a successful strategy for everyone in the long term. As 'positional' goods, like good jobs, become scarcer and competition for them drives up the price, parents have to make more and more sacrifices for their offspring, who need to be supported for longer periods so as to ensure they do not lose out in competition with others. And at the end of the day, nothing can be guaranteed. Even a university degree does not automatically provide a satisfactory return on the family's moral, cultural and financial investment, since a good job may never materialize.

In addition, it is doubtful whether such striving for advantage, apart for its overall social effects, is even very good for the internal democracy of the family. Most couples in the study opted for a strategy where the man became the careerist and the wife the secondary earner who arranged her paid and unpaid work activities in a way that supported her husband. As the authors point out, each career-oriented father is forced to keep his job longer, which means that 'the vicious circle of prolonged dependence is given an extra twist' (Jordan *et al.* 1994: 219) since access to good jobs for their offsprings' generation is blocked for longer. Thus both the wife/mother and offspring are increasingly dependent on the husband/father, which has major implications for power relations in the family. Daughters, in particular, may lose out. Since middle-class families are equally ambitious for their daughters as for their sons, daughters are likely to experience a prolonged dependence before they can leave home, only to be thrust back into dependency at a later stage, when in the interests of the family they take a back seat to their future husbands in career terms, with whatever autonomy they achieve dependent on the survival of the marriage.

Concluding comment

The family contributes to social inequalities, but this is not all that can be said about it. The tendency for parents to seek advantages for their own offspring is unfortunate from a democratic perspective, but there is a world of difference between the loving, child-centred, liberal family where this is experienced as a contradiction, and a traditional authoritarian or 'sick' family where children are barely able to develop their own self-identity let alone have pangs of conscience about their contribution to the oppression of others.

State institutions such as the school should therefore support parents in their attempts to produce ontologically secure, autonomous learners who are also good citizens. Education for parenthood where the focus is on the future generations of parents is one way of doing this. In general, schools and other institutions need to bear in mind a vision of the family ideal in a democratic society and become more aware of how their actions either support or undermine this ideal. Family policy can never be value-free (see Fox Harding 1996); it always contains assumptions about what the family should be like, even if these are not always made explicit.

If we are to take the idea of support for families seriously, all social policies must be considered in terms of their family effects. These include the unintended effects of policies which do not deliberately incorporate family considerations (for example, economic policies), as well as the intended and unintended effects of explicit family policy. It follows from this that any intervention to improve the condition of the family must look at 'needs' across a wide front and at the actual and potential impact of a wide range of policies. Thus in relation to schools everything that occurs in school from taking the register to teaching sex education, from teaching parenting skills to pupils to involving parents in the teaching of reading, should be scrutinized for its family effects. The criteria for judging the effects of any action in school will revolve around the extent to which it fosters the capacity for learning, autonomy and citizenship for all, not just a selected few. Schemes which involve only a minority of parents or pupils would be critically examined to see what hidden messages were thereby conveyed to non-participants. Appropriate action would vary according to political and historical circumstances and current perceptions of the nature of families and family life in the local community or communities. Sometimes it would be direct and sometimes indirect, but it would always be a question of working with families, warts and all, to secure improvements.

9 | Reworking the work ethic

Introduction

In a democratic society, the hope is that all citizens will have jobs which are worth doing, both in terms of their own interests and desires and the interests of society as a whole. To advocate work as a creative, meaningful, self-fulfilling and socially productive activity requires us to see it as a virtuous activity rooted in the identity of people as moral beings and thus to argue for a version of the old idea of a 'work ethic', albeit one reconstructed in accordance with the cultural understandings and the social reality of contemporary society. The central feature of the work ethic is the idea that work is valued in and for itself, irrespective of any financial benefit which may accrue to the individual. A worker who subscribes to the work ethic is self-motivated and will not need to be coerced or enticed into doing a 'good job', since it is intrinsic to his or her self-identification as a moral being that the work done is socially necessary and carried out in accordance with certain standards.

This contrasts with the view that in contemporary society the work ethic is in decline and that this is no bad thing because there will be less work in the future as society becomes more leisure-dominated (see Watts 1983). The view taken in this chapter is that work as creative effort is and will always be a necessary and desirable social activity, even if it is unpaid and regarded as a leisure activity. The work–leisure dualism is clearly only helpful when work means employment and leisure is time off work. But in the present circumstances, there are new possibilities in both paid work and leisure for endeavour to be informed by a new work ethic. What hopefully will be in terminal decline is a version of the work ethic where duty is emphasized rather than rights, coercion and control at the expense of freedom of choice, and employment as opposed to a wider definition of work.

The main purpose of this chapter is to explore some of the ways we need to think about work if we are to teach it as a 'good' for the self and society. The social, cultural, technological and economic developments of 'new times' have led to enormous changes in the kind of work people do, and this has given rise to opportunities for a new relationship between the self, work and society which can be culturally enriching for self and community, but which also carries with it certain dangers. I shall begin by explicating the work ethic and some of the ideas associated with it, with a brief reference to its historical origins and the interpretations of various social analysts, in particular those of John Dewey. I shall then go on to examine the ways in which these ideas might be applied to teaching and learning about work in a school context. This will involve looking at the informal and the formal level of the curriculum, and addressing questions to do with the way we expose pupils to various meanings of work, what it means to do 'good' work and what alternative teaching approaches might be envisaged.

Religion, the work ethic and the rise of capitalism

In its modern form the work ethic has been associated with the rise of capitalism (see Weber 1930) but it is important to remember that the idea can be traced back to pre-modern times, where it had a distinctly different meaning. In medieval society, work had its place within a social system conceived as a whole in which activities were related to a hierarchy of functions, each of which had value at its own level, as long as it contributed to the common purpose of society as defined by the Church. Thus every individual's work had a moral significance and was a 'holy' business, carried out for spiritual purposes. What we would now describe as economic activities were included under this moral umbrella, but they were not ethically equivalent to each other. Some economic activities were distinctly more 'perilous to the soul' than others and the more pecuniary the motive the more 'dangerous' the activity became. For medieval thinkers such as St Thomas Aquinas labour was a noble and honourable activity, but trade was more suspect and finance, whilst not exactly immoral, was a high-risk activity from a spiritual point of view.

All this was to change in the three centuries from the later Middle Ages to the early eighteenth century as a new version of the work ethic gradually formed under the impact of economic and political changes in the period of the Reformation. It was the Reformation which fostered the work ethic in a manner that made it compatible with a developing economic system where making profits and accumulating capital were the very lifeblood, namely capitalism. Both Weber (1930) and Tawney (1938) have charted this developing and mutually confirming and reinforcing association between religious nonconformity and capitalism, as expressed for example in the social psychology of members of religious movements like Puritanism. For Tawney (1938: 229), it was the 'moral self sufficiency' of the Puritan which 'nerved his will but corroded his sense of social solidarity' and made capitalist relations more acceptable by blinding him or her to the social injustices which were a consequence of economic activities. This individualism stemmed from a view of the individual believer as one who had a responsibility for his or her own spiritual development and needed no intermediaries between himself or herself and God with whom a personal relationship was established through the individual's own efforts.

It is the individualistic and ascetic view of the work ethic which, in its secularized form, is bequeathed to us today. From a capitalist perspective it has a number of advantages. Work is seen as a social duty, it staves off idleness, fosters thrift and sobriety and contributes to social order. It is regarded as a central life activity which individual workers have, in a sense, chosen for themselves, the contract with the employer being analogous to the contract with God, since 'God hath given to man a reason for this use, that he should first consider, then choose, then put into execution . . . ' (Steele, writing in 1684, quoted in Tawney 1938: 240). It is thus also, to quote Noon and Blyton (1997: 48), a 'conscientious endeavour' involving 'disciplined compliance'. In sum, Noon and Blyton (1997: 48) point out, what all this boils down to in modern times is a version of the work ethic which involves 'the belief that it is the duty of everyone to treat productive work as their central life activity and to perform it with diligence and punctuality under the direction and control of managers'. It assumes a view of self-in-the-world where, like the Puritans, one takes the existing set-up for granted, being focused rather narrowly on the self, one's immediate environment and one's day-to-day existence rather than on wider issues and the 'big questions' about the overall purpose of work. The Puritans, of course, *did* attend to higher moral imperatives, but only in so far as the self in relation to God was concerned, which in effect meant taking little interest in the details of the impact of their activities on society generally.

Alienation and false consciousness

But to describe the 'work as life activity' approach of the Puritans as informed by a work ethic – even in such an attenuated form – is perhaps still to give it too much credence. For Marxists, Christian socialists and other critics of capitalism, the mode of work in capitalist society was the very antithesis of its meaning in the moral tradition referred to above. Under capitalist economic conditions, to do work or to be in work was to be in a social relationship 'with some other who has control over the means of productive effort' (Williams 1976: 280) and where endeavour was not an expression of a mutually fulfilling relation between people but was alienated labour which left 'no other nexus between man and man than naked self interest, than callous cash payment' (Marx and Engels 1970: 82). For Marx this cash nexus stood over and above human beings, determining their actions and their psychology in a way which prevented them realizing their 'species powers' (that is, their human qualities). In this way, human beings became estranged, separated or alienated from their life and work activity, from their products, from their fellow men and from their 'species being'. They were estranged from their work over which they had little control, from the objects they produced which had little personal significance for them, from their fellow human beings with whom they were in competition and from their own capacities and sense of agency which were constrained by economic imperatives.

Of course, in the Marxist version of alienation and some other versions – that of Fromm (1971), for example – which interpret alienation as endemic to work in a capitalist society, 'being estranged' is viewed as a state of being which people are not necessarily able to articulate fully. They may, of course, experience feelings of alienation – they may feel their work is a meaningless activity, feel dominated by the boss, have conflictual relations with other workers and feel bored and stultified rather than fulfilled by the daily grind of work – but equally they may feel happy or reasonably contented with their lot and not at all alienated or estranged. For the Marxist, the latter would be a form a self-deception or false consciousness.

False consciousness is an unfashionable term, but in the context of a discussion of the self and work it still retains its usefulness as an analytic tool. We know the self has hidden depths and that the individual's understanding of the self cannot be grasped in its totality at the level of consciousness (see Chapter 2). However, like the Freudian concept of unconscious motivation, false consciousness is vulnerable to the charge that it fails to provide a means whereby hypotheses about events in the world can ever be proved right or wrong. If we hypothesize that worker X is alienated, then the evidence can take the form of either X's avowals as to feelings of alienation, or denials of such feelings – it being assumed in the latter instance that the worker has a false consciousness. Thus we do not have to search far for an interpretation which can 'explain away' any finding we may come up with. But there is only a risk of 'bad' explanation if we adopt a determinist model of the impact of social forces on a person's psychology. If on the other hand we assume the worker is a moral agent, then we have to acknowledge the possibility that the meaning attributed to work by an 'objectively' alienated worker may in fact be genuine, just as we have to acknowledge the possibility that it may be 'false' (Lukes 1977). There is nothing inherent in the concept of false consciousness that prevents us treating the person as an agent and asking questions which can be subjected to an empirical test. I shall return to this later in the discussion of teachers' work.

Work and education

Self-centredness of the Puritan kind, however, was not an inevitable accompaniment of the development of individualism, since, as the history of Western society has shown, there was an alternative path for the 'freed spirit' of the individual – one which opened the way towards a more socially oriented and democratic character structure. In this connection it will be useful to look at the views of John Dewey, who has provided one of the clearest statements of a modern ethical view of work and the relationship between work and education. Like the Puritans, Dewey interpreted work as a 'calling' or a vocation, but his definition of this was secular and humanistic. For him a vocation was any purposeful and continuous activity which involved a service to others and also engaged 'personal powers' in a way that fostered growth of the individual (Dewey 1933: 350–60). The opposite of 'vocational' was not 'leisure' or 'cultural' activity, but activity that was aimless, capricious and involved 'parasitic dependence' on others rather than 'cumulative achievement in experience' for the individual. His definition thus referred to a person's role in society (service to others) as well as to their development and growth as an individual. Vocational activities were thus educational and vice versa. There was a continuity between the vocationally oriented activities or occupations of pupils in school (educational activities) with adult occupations; as well as continuities between paid and unpaid work, and work that was 'economic' in a conventional sense and other types of work, which included nearly all activities in pursuit of social roles, including those carried out in institutions such as schools. For him an occupation was vocational in the sense that it was socially useful and growth-enhancing and thus educational for the individual, and education through engagement in occupations was like 'good work' at any age – there was no basic difference between a 'calling' as a child and one as an adult.

This ethical view of vocational education was accompanied by an analysis of 'dangers and opportunities' for its realization in the 'current context', that of the early twentieth century. The opportunities were, in general terms, very similar to those a pragmatic and optimistic person of liberal democratic persuasion might identify today. Dewey felt that there was 'increased esteem' in a democratic society for manual labour and whatever else had to do with 'rendering tangible services to society'; there were 'better moral sentiments' involving a new valuing of social responsibility and personal capacity (Dewey 1933: 366). Similarly, the growth of technology and the stimulation of science by the economic revolution had increased what Dewey described as the 'intellectual possibilities of industry', although current industrial conditions tended, for the great mass of workers, to make industry less of an educational resource. Advances in the psychology of children's learning were in line with the increasing importance of industry. 'It reveals that learning is not the work of something ready-made called mind, but that mind itself is an organization of original capacities into activities having significance' (Dewey 1933: 368). Play and work were thus not radically different activities; the passage from one to the other was to be gradual and no radical change of attitude was required.

Dewey also, of course, saw various dangers in the prevailing conditions. The industrial regime as currently in operation was divisive and feudal. In the following well-known passage the implications for schools are spelt out:

> any scheme for vocational education which takes its point of departure from the industrial regime that now exists is likely to assume and perpetuate its divisions and weaknesses and thus to become an instrument in accomplishing the feudal dogma of social predestination. Those who are in a position to make their wishes good, will demand a liberal, a cultural occupation, and one which fits for directive power the youth in whom they are directly interested. To split the system and give to others, less fortunately situated, an education conceived mainly as specific trade preparation, is to treat schools as an agency for transferring the older division of labor and leisure, culture and service, mind and body, directed and directive class, into a society nominally democratic.
>
> (Dewey 1933: 372)

A curriculum which acknowledged Dewey's view of the link between education and work would offer an immediate challenge to both the traditional liberal and vocational curriculum as conventionally understood. It would include

> instruction in the historic background of present conditions; training in science to give intelligence and initiative in dealing with material and agencies of production; and the study of economics, civics and politics to bring the future worker in touch with the problems of the day. . . . Above all, it would train power of readaptation to changing conditions so that future workers would not become blindly subject to a fate imposed upon them.
>
> (Dewey 1933: 372)

It is this emphasis on worker empowerment – on making workers critical – which has been interpreted by some (see Lewis 1994) as an aspect of Dewey's model of vocational education which is more radical than 'mere shifting from job-specific to generic vocationalism' (Lewis 1994: 213).

Schools, work and the curriculum

It is evident that Dewey's view of the work ethic is very much in line with the kind of approach to work that a curriculum for life in reflexive modernity should foster. His thought is clearly consonant with that of the 'progressives' (be they liberals or 'trainers') of the current period and is grounded in similar assumptions about the need for a critical vocationalism. In fact it is probably true to say that contemporary analyses (particularly those carried out by educationalists) of the vocational–liberal education divide and the proposals for overcoming this – indeed, the fact that it is regarded as a 'good thing' that it should be overcome – not only rely heavily on Dewey's ideas but in some respects are not much of an advance on his position.

The purpose of what follows is to explore, in the light of Dewey's analysis, some of the opportunities for a successful reconstruction of the work ethic through curriculum development in schools, in relation to both the informal and formal aspects of the curriculum, as well as to identify some of the limitations of current approaches. The questions posed are: what do schools teach about work, how do they teach it and in what ways do they need to think about work in order to develop an appropriate work curriculum? Pupils and teachers need to be knowledgeable about current work practices, but they also need to be able to make judgements about how principles derived from a broader understanding of work might be applied to themselves and their own situation.

The informal curriculum

Pupils experience something which is called 'work' from the moment they enter school, where the play–work dualism soon becomes apparent. School is the first experience of having to do work – unless, of course, certain activities in the home have been identified as work, for instance housework (see Leonard 1990) – and of being on the receiving end of someone who is doing paid work. For the most part the idea of what is considered to be 'socially necessary' about work is not seriously challenged. It is experienced as essentially an activity which is carried out for instrumental reasons and does not involve the 'real' self. Evidence for this comes from a variety of sources, in particular from sociological studies in the ethnographic tradition. In his review of studies in this area, Peter Woods (1990) has noted that although there is no simple relationship between teacher intentions and pupil actions, the message conveyed to pupils is that work has no intrinsic satisfaction; it is a question of 'buckling down' and learning good work habits. Categories used to describe pupils typically include terms such as 'idle', 'lazy', 'good worker', 'industrious', 'needs to work harder', 'more effort required'. Pupils rarely claim to value 'work' as much as they do other activities, such as 'mixing with friends' or 'sport'. Those activities which involve the 'real' self are not considered to be work. This carries over after school or college, where the only difference is that work is paid for. Sometimes work may be interesting but, whether interesting or not, it is a common perception that existing forms of work have to be done if society is to survive and the individual is to make a living.

Teachers are often conscious of contradictions in their work practices which stem from the need to retain a certain kind of professional identity and moral commitment in what is often an alienating school environment. They often find themselves having to balance what they perceive as their pragmatic with their paradigmatic concerns (see Hammersley 1977b) – the former are to do with ways of accommodating to the current situation and are often in tension with the latter, which relate to educational ideals: 'how teaching ought to be, how it could be in ideal circumstances' (Hammersley 1977b: 38). It is in coping with the pressures emanating from this tension between their different concerns that teachers' work is accomplished and the meaning of work in schools constructed. Any formal curriculum input about the nature of work would have to take account of this informal curriculum, which in Foucauldian terms may constitute a 'contradictory discourse' about work. In particular, it is important that the so-called work-related curriculum is developed with due regard to the various interpretations of what in the sociological literature are described as teacher 'survival strategies' (see Woods 1983) – the kinds of skills teachers and other workers need to 'get by' in jobs which have little personal meaning (often, in the case of teachers, a 'lost meaning'), and over which they have little control.

We need to bear in mind here the idea of false consciousness discussed earlier. When we examine the work situation of any particular group of teachers matters are usually never clear-cut. In the Menter *et al.* (1997) study referred to in Chapter 4, primary school teachers' responses to recent educational changes varied according to whether they originated in the 'public' or the 'private' selves of the individuals concerned. Those which derived from the former tended to be more positive about the changes than the latter, which were disclosed when teachers were speaking 'confidentially about their private perceptions of changes' (Menter *et al.* 1997: 100). The tension between these two versions of the self was clearly the source of much stress. The positive and public account revolved around the idea of accountability, particularly in relation to parents, and the idea of consistency in provision across schools and local education authorities, both of which were supported in principle by the teachers. But, as Menter *et al.* (1997: 110) suggest, 'the negative aspects were presented by the teachers as an introduction of overburdening administration and a reduction and a waste of teaching time, which had led to a lowering of standards because topics were dealt with more superficially than before'.

A key question here is whether to interpret the teachers' accounts as an example of the inevitable strain experienced when adapting to a new role or as a reflection of increasing alienation and demoralization. The strength of the false consciousness view of alienation, as stated above, is that it requires us to be cautious about expressions of satisfaction and always to look critically at the surface features of teacher consciousness. Menter *et al.* themselves certainly seem to take account of this in the distinction they make between private and public versions of teachers' responses. But educational researchers cannot avoid taking up a value position here. The point is whether the 'new' self of teachers who became thoroughly socialized into the new role would be a 'better' or 'worse' self from an educational viewpoint. It is clear that for several of these teachers the move away from 'traditional child-centred and teaching-oriented professional identity' (Menter *et al.* 1997: 115) towards the new collaborative, co-ordinating, managerialist professional identity would not seem to represent an improvement. Had they used the term, they would clearly have seen this as an increase in alienation, and, in so far as we held the same educational values as they did, we would probably have agreed with them. The new role seems to lessen autonomy and seems to be about contrived rather than genuine collaboration.

At the same time, however, our value position also requires us to make judgements even in situations where no feelings of alienation are expressed either by the public or the private self, since it could be the case that both selves interpret and incorporate change in ways which result in less autonomy and more alienation. How could we make such judgements? Our analysis might perhaps deploy reference points grounded in the cultural expectations of those – maybe teachers in other schools in a contemporary or historical context – who had more experience of the quality of education that could be achieved in schools which were more democratic. Thus it is not that the empirical world is ignored but that the experience of others beyond those in the field of investigation are taken into account. Individual teachers will be positioned differently with respect to cultural ideals, but membership of a putative democratic society provides everyone with certain options and resources for the realization of a new consciousness. Of course, the creation of a new consciousness is not the same as making explicit and bringing to the surface, as it were, what is already there. For many, awareness of alienation could follow from an acknowledgement of certain aspects of the self which had, for one reason or another, remained suppressed. It is a commonplace that there are many aspects of the self not always available to consciousness. It is not untypical for people to be surprised by their reactions to certain events, and to acknowledge subsequently that they had discovered aspects of themselves of which they were not previously aware.

However, although terms like alienation and false consciousness are difficult to define and apply, this should not weaken the assumption that how teachers feel about their work and how they accomplish their work roles will contribute to the curriculum by conveying meanings about the nature of work to pupils. This implies that, to take two extreme but relevant examples, the job satisfaction of the most outwardly satisfied teacher may be interpreted by pupils, as it may also be by colleagues, as an expression of alienation, and this may be the truth of it; and similarly, that the unhappy teacher may in his or her day-to-day relations with pupils paradoxically communicate a real sense of what non-alienated work means.

The formal curriculum

There are many aspects of the formal curriculum in schools which might be relevant here, but I want to focus on a development which directly addresses the theme of work, namely the so-called *work-related curriculum*. For the purpose of our discussion here, I want to concentrate on two areas: first, knowledge and understanding of the 'world of work', particularly work defined as paid employment; and second, the acquisition of core skills which are thought to be important for all workers in present day society.

Understanding the world of work

In recent years there has been a growing consensus about the need to construct a work-related curriculum as an integral aspect of the formal curriculum (see Saunders *et al.* 1997). Properly contextualized rather than merely 'bolted on', it would interact with the general curriculum in a way that was mutually enhancing and enriching. One of the clearest statements of this view is that of Spours and Young (1988). In arguing for vocational aspects of academic learning, the authors propose that 'the demands of working life' be regarded as a new educational principle and that from age 14 onwards 'work' should move to the centre of the curriculum and be integrated with and informed by the academic curriculum. Although they recognize that work can be defined in various ways, they consider that 'the concept of work cannot escape being about future employment and preparation for it' (Spours and Young 1988: 9). Consequently, they envisage the application of academic subjects to the study of work mainly in the paid employment sense of the term. Such an application would facilitate the progressive development of academic subjects through a 'dialogue with productive life' (Spours and Young 1988: 5) and bring to the study of work the morally informed, systematic enquiry and bodies of knowledge associated with subject disciplines.

This approach to the work-related curriculum is open to criticism on a number of counts. For instance, it focuses on paid work and the 14+ age group to the exclusion of other forms of work and younger age groups. This may be justified on the grounds that it is the best place to start given current understandings of the meaning of work and expectations of both pupils and teachers, as well as interested third parties like parents and employers. However, the main problem is that it does not sufficiently problematize the notion of the 'academic curriculum' with which the work-related curriculum is supposed to be integrated. In advocating a dialogue between the academic disciplines and productive life, the power of existing subject disciplines to alienate pupils seems to be underestimated. With the central subject pillars of the National Curriculum intact, there is every danger that a 'vocationalist' initiative of this nature would lead to the cart being put before the horse. Whilst the ostensible aim would be to teach about work and foster a critical disposition towards paid employment, the real aim of subject teachers might merely be to incorporate this new theme into the existing set-up rather than to use it as a spur for genuine dialogue.

The capacity of the subject-based curriculum to impede genuine dialogue and subvert the aims of the work-related curriculum has been demonstrated in several studies. A pertinent historical example would be the Technical and Vocational Education Initiative, which, though it preceded the Education Reform Act (1988) and the establishment of a National Curriculum, encountered various forms of resistance emanating from the subject specialists of the traditional curriculum. Studies (see, for example, Dale *et al.* 1990) have shown that responses to TVEI were various, but there were certain general tendencies:

- High-status subjects such as science and maths often did not become involved.
- The focus of new courses was often on the 'less able', thus limiting the impact of change and reinforcing class reproduction.
- Traditional subject teachers often resisted new courses which attempted to break down the barriers between subjects – an example is the creative arts course which attempted to integrate drama, art, music and home economics.
- In general, the initiative did not remove the distinction between high-status and low-status subjects.

In a recent assessment of the impact of the work-related curriculum on young people's conceptual understanding of work, Saunders *et al.* (1997) note that the use of 'real-life' contexts – for example, work experience placements – have not realized their potential because they have been divorced from the main curriculum framework; and that, despite the intentions of the National Curriculum Council (NCC 1991) and others to incorporate economic and industrial understanding as a cross-curricular theme within the National Curriculum, there has been little to show for it. Subject specialists themselves have been unwilling and often unable, because of syllabus and exam constraints, to alter their practices in ways which can accommodate new content and the new experiential approach to learning which goes with it. As recent research findings have shown (Whitty *et al.* 1994), whilst there is support amongst teachers for cross-curricular issues at the level of rhetoric, in practice the subject culture of the National Curriculum is still dominant. Between the ages of 14 and 16 there have been some changes as a result of the introduction of so-called 'vocational' options, but the direction taken has been defined almost exclusively in terms of the development of 'skills' rather than education in a broader sense. Such reforms as there have been, as well as those anticipated by the Dearing (1996) proposals, are of the 'bolt-on' variety and do not involve a complete rethink of the National Curriculum.

Key skills and general education

As Saunders *et al.* (1997) point out, the aim to foster 'key skills' is associated with the idea of education for adult life as well as skills specifically for work. In some ways what is being proposed is an extension of the approach discussed above and represents an attempt to alter both the formal and informal curriculum through the introduction of an alternative content and methodology. A broader definition of work, to include 'social and life skills' rather than just skills for paid employment, is being deployed here. From a democratic educational perspective, the hope might be that such skills would play a role in the reconstruction of work, whether paid or unpaid, and its transformation into an activity informed by an alternative work ethic. If students learned that 'good' work involved the use and development of such skills, their expectations would be raised and they would be critical of jobs where there was no opportunity for such development.

The idea of 'core skills', or 'key skills' as they are now called in official discourse (see Dearing 1996) has become central to policy debates in the area of post-16 education and training (Green 1997). Although bodies such as the Further Education Unit (FEU), the Confederation of British Industry (CBI) and the Qualifications and Curriculum Authority – the successor organization to the School Curriculum and Assessment Authority and the National Council for Vocational Qualifications (NVCQ) – have produced different definitions, there has been common agreement about the possibility and desirability of identifying skills or competences in certain key areas, such as literacy, numeracy, information technology (IT) and problem-solving – all essential requisites for flexible adaptation and functional efficiency in a rapidly changing economy and society. Such bodies have been supported by those who want to reform the current A-level exam to encourage more breadth and balance in the academic curriculum (DES 1988; FEU 1990); by adherents of competence-based vocational education as a means of achieving transferability (Jessop 1990); and by those concerned with a unified post-16 curriculum as way of bridging the vocational–academic divide (Spours 1995).

In the light of our concern for an autonomy-enhancing curriculum, it is important to note that most proposals for key skills include a 'personal effectiveness' or 'personal skills' element. In 1989 the CBI produced a document *Towards a Skills Revolution* which referred to 'effective communication' and personal and interpersonal skills'. In the same year, John MacGregor, the then Secretary of State for Education, asked the School Examination and Assessment Council, the NCC, NCVQ and FEU to define core skills in six key areas, one of which was 'personal skills'. And personal skills – which would include such skills as 'improving one's own learning' and 'working with others' – are amongst the mandatory units of the General National Vocational Qualification (GNVQ, see below). Indeed, some commentators have seen the notion of personal effectiveness and personal autonomy as a theme in post-16 education which has of all key skills the greatest potential for integrating the vocational and the academic curriculum (Hodkinson 1989).

Critique: the case of GNVQ

In evaluating the key skills approach, the rhetoric of personal effectiveness and personal skills is a good place to start, and a pertinent example is the GNVQ. The overall aim of the GNVQ is to provide a high-quality vocational alternative, based in school or college, to the traditional academic route of GCSE through to A level. It was conceived in response to misgivings about National Vocational Qualifications (NVQs), particularly the latter's association with a narrow and over-specific range of job-related skills. The GNVQ at advanced level is supposed to be roughly equivalent to two A-level passes, whilst at the intermediate level the aim is to provide a qualification equivalent to four A–C pass grades at GCSE. At intermediate and advanced levels four types of unit are involved – mandatory, optional, core and additional – the first two of these representing the knowledge as well as the skills considered by employers and professionals to be essential for entry to and performance in an occupational area. Although NVQ and GNVQ share the same competence-based framework, GNVQs are broader-based with a more flexible structure and a greater emphasis on self-directed learning techniques which enable students to demonstrate their abilities over a period of time and to some extent to work at their own pace. Students are encouraged to gather evidence for portfolios and to plan their own work, and are provided with scope for self-evaluation.

At the level of rhetoric there is certainly an emphasis on the development of the student as a self-regulated, autonomous learner (see NCVQ 1995), but in practice the various constraints – a demanding assessment schedule, an excess of paperwork, the large amount of course work, outcomes which are still too specific and prescriptive, a jargon-ridden language of assessment (Spours 1995) – minimize the possibilities for the exploratory and reflective approach to learning which one would expect of the autonomous learner. Students are not in fact treated as if they were effective individuals pursuing their own goals (FEU 1994) but more as deferential workers who can follow instructions, carry out routines in an efficient and orderly way and conform to set procedures for problem-solving (Spours 1997). Moreover, although students are often asked to display 'confidence in analysis, understanding and creativity' (see Ofsted 1994: 18) there is no scope for this to go beyond the parameters of the employer-dominated discourse. Consider the following example of a a student's work which is cited by the inspectors as an example of good practice:

Jane's Advanced Business portfolio addressed the full range of these skills and understanding in a report produced for a local building company. Her assignment was to act as a systems analyst making proposals to the company about how they could improve their competitiveness through the use of computer and IT systems. She was asked to consider the company's operational and financial efficiency. Her report was presented exceptionally well but behind this was evidence of detailed and careful analysis of how, for example, the company's payroll system could be more efficient if it used an IT based programme. Jane based her judgments on clear and comprehensive knowledge of the company and had tested out all the stages of the proposal. The assignment had been well designed and well matched to the time available, the scale of operation in the company and the ability of the student. It had also grown out of a good level of respect and cooperation between school, student and company that encouraged high expectations, which were fully realized.

(Ofsted 1994: 18–19)

Whilst no doubt various skills and qualities were displayed here, this example gives cause for concern from an educational viewpoint. Clearly, there are values underpinning this activity (efficiency, competitiveness) but there is no evidence that the student has reflected upon these. Systems analysis can be carried out from a variety of perspectives but the student does not seem to have been encouraged to think about different approaches or to think critically about the particular model she is using. The use of IT shows the danger of treating this as a 'core skill' as opposed to a cross-course theme which needs to be known and understood in a broader and more interconnective way. How did the application of IT affect the way work was structured? How did it affect the experience doing work? If it did not involve deskilling and job losses, as so many applications of IT have done, what were the social and economic consequences of applying it in this particular instance?

An alternative perspective

The fate of GNVQ is still in the balance, but it seems clear that at root the problem here is that the skills- or competency-based approach to teaching for autonomy and self-regulation will just not do. It is based on a view of the self which is 'thin' relative to the kind of reflexive, critical and creative agent which, I have argued, is the ideal self of 'new times'. Similar points could be made about most other key skills. In relation to the goal of bridging the vocational-academic divide, they seem to add up to a programme of training which cannot deliver a coherent set of aims and objectives for a unified curriculum or serve as a common core which would provide learners with a broad and balanced education.

So what is the alternative? In the view of one influential commentator, what is required is a well-thought-out programme of continuing general education, similar to that taught on many vocational courses in other European countries and Japan. For Green (1997: 19) 'the core skills paradigm represents an impoverished form of general education which is neither delivering minimum basic skills . . . nor even attempting to impart a foundation of scientific and humanistic culture adequate to the demands of active citizenship in modern societies'. The solution is for all post-16 courses to have a mandatory minimum core curriculum of general education which should include:

> at the least, English/communications; mathematics/numeracy; and some form of civic or citizenship education which would have as its aim the cultivation of political literacy, environmental awareness, international understanding and social responsibility. Ideally, it would also include a science and a foreign language.
>
> (Green 1997: 20)

These would be constructed as modules which would provide a common core across the different vocational pathways and would assist the process of transfer and progression.

Green's proposals have a number of strengths. Unlike Spours and Young's approach, his proposals for a general education go beyond the traditional subject curriculum and, if taken up as a common curriculum in schools, would in effect be an alternative to the present National Curriculum. Does this approach really bridge the vocational–academic divide? Yes, potentially, but it depends on how courses are taught and whether the content of general education courses is appropriate. The pathways he refers to reflect different career trajectories either with respect to content (engineering, languages, business studies) or form (the university route, further education, on-the-job training), but unless steps are taken to integrate the different components, these pathways could easily be viewed as the main vocational and career element, thus leaving general education as high, dry and disconnected as liberal education always has been in a training context. And whilst the omission of areas such as 'personal effectiveness' and 'life and social skills' is certainly justified in view of the impoverished view of the self and the restricted model of learning they have usually entailed, the baby does seem to have been thrown out with the bathwater. Self-reflexivity and personal relationships – the social psychology of the individual learner – move out of focus as specific topics in Green's model. It is precisely these themes, I would argue, which, if properly addressed, would provide the greatest scope for integrating different parts of the curriculum in all phases of a person's career and for developing a pedagogy which involved connecting with the priorities and concerns of individuals.

Concluding comment

The Puritan work ethic and a work ethic for 'new times' have in common the imperative to recognize work as an expression of people's identities as moral beings, but the latter will be different in at least two important ways. First, a person today is likely to have more than one 'calling' in their working life, either currently or, more typically, throughout their active life. Thus, they would have to be flexible and adaptable in terms of practical and intellectual skills, but (more importantly, I would argue) they would have to develop their capacity for transferring commitment from one job to another and also, at a deeper level, to become more aware of the various problems and dilemmas intrinsic to the process of becoming morally committed – for example, the renewal of trust, the transfer of loyalty, the need for a period of adjustment.

Second, they would have to become more critically aware, both in relation to their own self projects and the needs of society generally, of a wider range of issues and dilemmas derived from the experience of living in 'new times'. A series of questions would need to be generated. Is the job worth doing? Is it socially necessary? Would I do it if I didn't have to do it? Is it damaging to the social and material environment? Is it culturally enriching? Do I have any control over it, that is to say, over what is produced and over the production process? What does doing this job create in the way of social relationships between myself and others in the workplace? Am I exploiting others and/or being exploited by them? Do I see others as competitors? What is the job doing for me personally? Is it improving me? Is it making me a better person? Is it helping me to develop my talents? Is it giving me an identity I can live with?

10 | Science and the risk society

Introduction

A key characteristic of reflexive modernity is uncertainty with respect to all those modernist institutions and belief systems rooted in the Enlightenment tenets of Truth, Progress and Science. These 'old truths' have given way to doubts and anxieties about the nature and validity of natural scientific knowledge itself, the Big Science, which might be thought of as the core domain of modern knowledge. Nowhere is this more evident than in concerns about the questionable role of science and technology in relation to environmental degradation and ecological disaster. What was once considered a 'source of safety' has now become a 'source of risk' (Irwin 1995: 61). It is not just that scientific knowledge can no longer be relied on as a secure base for decision-making but that threats to the environment are actually produced by developments in scientific and technological practices. We live in a period where uncertainty is 'manufactured', to use Giddens's (1994: 4) term; that is to say, it originates not in 'natural' happenings but in the scientific and technological activity of society itself. Science is both a creator of problems and the claimed solution to those problems.

The notion of risk society, however, refers to more than the pervasiveness of concerns about those high-consequence risks which threaten human survival, such as the threat of nuclear war, ecological catastrophe or incurable disease. To live in this kind of society means to adopt a certain kind of attitude towards everyday existence, one that derives from an awareness of 'possible worlds' and of ways of knowing. The knowledge required for daily life is of the 'life world' variety where there is no 'quest for certainty' or seeking for 'the truth' but merely the hope of a reasonable chance to fulfil one's aims. As the sociological phenomenologist, Alfred Schutz (1971a: 72–3) puts it:

> Our knowledge in daily life is not without hypotheses, inductions and predictions but they all have the character of the approximate and the

typical. The ideal of everyday knowledge is not certainty, nor even probability in a mathematical sense, but just likelihood. Anticipations of future states of affairs are conjectures about what is to be hoped or feared, or at best about what can be reasonably expected.

In the period of reflexive modernity, more people are guided by this interpretation of the way knowledge works in everyday life. They do not 'take life as it comes' but are aware of the need to construct it for themselves – to 'realize their dreams', to fulfil themselves and to 'make it happen' – and to acquire and use whatever knowledge they need to achieve these ends. They know that risks are always involved. Knowledge still has its 'cookbook', taken-for-granted elements for dealing with the routines of daily life, but there is more emphasis on the reflective mode as existing patterns become transformed with increasing rapidity in contemporary society. The role of expert and the role of formal knowledge change. Like informal everyday knowledge, there is no longer any 'quest for certainty' and, as expertise becomes more differentiated and specialized, the less capacity there is for anticipating consequences outside the specific area of application.

Risk should not be a problem for democratic educationalists since it is an intrinsic feature of open learning communities. It is not a question of eliminating risk but of giving students more opportunities to develop strategies for coping with it. Of course, for many pupils life is less about being creative in a risky world and more about being constrained by the foreseen and unforeseen consequences of others' actions. In democratic communities, it is these anti-democratic and anti-educational elements which need to be removed, not risk itself.

The problem with Big Science is that it impedes the development of a more person-centred and community-oriented approach to the resolution of problems which is the most desirable mode of operation in the risk society (see Beck 1992). As a highly prestigious form of knowledge, it is used to legitimate policies which would otherwise be given a rough ride by the populace, and to silence oppositional 'voices' by giving false reassurances that problems can be resolved by the simple application of its truth. Such uses are, of course, challenged in various ways in different circumstances by different groups, but what really needs to occur is an increase in the reflexivity of all parties. Professional scientists and the teachers of science need to acknowledge the fallible and provisional nature of their discipline and its groundedness in a community of practice; students and the public generally need to be more aware of what they can expect of science and how they can make appropriate use of scientific knowledge – that is, they should not look to it for definitive answers or even for always posing the right questions.

Of course, acknowledging this alternative view of science as fallible and provisional does not imply its devaluation. It is not a question of somehow downgrading or ignoring science, but of ascertaining its appropriateness as a resource in particular circumstances and contexts. Just how helpful it will be will depend on a number of factors, such as whether the content of a particular scientific discipline is relevant to the problem addressed or whether the communities concerned are capable of generating mutually beneficial dialogue. But in the risk society the deployment of scientific knowledge will always entail risks. Science assists the process of calculation in a calculated risk but is itself an example of knowledge the very construction of which involves risk assessment – making predictions, evaluating evidence, drawing conclusions based on judgements, and so on. Just as risk and reflexivity are 'hazardous' but progressive characteristics of today's world, so science can be seen as both a threat and a help to the development of a democratic learning society.

'Good' science: a community model

Fortunately, we do not have to look far for a model of science which acknowledges that science, like all knowledge, is rooted in the practices of communities, is provisional and inevitably includes a component of 'risk'. Most scientists and educationalists are familiar with the model elaborated over 35 years ago by Thomas Kuhn in his book, *The Structure of Scientific Revolutions*, where it was proposed that science was paradigmatic and that progress and development were not so much a reflection of the 'discovery of truth' as of a paradigm shift or 'revolution', as the 'world view' (Kuhn 1970: 111) of one community of scientists gave way to that of another.

In thinking about the science 'curriculum for life' this is an obvious place to begin, and what follows is an attempt to spell out the educational implications of this community model of science. But before doing this, I want to clarify certain features of the model which are particularly germane to the argument of the book. It will be suggested that for the purposes of teaching we need to be aware of paradigms not just as closed systems of thought but also as open community projects underpinned by certain values, and just as embedded in social and political contexts and just as vulnerable to corruption and distortion as any other form of social practice.

For Kuhn (1970: 182), a paradigm was what members of a scientific community had in common which accounted for the 'relative fulness of their communication and the relative unanimity of their professional judgement'. Paradigms have the following characteristics:

1 They are 'living traditions' with their own situated (and thus socially constructed) rationality embodied in a community of persons and reflected in 'symbolic generalizations' (Kuhn 1970: 182), models, 'exemplars' (Kuhn 1970: 198) and values held in common.

2 Although they are incommensurable, this does not mean there can be no communication between them. In the case of a communication break-down, as Kuhn (1970: 202) acknowledged, participants can 'recognize each other as members of different language communities and then become translators'. A 'good' scientist should welcome communication between paradigms because it is one of the ways that 'scientific revolutions' (Kuhn 1970: 92) occur.
3 They have their own values and boundaries but reflect the wider values of the community of scientists where the 'risk' mentality required by science stems in part from the tolerance of individual variation and non-conformity characteristic of democratic society as a whole.
4 There are values externally and contingently related to paradigms which may have a distorting or corrupting effect on them.

The first characteristic embodies the idea of science as a 'world view' rather than a way of thinking which assumes the absoluteness of truth. It is a view which constructs the individual scientist as an agent operating within a culturally and historically located community of practice. The practice in which he or she is engaged is one which deploys 'symbolic generalizations' (laws and concepts) and models (explanatory frameworks, metaphors and analogies) which are interpretations of nature rather than theory-free descriptions. 'Exemplars' refer to historically concrete problem-solutions which any specialist group of scientists recognize as definitive of their field of enquiry. Moreover, conceiving of such knowledge as the provisional, historically located 'working' knowledge of a community suggests a potentially more tolerant and sympathetic attitude to other forms of knowledge; if nothing is 'dead certain', then other views might need to be taken seriously. This seems compatible with a democratic, non-hierarchical, pluralist approach to knowledge. It further suggests the potential value of 'conversations' between different paradigms – see point 2 above – including, I would argue, those that involve dialogue between the high-status, formal knowledge of science and the common-sense knowledge of everyday life – a point which will be taken up again later.

With reference to point 3, although Kuhn had in mind a view of scientific practice as differentiated into a number of separate communities with regard to symbolic generalizations and models, in relation to values he is clearly referring to a wider notion of community which embraces 'natural scientists as a whole' (Kuhn 1970: 184). Unfortunately, Kuhn's discussion of values is for the most part too sketchy to be of much use to the teacher or learner. He mentions shared values about the nature of prediction, and about the need for theories to permit puzzle formation and solution, and to be 'simple, self consistent and plausible'. Tantalizingly, he refers to 'other sorts of values' relating, for example, to whether or not science should be 'socially useful', but he does not elaborate on this. However, he does provide a fuller statement on one aspect of shared values which is highly relevant to a reflexive pedagogy in science – namely, that 'values may be shared by men [sic] who differ in their application' (Kuhn 1970: 185). Although commitment to shared values is both 'deep and constitutive of science', he stresses that it is often the case that the application of values is 'considerably affected by the features of individual personality and biography that differentiate members of the group' (Kuhn 1970: 185). For Kuhn this individual variability in the application of shared values is highly significant; indeed, it gives rise to the 'risk' element which is so essential to scientific activity that 'revolutions' would probably not occur without it. As he puts it:

> The points at which values must be applied are invariably also those at which risks must be taken. Most anomalies are resolved by normal means; most proposals for theories do prove to be wrong. If all members of a community responded to each anomaly as a source of crisis or embraced each new theory advanced by a colleague science would cease. If, on the other hand, no one reacted to anomalies or to brand new theories in high-risk ways, there would be few or no revolutions.
>
> (Kuhn 1970: 186)

Kuhn's idea of community enables us to go beyond the particular to the universal, albeit one that is 'bounded' rather than 'unbounded', a contextualized not an abstract rationality. The valuing of the individual in scientific communities is a reflection of the values of democratic society, and likewise doing 'good' science contributes to the construction of such a society. It thus seems a logical extension of Kuhn's position that the 'good' scientist would inevitably be concerned with social and political issues, such as environmental issues, since his or her very practice would reflect, reproduce and be dependent on the realization of the values of a particular kind of society. To teach science, or more precisely what it means to do 'good' science, therefore, is in part to teach about the need for social and political awareness as an intrinsic part of the process.

'Distortion' (point 4) is of concern to the Kuhnian scientist because it is a violation of the values of 'good' science. This is in line with the position taken in this chapter that it is possible to distinguish between 'good' and 'bad' science and which is opposed to the thesis that science itself – even in its 'pure' form – is somehow the cause of the problems faced by societies in the current period. 'Good' science may have negative consequences, but these are an unforeseen and an unfortunate by-product of an activity which at its best does have an in-built ethical concern about the nature of its impact on the environment and the wider community. The 'good' scientist will want to ascertain whether a particular instance of what might be thought of as a negative consequence of scientific activity is 'innocent' or the result of a corruption or distortion of his or her practice.

Educational implications

In what follows the educational implications of the above view of science will be discussed under three headings. The first, *science as a way of knowing*, relates to the first characteristic of Kuhn's paradigm; the second, *science as cultural communication*, to the more outward-looking role of the scientist and his or her location in a wider community; and the third, *science as an expression of interests*, to those structural sources of motivation which often distort the work of scientists.

Science as a way of knowing

In teaching science as paradigm we clearly do not want to portray scientific knowledge as ' "truth" unproblematically revealed by observation and confirmed by experience' (Millar and Wynne 1988: 396), but rather to teach, as Driver *et al.* (1994: 6) put it, that 'learning science means being initiated into scientific ways of knowing . . . the ideas and practices of the scientific community and making the ideas and practices meaningful at the individual level'. The teacher will want to foster an approach where learning takes place at two levels: the student will be learning about the specific content (concepts in a particular field of enquiry) but will also be learning that 'doing science' means developing shared meanings and common frameworks for observing and interpreting the world.

It is a question of enabling students to get a 'feel' for the language and practice of science (see Sutton 1992) through a pedagogical dialectic that positions them both as active constructors of meaning and as inductees into a scientific community which holds in common certain 'components of a disciplinary matrix', to use Kuhn's (1970: 187) phrase – in particular, the 'exemplars' which Kuhn felt were more definitive of the field of enquiry than other components. Learning to work within the paradigm, certainly in the early stages, involves 'doing problems' rather than learning theories because otherwise laws and theories would have little meaning. It is more a question of modelling problem-solving on previous solutions, with only minimal use of symbolic generalizations. For Kuhn (1970: 190) one learns from solving problems 'to see situations as like each other, as subjects from the same scientific law or law-sketch'. This process is essentially 'personal', includes an affective as well as cognitive component and involves what Polanyi (1966) described as 'tacit knowledge' which we develop through doing science rather than learning rules about how to do it (see Wellington 1994).

The teacher's *stance* towards knowledge is particularly important. It should convey a sense of the fallibility of scientific knowledge, its hypothetical nature and the way it can stimulate curiosity and further thought. It is not just a question of transmitting facts but of giving a demonstration of how pupils should use their minds in 'doing science'. As Bruner (1986: 127) suggests, pupils are not just 'informed' but are asked to participate in 'negotiating a world of wonder and possibility . . . and the materials of education are chosen for their amenableness to imaginative transformation and are presented in a light to invite negotiation and speculation'. He gives the following famous example:

> Stance marking in the speech of others gives a clue about how to use our minds. I recall a teacher, her name was Miss Orcutt, who made the statement in class, 'It is a very puzzling thing not that water turns to ice at 32 degrees Fahrenheit, but that it should change from a liquid to a solid.' She then went on to give us an intuitive account of Brownian movement and of molecules, expressing a sense of wonder that matched, indeed bettered, the sense of wonder I felt at that age (around ten) about everything I turned my mind to . . . In effect, she was inviting me to extend *my* world of wonder to encompass *hers*. She was not just *informing* me. She was, rather, negotiating the world of wonder and possibility. Molecules, solids, liquids, movement were not facts: they were to be used in pondering and imagining.
>
> (Bruner 1986: 126)

Miss Orcutt is making an attempt to connect with students' existing knowledge (about the difference between a liquid and a solid), but she is also trying to connect with what she anticipates as their sense of wonder. She could be wrong – after all, not all students will wonder about this phenomenon and not all will be as captivated as the young Bruner. But she is not working in the dark; the good teacher knows her students, knows what interests them and knows what is likely to stimulate their imaginations. Her knowledge therefore is not just about their cognitive but about affective and motivational dispositions. And the process is two-way. If students have got to know Miss Orcutt, they will know that she does not just express a sense of wonder about 'any old thing'. They might know from past experience that when she talks in this way, there must be something in it, something interesting to anticipate. They may think that the change from liquid to solid is unremarkable or they may (if very young) not know the difference between liquid and solid, but she encourages commitment and engagement by the way she models for them her own internal dialogue. And of course, as Bruner acknowledges, students are not being asked to wonder about the 'wonders of nature', but about human interpretations – if, in language, 'liquid' and 'solid' were not distinguished as 'different' then indeed there would be nothing to pick out as unusual, let alone wonderful, in the flow of events.

Science as cultural communication

But there is more than this to becoming a participant in a community of scientists. 'Good' scientists in a democracy, as academic pluralists and non-absolutists, would acknowledge the scientist's voice on practical issues as one amongst several to be heard and not necessarily the most authoritative. They would recognize the importance of communicating with others from other branches of science or from other formal disciplines as well as with 'lay' persons who spoke from common-sense understandings of problems and issues. They would be concerned about the social consequences of their scientific activities, and would try to make sure that their work was not misapplied or used inappropriately, but they would also acknowledge that they could never be certain about the consequences even of what might seem to be appropriate applications of their knowledge and that this was also always a matter of a concern for them.

For the educationalist it is important to convey to the student that learning science does not usually involve a process where 'false' old knowledge is replaced by 'true' new knowledge. What takes place in a teaching and learning context is more like a conversation between paradigms, where a student's own conceptions may merely derive from a different paradigm rather than what may be deemed as an inferior way of looking at the world. Of course, conversations in such contexts are not always conversations between different paradigms. A student's everyday concepts might not derive from an alternative paradigm to formal science, but represent a watered down or 'false' version of concepts which would be acknowledged as more precisely and accurately defined in the formal way were the student in a position to judge this.

A good starting point here for the educationalist might be to treat science not as a 'superior' way of knowing but as a culture and, in the case of the novitiate, a kind of foreign culture with a language that had to be *translated* into the informal common-sense language of students, even though, like all foreign languages, it contained words and phrases which sometimes had no equivalent in the host culture. In this context, following Aikenhead (1996), we might consider the role of the teacher as 'tour guide'. The idea is that students should be encouraged to 'cross the border', from the cultural context of their everyday world into the unfamiliar territory of the 'foreign' culture of science. Students would be helped to feel that the school programme was taking them back and forth from one culture to another. Students are not coerced into assimilating the subculture of science, but are encouraged to feel that they can borrow or adapt concepts from this culture according to what seems appropriate in relation to their own projects and concerns, what Aikenhead (1996: 27) describes as 'autonomous acculturation'.

In border crossings students would have to acknowledge that there was an alternative culture and that learning about it meant developing a new vocabulary, but that this did not necessarily require them to suppress or expunge other cultural meanings; that it was a question of concept proliferation rather than concept diminution, of language enrichment rather than impoverishment. As Aikenhead (1996: 28) points out: 'If students are going to cross the border between everyday subcultures and the subculture of science, *border crossings must be explicit* and students need some way of signifying to themselves and others which subculture they are talking in, at any given moment'. This clearly requires the kind of distancing from both cultures which is a feature of critical reflection on paradigms. Students in fact are not being encouraged to 'go native', but to take on board the ideas of the new culture in a more deliberate and self-conscious way.

Aikenhead gives an example of this new kind of teaching approach. Students' understandings of *mixtures* are likely to involve a number of common-sense concepts which derive from family beliefs. Having articulated these beliefs, students go on to discuss examples like milk, where

> guided by the teacher who introduces the dichotomous concepts 'heterogeneous' and 'homogeneous' mixtures, students conspicuously cross the border into the subculture of science, only to discover the contradiction that homogenized milk in the everyday world is not a homogeneous mixture in the subculture of science. One explicit objective . . . is to learn that language used in subculture science is tied to scientific classification schemes, which may or may not correspond to common-sense language, and therefore to cross the border from everyday subculture into subculture science is to change completely one's personal orientation to language. Classroom content would include other discrepancies in language besides 'homogeneous milk'; for example, 'energy conservation' has opposite meanings in commonsense and science language registers.
>
> (Aikenhead 1996: 29)

In some cases, as the research of Aikenhead (1994) has shown, common-sense ideas about mixtures, for example, could be richer and more complex than the scientific classification of heterogeneous and homogeneous. Moreover, the reason why students resisted the heterogeneous construct was not that they did not understand it but that it proved less useful than their common-sense understandings. Nevertheless, Aikenhead feels that students can often benefit from being familiarized with the scientific version, though which aspects of this will be relevant will depend on the circumstances. For instance, if the concern is to learn more about pollution in water and air then classification schemes used in science (such as emulsions, suspensions and colloids) may provide a useful framework, but it would not be necessary to learn about molecular theories, structures and forces.

This approach leads naturally to a more critical appreciation of the role of science in a practical context. Students are encouraged to see their own knowledge as valid and to appreciate the contribution of formal science, but it is only a short step from here to greater reflectiveness about the types of knowledge appropriate for illuminating and resolving issues in relation to any context of concern. In schools these matters are often dealt with by adding a 'social dimension' (for example, Science, Technology and Society initiatives) to the mainstream science curriculum, but, as Millar and Wynne (1988) point out, this is usually merely to 'bolt on' a feature which should be seen by teachers and learners as intrinsic to the process of 'doing science'. The problems of real life are multi-faceted and situated in a context where there are usually different interpretations of what exactly the problems are and what should be done about them.

In considering these matters further, it will be useful to examine some of issues to do with the public understanding of science which illuminate the political aspects of the relationship between formal and informal forms of knowledge in social and cultural contexts. In professional circles, it is typical for the 'problem' to be defined as one to do with the public's scientific ignorance and failure to appreciate the contribution of science. But, as sociologists like Irwin and Wynne (1996) have pointed out, it is the scientists' own attitudes which are really to blame. When they should have been examining their own beliefs and practices, and the way they communicated their knowledge to others, they have tended to see the problem as existing 'out there' in society at large in the incapacities of others. This lack of reflexivity on their part is borne of a certain arrogance underpinned by a number of assumptions about the role of science which are highly questionable – the assumption, for example, that scientific knowledge is inherently superior to common-sense beliefs, or that the application of science will inevitably be positive and result in an improvement in the quality of life.

A more reflexive approach would mean a more critical orientation to the nature of scientific expertise and its impact on society. Scientists or representatives of the scientific community would have to develop a more detailed understanding of just how science was actually taken up in the public domain. It would involve taking a close look at how differences in take-up were related to differences in the the way science was interpreted in terms of the social and cultural knowledge of the individuals and communities concerned. Scientists would be required to probe their own assumptions about the nature of society and to develop an awareness of the various ways in which the social world might be interpreted; in short, to adopt a more sociologically sophisticated approach to the way scientific knowledge interacted with common-sense cultural knowledge. In pursuing this, it would become evident that nothing was ever as straightforward as the top-down dissemination of expertise model of conventional public education in science would suggest. It is often the case, for example, that the practical knowledge of lay persons is more relevant and more reliable in particular circumstances than that derived from formal science; that the claims of scientific knowledge are often derived from laboratory science, which leads to not only false but even dangerous conclusions when applied to the 'real' world; and that the distinction made between science and non-science, a reification so typical of the traditional model, leads to a misrecognition and downgrading of the knowledge actually used by communities in attempting to resolve their own problems.

In general, in order to appreciate the contribution of science to the resolution of social and environmental problems, we have to understand the social and cultural context in which the scientific knowledge will be deployed. If there is concern about the use of a scientifically created product, for example, then we have to know how it will be used or how it is likely to be used and often why it will be used in a particular way. The history of scientific interventions is full of examples of how the powers that be have lacked such understanding. Irwin (1995), in his analysis of the conflict between farmworkers and the Advisory Committee on Pesticides (ACP) over the use of the pesticide 2,4,5-T showed that expert accounts were inadequate because they failed to draw on the everyday knowledge of the farmworkers. As one of the latter put it: 'They [the experts] may know the risks of 2,4,5-T. They may handle the stuff properly. They tell us we're all right if we use the spray normally. But have they any idea what normally means in the fields?' (Irwin 1995: 112). The farmworkers could also identify a variety of spraying conditions and circumstances of operation (equipment that was not adequate, long distances from washing facilities, drift on to other fields, for example) which were not taken into account by the experts. The former were also operating with a social model of farming (involving, for example, isolated workers dependent on one employer for housing and wages) which was different from that of the ACP.

None of this means, of course, that local occupational communities cannot themselves be mistaken in rejecting formal science. Moreover, instances where science has played a 'positive' role may be under-reported since it is only when the intervention of scientists has been experienced as a problem (for example, as a source of pollution or some other kind of threat to the environment) that the issue of the relationship between formal science and the informal knowledge of communities becomes visible (see Mulkay 1997). It is also possible, of course, that both sides may be 'right' or that both may be 'wrong'; both may have a good working knowledge of the social and cultural context, but both may also have 'blind spots'. It is not just the 'outsider scientists' who misrecognize or misunderstand community mores. The prejudices of members of local communities may prevent the communities themselves from appreciating the perspectives of certain minority groups in their midst. And the situation becomes even more complex if we acknowledge that the so-called informal knowledge of lay persons has often already incorporated formal scientific concepts. In one of the case studies reported by Layton et al. (1993), the parents of children with Down's syndrome were critical of medical knowledge not because it was scientific per se but because it was irrelevant to their particular needs and was the wrong kind of scientific knowledge. The authors' conclusion that 'the practical knowledge the parents had constructed was a powerful alternative to the "high science" of Down's syndrome available from medical and other experts' (Layton et al. 1993: 57) ignores the fact that the parents' knowledge itself was clearly grounded in a form of formal knowledge, in this case social scientific knowledge, already available to them as common sense. As the authors point out, many parents were critical of the stereotyping of Down's children – one is quoted as asserting 'there's just as much a difference in Down's children as in the general population. I'm sure there must be as much a spread of intellect and whatever as there is within the population as a whole' (Layton *et al.* 1993: 46). This is common sense, but it is clearly common sense of our times. Not only is the general direction of thinking in tune with the findings of research on Down's syndrome, but this particular parent even deploys the language of social science ('spread of intellect', 'general population'), terms which were originally technical but are now arguably common parlance.

Science as an expression of social interests

Interests are always at work in social action, and critique involves distinguishing legitimate from illegitimate interests. Such distinctions are not always as straightforward as one might think. Political interests, for example, are often cited as illegitimate because they 'interfere' with the integrity of scientific practices, but this is not necessarily the case, since certain political forms enable such practices to become established in the first instance and may be indispensable for their continuance. A genuinely democratic political framework would 'free' the scientist to do proper science as much as it would 'free' other citizens from the domination of Big Science. The interests of lay citizens and professional scientists in democracy and science would be pursued with vigour in the 'good' society to which they could both make a positive contribution. But there are other interests that are more corrupting and undermining of this society and its science. These are typically associated with economic or bureaucratic imperatives, which lead to the violation of both scientific and democratic norms and result in 'distorted' science.

The distorting influence of big business and powerful *economic* concerns has been well documented in the research literature. A recent example is provided by Levidow (1997) in his analysis of the relationship between scientific/technological and commercial interests in the agricultural biotechnology industry. As he points out, insecticidal genetically modified organisms have been considered a benign substitute for chemicals, but like other products they have been developed as part of the so-called 'value added' approach to genetics which involves the search for genes that can improve the market value of products, even where there is already an effective product in existence. The problem is predefined as one to do with genetic deficiency rather than in terms, say, of the organization and design of agricultural production. In this, as in other cases, most funding for research and development (R&D) has been for these 'genetic fixes', since they are regarded as the best way forward for crop improvement and the efficiency of agricultural practices, rather than the alternatives which would involve focusing on the intensity of farming methods, the use or lack of use of local resources and flaws in agricultural design. Levidow (1997: 116) concludes that in this context

> biotechnology education faces political choices . . . Either it can promote the genetic-reductionist account of problem-setting which dominates biotechnology R&D. Or, alternatively, it can strengthen people's capacity to engage in the wider public debate – as regards what features of 'nature' we should value, what agricultural and social order we should promote, and for whose benefit.

Of course, many situations are not as clear-cut as this. In the cases described by Levidow it is evident that there was no opportunity and no apparent will for an alternative to the genetic reductionism advocated by the dominant commercial interests to be considered. But it is often more difficult to ascertain the role of 'outside' interests in the construction of scientific agendas, and the scale of their impact on scientific decision-making cannot be read off from merely identifying their presence. We can only make judgements after 'closely observing' how scientific practice is actually accomplished in particular contexts.

As far as *bureaucratic* interests are concerned, these often find expression in the manner of organization of the teaching and learning of science in schools. Thus, emphases are placed, implicitly and/or explicitly, on the need for a hierarchical relationship between formal and informal knowledge, which translates into a transmission model of teaching; for relationships to be depersonalized, for pupils to be 'typed' and anonymized, for learning to be conceived as neutral and 'objective' and for procedural rules to be established which constrain interaction within tightly defined roles. These bureaucratic interests in fact derive from a rationality which has affinities with the positivist epistemology of Big Science, and it is scarcely surprising therefore that the latter finds a 'natural home' in bureaucratized schools.

But schools are not all of a piece in this respect, and bureaucratic imperatives are often contested. Teachers and pupils frequently find themselves wrestling with contradictory discourses which can be traced back to the tension between bureaucratic and democratic features of school life. In Edwards and Mercer's (1987) examples of science lessons teachers' attempts to operate on the principle that children should learn from experience through engagement in practical activities is in tension with the procedural rule that the teachers have to retain a very strict control over lessons. This may result in an emphasis on small-group work and practical activities justified in terms of the former principle but in fact guided predominantly by the latter, so that the learning that takes place is superficial as the focus shifts from activities and experiences producing genuine understanding to those driven by the need to 'get through' what has been planned for that particular lesson. Consequently students' grasp of important concepts is essentially 'ritual' rather than 'principled' (Edwards and Mercer 1987: 92).

In their study of writing in school science, Sheeran and Barnes (1991) found that impersonal language continued to be favoured by science teachers in their sample, despite the various changes in teaching methods which had occurred in recent years. The teachers justified this in terms of its being an aid to the development of thought processes and an important aspect of learning to 'do' science, since impersonal language was associated with adopting a scientific perspective. But as the researchers' analysis of scripts showed, the use of personal, expressive language was not in fact the reason for students' failure to adopt a scientific perspective, and the use or non-use of impersonal language was not necessarily the most relevant issue. The authors concluded that in order to be judged favourably by the teacher, children had to follow rules on the use of impersonal language, a number of which had nothing to do with science but reflected the kinds of communication skills children needed to be successful students in a bureaucratic context. The root cause of differences in performance between students lay in their differing capacities for identifying ground rules and acting upon them appropriately rather than in differences in their abilities to understand and explain scientific concepts.

Concluding comment

However, if subject disciplines are taught as paradigms and schools are debureaucratized, then perhaps we can agree with Aspin and Chapman (1994: 160) that exposure to the liberal democratic procedures and relationships within subject disciplines will give rise to 'the greatest possibilities for growth into the democratic mentality'. Participation in the practice of 'good' science is to 'do' both the subject and democracy. It implies contributing to the life of a 'living tradition' and to the realization of one's own goals, but it also means contributing to the construction and sustainability of democratic life for all in the risk society.

As part of the curriculum for life, the science curriculum would be the same for all students whether or not they intended to become professional scientists or specialists in particular disciplines. Scientific literacy must involve more than just learning the 'basics', if by that we mean understanding a few basic concepts and methods, and should encompass all the aspects discussed in this chapter. This puts any call for specialist science curricula in the school or college phase into perspective. A specialism can only ever be justified if it is additional to rather than a replacement of what students or pupils would be expected to learn in general science as part of a common curriculum, which, as indicated above, would be a broad curriculum encompassing all facets of science as a community of practice.

Scientific practices are closely associated with the dynamic of social change, with the speed and form of change and new possibilities for creating new worlds and new ways of living in a global context. They are also associated with various anticipated and actual dangers which are experienced as 'threats' not only to democratic ideals but also to the very existence of life itself on the planet. Those who become professional scientists have an awesome responsibility, but all citizens have a responsibility as well as a right to develop their capacity for making judgements about 'risk' and this entails serious engagement with the practices of formal science. All citizens would recognize the value of science and its potential usefulness in exploring a whole range of environmental issues, including those where its usefulness was not always obvious or uncontroversial. They would know that a pluralist approach to knowledge does not imply that scientific knowledge can *never* be the most relevant or useful and that, in certain circumstances, it may be indispensable.

11 | Schools for a democratic learning society

Introduction

The rationale for the 'curriculum for life' is derived from an analysis of contemporary society and 'what needs to be done' to realize democratic goals in that society. The themes which have been explored are relevant to this project in two ways: first, because they are assumed to reflect the current and future concerns of citizens; and second, because they are thought to be particularly significant for the achievement of a democratic learning society at this historical juncture. In teaching them one inevitably has to address the tension between diversity and commonality. Indeed, one of the important aims of the curriculum is to show how diversity and difference can be expressed and appreciated through cultural development, whilst at the same time recognizing the importance of the growth of a common understanding based on democratic values.

The 'curriculum for life' is inevitably an *integrated* curriculum, since its rationale dictates that each theme can only be taught and thought about in a way which links with all the other themes. Alienation at work, for example, assumes an understanding of what it means to be morally committed and this entails an adequate sense of self, which in turn is dependent on the way 'nurturing' has taken place in families. It is also a relatively *non-prescriptive* curriculum. The themes are broad enough to accommodate a wide diversity of content, and the actual selection would depend on what was considered appropriate for the particular students and teachers involved. Education for self-identity could be taught informally or formally through content drawn from literature, art, history or social psychology; collaboration through English or personal and social education or practical community projects; cultural politics through school councils or formal political education; the family through reflection upon home–school contacts or through specific topics in social science; work through work experience or programmes in economic and industrial understanding; science through formal science or environmental projects; and so on.

The process of teaching would involve encouraging pupils not to treat these themes as reified bodies of knowledge to which they were committed only in the limited sense of being sufficiently *au fait* with them to pass exams. The central responsibility of teachers would be to nurture a 'love' of learning in the practices associated with each theme which would last a lifetime. The routine day-to-day language exchange between students and teachers would have to involve the construction and reconstruction of a language 'fit for intimacy', since conversational exchanges in the classroom should reflect the aim of modelling the 'closeness' required to identify with the practice as a morally worthy activity. The student is encouraged to build creatively and critically on existing knowledge and experience, but creativity also requires the emotional and moral engagement of the self, and that presupposes the development of a multiplicity of shared meanings between teachers and pupils which make the experience 'personal' as opposed to 'impersonal'.

No subject or disciplinary framework or cultural process stands 'outside' these considerations. They are as relevant to science as they are to studies of family life or self-identity. Students learn how to do science, but they also learn how the process of learning science can contribute to self-knowledge and their understanding of how to participate in the intimate relations of a learning community. Science teachers have to show that it is as important to themselves as teachers as it should be for the students that science should 'speak' to them; that is to say, it relates to both teachers and students as participants in an already developing framework of meaning which enables it to be judged as a worthwhile form of life. 'Loving' science teachers care that their students should become 'close' enough to the human practice of science for them to 'feel' its significance for human living and for their own lives. They will want to foster feelings in their students similar to those experienced by the narrator in Willa Cather's novel, *My Antonia*, (first published in 1918: 'We left the classroom quietly, conscious that we had been brushed by the wing of a great feeling' (Cather 1980: 265). Practices constitute the meaning of life; there is nothing 'beyond' them which validate one's existence as defined by them. Science well taught should contribute to the student's sense of identity – that is, to their knowing where they stand, knowing the commitments and identifications which frame their horizon 'within which [they] can try to determine . . . what ought to be done, what [they] ought to oppose . . . what is good and valuable on a case by case basis' (Taylor 1989: 28).

A way forward

In the light of this understanding of the human relations required for 'good' learning in classrooms, I shall conclude this book by putting forward some tentative proposals for school reform. Clearly, the primary need is for a radical review of the existing curriculum, and the six proposals briefly discussed below would only make sense if they were seen as following on from this. At the outset, however, I need to make three background assumptions explicit. The first is that education for the learning society is a lifelong experience, but that the formative years of childhood and adolescence are still the most important period as far as direct intervention by governments is concerned. All children and young people go to school. In the post-school period and for the rest of life, provision will inevitably be a mix of the public and the private, and, as people go their myriad ways, inevitably more haphazard and beyond any kind of central control. Governments will still have a responsibility to provide lifelong learning opportunities for their citizens, but their greatest responsibility must surely be to ensure that all of them have a good start in life? This means developing educational systems which give equal opportunities to all citizens to acquire and develop the necessary capabilities for life in democratic learning societies. It is imperative that these systems do not close things down for students but open them up, so to speak. No one should leave school feeling a failure or feeling that what they have learned in school has been a waste of time, and everyone should be both willing and able to continue their education.

The second assumption is that this curriculum can be realized in the institutions we call state schools – schools that would certainly need to be radically reformed, but schools nevertheless. The idea of school itself is thus not challenged; nor is the idea that the school system should be state-controlled and state-run. For governments wanting to intervene to empower all citizens for the democratic learning society, a proper system of state schooling is considered to be, certainly for the foreseeable future, the most realistic and the most desirable option. Although the overall thrust of the argument in this book has been highly critical of schools, none of this is to suggest that things could be radically improved if the system was privatized or deschooled. Wholesale privatization inevitably allows market forces to rule and this can only mean the production and reproduction of inequality and ultimately a diminution in freedom for all. Deschooling assumes that schools themselves *qua* schools are the main problem, but most of the reforms historically advocated by deschoolers – a more personalized curriculum and humanistic pedagogy – seem realizable through reforms which debureaucratize schools and reprofessionalize the teaching workforce. And so, in advocating these proposals, no alternative is envisaged to the state school where attendance is compulsory for a given period and teachers are professional educators employed by the state.

Third, it is assumed that the secondary phase of education is the crucial phase for intervention at the present time. This goes against the grain of many current policy initiatives, which are premised on the view that standards are too low and that to raise them we need to begin at the beginning, so to speak, and focus on the 'basics' of primary education, such as literacy and numeracy. No doubt things could be improved in this phase, but the view taken here is that the extent of the decline in standards has been exaggerated and in any case it is in the secondary rather than the primary phase where children are really 'turned off' school. On the whole, primary schools produce many active and happy learners whose decline in enthusiasm is a familiar and depressing feature of life in secondary schools.

A new teacher for a new curriculum

The key to 'good' schools is 'good' teachers, and so my first proposal will address the question of the kind of teacher we need for teaching the 'curriculum for life'. To begin with, one would hope that teachers themselves were morally and intellectually engaged in the 'curriculum for life' and were themselves lifelong learners in relation to the themes discussed in this book. It is difficult to see how they could teach this curriculum as a 'curriculum for life' without being so engaged since the contradiction would be obvious to themselves as well as their pupils. Clearly the curriculum would not be 'for life' if teachers did not treat it as such in relation to their own lives. It follows from this that if pupils are to get the message right then teachers' personal involvement in this curriculum must in some way be communicated to them, and the best way to do this is for each teacher to be involved at some level in teaching the 'whole' curriculum.

It is self-evident that the curriculum envisaged would be impossible to teach unless teachers knew their charges extremely well. The personal nature of much of the material, the focus on close relationships in the family, the critical engagement with pupils' own culture and so on would require teacher–pupil relations of a mutually intimate and trusting nature. Teachers would have to recognize the uniqueness of each pupil's individual expression, yet be aware of the limits of their own knowledge of the pupil and accept that it was neither desirable or possible to know their charges 'through and through'. They would have to develop insights into the constraints of race, class, gender and other structural factors; and to recognize that both they and their pupils were always and already in a state of 'becoming'. At the same time, they would know that it was necessary at certain times to allow pupils to experience other kinds of relations of a less close but still personal kind with themselves and also with other teachers in the wider community of the school. They would have to recognize when it was appropriate to make links between justice and fairness in personal relations and the idea of social justice in society as a whole. And they would have to do all these things in full knowledge of the potential dangers – the possibility of the relations established being too intrusive, involving an unacceptably high level of surveillance or fostering a high level of dependency.

This sounds a tall order, but if we are serious about education for citizenship in a democratic learning society it reflects a necessary stance for all welfare state professionals, as appropriate for the ideal teacher as for the ideal medical practitioner, social worker or psychologist. Teachers would be teachers but this would automatically include being a 'personal tutor' and thus there would be no differentiation between the pastoral and the academic role, as in the present system. Thus the new teacher for the new curriculum would not be a subject specialist but a *polymath teacher-tutor* whose role would be to establish close relationships with each of his or her pupils as individuals and facilitate their learning in all areas of the 'curriculum for life'.

The organization of teaching and learning

The second proposal relates to the way teaching and learning should be organized in schools. Teacher-tutors could be grouped into teams in a similar fashion to the model advocated by John Adcock in his book, *In Place of Schools* (1994). There are a variety of possibilities here, but the basic idea is that pupils would be attached to teams consisting of five teachers each of whom would be responsible for the education of 20 pupils in one age band for at least one year. Teams would be responsible for 20 pupils in each age group of the five years of compulsory secondary schooling, a kind of school within a school. Although pupils in a year group would be taught in the main by one teacher, they would also be taught or supervised regularly by other teachers in the team, who would, of course, either be their future teachers or ones who had taught them previously. To release individual teachers for intensive one-to-one contact or small-group work or for other activities such as home visits, cross-age groupings could be organized where appropriate, perhaps involving peer tutoring or team teaching and almost certainly making used of IT-based independent study programmes. Clearly other kinds of arrangements might be possible (for example, involving horizontal as opposed to vertical organization and various permutations of these), but the basic unit of teaching and learning would be the same – teachers working in small collaborative teaching teams, pupils working in collaborative groups and receiving individual attention through a system of personal tutoring in all areas of the curriculum.

Adcock, of course, is describing an alternative which does away with schools altogether, but most of his ideas can be adapted for a school context. In his deschooling model, parents would initially choose a particular panel (his word for what I have called a team) from a range on offer. In a comprehensive state system, this choice should not normally be available because all schools should be able to meet the standards required by the teaching profession and the state. But things can go wrong in practice and a change of team might be thought to be desirable. This might involve 'transfers' of teachers or, more commonly, pupils, who in consultation with parents and tutors could individually opt for a different teaching team. Since there would be a number of such teams in any one school, there would be plenty of choice available. If this did not resolve the problem then parents and children could just request a change of school.

The good polymath teacher-tutor would need to be a flexible, adaptable person, capable of working in a team, making the appropriate kind of personal relationships with pupils and confident enough to experiment, to take risks, to innovate and to pursue all the other activities of the reflective, collaborative practitioner discussed in Chapter 4. It follows from this that he or she would need to be regarded as an autonomous not a managed professional whose relations with other teachers were collegial. This model is, of course, completely out of kilter with a hierarchical organization of staff in schools. Democratic schools would have no heads or deputies or even team leaders of any kind who were permanently positioned in such roles and paid accordingly. All responsibilities would be shared. Obviously, the school would have to be managed; but this management function would need to be examined closely to see what it actually entailed over and above routine administration in a situation where most decision-making had been devolved to teams acting collaboratively and democratically, internally and in relation to each other. Resources should be shared equally between teams unless a collective decision was taken on educational grounds for a differential allocation.

School and the family

Adcock also feels that family- and home-based education is an integral part of the learning process. This would connect with the analysis of the family curriculum in Chapter 8. Clearly, issues to do with the family, learning in families and the relationships between teachers and parents are of the utmost importance and have been underplayed historically for a variety of reasons. This is not just a question, as in the market model of education, of parents acting in the role of consumers but rather of them relating to teachers as genuine partners in the process of education. Education does not have to be home-based *as opposed to* school-based in order to achieve family involvement and accomplish the family curriculum. One of the problems with Adcock's model of home-based teaching is that it underestimates the huge differences between pupils in terms of social background and the capacity of their homes to promote relevant learning. Equipping all homes with studies and computers, for example, would be desirable, but far more difficult for the state to bring about than a reconstructed school system. However, even if it were possible to create a home-based system, it could never be a substitute for schools, which are in a far better position to provide a wider range of opportunities and a broader experience of life in a plural society.

Nevertheless, teachers in a new system should relate to parents in a more regular and more profound way than previously. This would seem to follow from the emphasis placed on the family as a major part of the curriculum. Of course, pupils would learn a lot about families in school – about their own kind of family as well as other kinds of families – but all this could be more engaging and stimulating if informed by insights gained by teachers as a result of developing closer relationships with parents or parent substitutes. This more intensive contact with the home should be as much a feature of home–school relations at secondary as at primary level. And so the third proposal would involve providing teachers with enough time to relate to parents in an educationally meaningful way. It would be part of the teacher-tutor's job to visit parents at home, at work or elsewhere on a regular basis, even if this meant doing evening work.

Assessment

Teachers would have greater scope for reflection and decision-making, but nevertheless the whole system would have to be monitored and the government would need to know that teachers were conforming to codes of practice laid down by the profession and approved by the state. Teachers would be expected to teach certain things, and pupils would have to be assessed and assessments made public at certain points. Summative as well as formative assessment would be needed, but there could be no blueprint for assessment ahead of establishing the alternative curriculum and polymath teacher-tutor system along the lines suggested.

However, it seems likely that a competitive public examination at 16+ would not be necessary (see also Hargreaves 1982). In an alternative system, the GCSE would soon be regarded something of a blunt instrument. Even in the present set-up, it has no intrinsic connection, in terms of actual content assessed, with the provision which comes after this age, unless the young person concerned is going on to study the same subjects at A level. The two subjects with by far the largest number of entries are English and maths, but in so far as these are tests of the 'basics' they could surely involve a simpler form of assessment, maybe as part of pupils' cumulative records of achievement? If a public exam were thought to be necessary, it should clearly be slimmed down (the equivalent of a maximum of five GCSEs), and be criterion-referenced and non-competitive, since its only purpose would be to ascertain whether a level of proficiency had been reached sufficient for the student to progress to the next phase.

Latterly the picture in the UK has become confused, not least because of government policy on league tables and its unhelpful conflation of the different purposes of assessment (see Noss *et al*. 1989), but there continues in many schools to be a focus on processes leading to the construction of records of achievement. These records differ from traditional reporting in several aspects, but above all in the way they attempt to involve the child in the process and to give a picture of the 'whole' child as an individual rather than as the sum of their academic attainments. Because they are based on an assessment model where assessment is regarded as an integral part of ongoing teaching and learning processes, they have functioned more as a strategy for introducing curricular and pedagogical change rather than just as an alternative method of assessment (Broadfoot *et al*. 1988). To what extent, in their present form, they are more controlling than autonomy-enhancing (Hargreaves 1989) is a matter of controversy, but at least at the level of rhetoric, if not always in practice, they place pupils at the centre of the learning process and their explicit aim is to facilitate pupils' reflection on that process. As such they are clearly consonant with the model of learning and the approach to the curriculum advocated in this book, and their development as a replacement for formal examinations would constitute my fourth proposal.

Information technology

The importance of IT to classrooms in 'new times' is easy to exaggerate, but nevertheless it will play a vital role. As indicated above, 'good' learning will be founded on the personal relationship between teacher and taught, which, if it is be educationally productive, should be reciprocal and intimate in a way that can only be achieved in face-to-face encounters. However, as fields of expertise multiply and the knowledge and experience of pupils become more varied, the teacher's generic knowledge and skills will almost certainly need to be supplemented by specialist knowledge in whatever area of enquiry may emerge as relevant. Such knowledge could be provided by properly designed, fully interactive computer programs which, in this function, would replace the specialist teacher. Computers have the potential to release teachers for precisely those activities which should be prioritized in the new curriculum, and they may even be indispensable for the realization of such a curriculum.

But there are still a number of questions to be asked. Will they, for example, be able to foster *authentic learning*? According to Bonnett (1997: 149), this requires

> relating what is learnt to one's own existence, to seeing how it should affect one's outlook and one's actions – in a way that properly acknowledges the element of personal responsibility that each of us has for how

we live our lives . . . It refers to the need for learners personally to evaluate what they learn so as to achieve a degree of authorship of their understanding.

It is evident that in their present form they tend to emphasize what Bonnett describes as *rational-calculative* rather authentic learning, reinforcing a way of thinking which is primarily technical as opposed to critical and ethical (see Apple 1992). But will this always be the case? Will IT always carry its own technicist 'hidden' curriculum, or can more dialogical, self-evaluative and reflexive modes of learning be built into programs? There are more questions here than answers at the present time, but there seems no logical reason why computer programs of the future will have to be restricted to only one model of learning.

The impact of commercial interests here cannot be ignored, since there clearly are large profits to be made from contracts to supply schools. The uncertainties about forms of learning are likely to be glossed over if the people who develop the software and hardware are also those who sell it for profit. The best way forward, and this is my fifth proposal, is for teachers to be involved at every stage of the process of creating and choosing programs, which would include not just being consulted about programs for general use but also being provided with the skills, facilities and specialist help to make their own programs.

The selection of teachers

The sixth and final proposal involves the establishment of a selection process that widens access to the teaching profession without a deterioration in quality. If all citizens become learning citizens and since to be a 'good' learner is to have the capacity to be 'good' teacher, it is likely that in future a greater proportion of the adult population will be suitable for formal training as teachers. At present, recruitment is hide-bound by selection criteria derived from the need to teach the current National Curriculum subjects to a particular standard. This gives rise to an excessively restricted field of recruitment in secondary schools, since one of the main criteria for selection is competence in one or more of these specialist subjects as measured by grades obtained on formal courses, especially those leading to the award of a degree. If these restrictions were removed the way would be open to widening access to include not only graduates with degrees in other subjects, such as psychology, sociology and politics, but also those active and responsible citizens without any formal qualifications at higher levels who might have an aptitude for teaching adolescents.

Widening access in this way should mean making the selection process more not less rigorous. It would not be enough for candidates to be chosen on the basis of exam grades or, for that matter, on evidence of prior learning or experience plus a one-off interview. Such are the moral qualities and skills required by teachers in 'new times' that teacher training institutions should operate their own selection procedures which should involve, amongst other things, the candidates being placed in practical situations for several days. They would need to be assessed through observation, interview and written tests designed to demonstrate their competence in a range of basic skills, their capacity for creative and critical thinking, their knowledge of the 'curriculum for life' and their ability to make the appropriate kinds of relationships with children and young people.

Concluding comment

Schools for a democratic learning society will be new kinds of schools but they will not be so different from those which currently exist that the changes envisaged will be perceived as too extreme. At least, this is the author's hope. Much of what is proposed has already been tried in one form or another, and has been unsuccessful or relatively so only because reforms have not gone far enough or have not involved 'whole school' and 'whole curriculum' change or have been carried out in an unfavourable context, against the background of a market-oriented national policy, for example. At a deeper level, I would suggest that the school and curriculum reforms proposed here, though radical, are by and large consonant with current needs, desires and values in the population at large. It would be surprising, therefore, if they did not have a measure of support. We are all part of 'new times' and cannot avoid experiencing the typical dilemmas, contradictions, hopes and fears that inevitably confront all of us in some form in the new era.

But human beings can change their destiny. They do not have to 'go with the flow', so to speak, of 'new times' in a way that moves them in the direction of realizing and embracing the 'good life' for all. They could equally opt for other strategies which are dysfunctional for democracy – ones that lead to the re-establishment of old power structures and hegemonic forms as a safeguard against further change. Like yearnings for democracy, these restorationist psychologies are equally well rooted. Those who cling to the traditional notion of achievement in schools, who use a rhetoric of collaborative management to legitimize undemocratic forms of school organization and reinvent bureaucracy, who define the learning society purely or largely in economic terms or who celebrate diversity and difference only to exploit them – all these and others may build on existing uncertainties and fears to fashion a society where the democratic ideal is more remote than ever.

References

Abbot, P. and Wallace, C. (1992) *The Family and the New Right*. London: Pluto Press.

Adcock, J. (1994) *In Place of Schools*. London: New Education Press.

Aikenhead, G.S. (1994) Collaborative research and development, in J. Solomon and G.S. Aikenhead (eds) *STS Education: International Perspectives on Reform*. New York: Teachers College Press.

Aikenhead, G.S. (1996) Science education: border crossing into the subculture of science, *Studies in Science Education*, 28: 1–32.

Apple, M. (1992) Is the new technology part of the solution or part of the problem in education?, in J. Beynon and H. MacKay (eds) *Technological Literacy and the Curriculum*. London: Falmer Press.

Arnot, M. (1984) How shall we educate our sons?, in R. Deem (ed.) *Co-education Reconsidered*. Milton Keynes: Open University Press.

Arnot, M. (1994) Male hegemony, social class and women's education, in L. Stone (ed.) *The Education Feminism Reader*. London: Routledge. Paper first published in 1982.

Aspin, D.N. and Chapman, J.D. (1994) *Quality Schooling*. London: Cassell.

Aviram, A. (1991) The paternalistic attitude towards children, *Educational Theory*, 41(2): 199–211.

Baker, D. and Jones, D. (1992) Opportunity and performance: a sociological explanation for gender differences in academic mathematics, in J. Wrigley (ed.) *Education and Gender Equality*. London: Falmer Press.

Ball, S. (1994) *Educational Reform*. Buckingham: Open University Press.

Ball, S.J. (ed.) (1990) *Foucault and Education*. London and New York: Routledge.

Barnes, D. and Barnes, D. (1984) *Versions of English*. London: Heinemann.

Barnes, D. and Shemilt, D. (1982) Transmission and interpretation, in B. Wade (ed.) *Language Perspectives*. London: Heinemann.

Barnes, D. and Todd, F. (1981) Talk in small learning groups: analysis of strategies, in C. Adelman (ed.) *Uttering and Muttering*. London: Grant McIntyre.

Barrow, R. (1984) *Giving Teaching back to Teachers*. Brighton: Wheatsheaf.

Beck, V. (1992) *Risk Society: Towards a New Modernity*. London: Sage.

Beck, V. (1994) *Ecological Politics in an Age of Risk*. Cambridge: Polity Press.

Bentley, D. and Watts, M. (1987) Courting the positive virtues: a case for feminist science, in A. Kelly (ed.) *Science for Girls*. Milton Keynes: Open University Press.

Berger, B. and Berger, P.L. (1983) *The War over the Family*. London: Hutchinson.

Berger, J. (1967) *A Fortunate Man*. Harmondsworth: Penguin.

Berger, P., Berger, B. and Kellner, H. (1973) *The Homeless Mind*. Harmondsworth: Penguin.

Bernstein, B. (1975) *Class, Codes and Control*, Vol. 3. London: Routledge & Kegan Paul.

Billig, M. (1985) Prejudice, categorization and particularization: from a perceptual to a rhetorical approach, *European Journal of Social Psychology*, 15: 79–103.

Bishop, N. (1996) Trust is not enough: classroom self-disclosure and the loss of private lives, *Journal of Philosophy of Education*, 30(3): 429–39.

Blagg, N., Ballinger, M. and Gardner, R. (1988) *Somerset Thinking Skills Course*. Oxford: Blackwell.

Bocock, R. (1986) *Hegemony*. London: Tavistock.

Bonnett, M. (1997) Computers in the classroom: some value issues, in A. McFarlane (ed.) *Information Technology and Authentic Learning*. London and New York: Routledge.

Borkowski, J.G. and Muthukrisna, N. (1992) Moving metacognition into the classroom: 'working models' and effective strategy teaching, in M. Pressley, K.R. Harris and S.T. Guthrie (eds) *Promoting Academic Competence and Literacy in Schools*. San Diego, CA: Academic Press.

Brell, C.D. (1990) Critical thinking as transfer: the reconstructive integration of otherwise discrete interpretations of experience, *Experience Theory*, 40(1): 53–68.

Broadfoot, P., James, M., McMeeking, S., Nuttall, D. and Stierer, B. (1988) *Records of Achievement: Report of the National Evaluation of Pilot Schemes*. London: HMSO.

Brown, G. (1984) Metacognition: new insights into old problems, *British Journal of Educational Studies*, 32(3): 213–19.

Bruner, J.S. (1983) *Child's Talk: Learning to Use Language*. Oxford: Oxford University Press.

Bruner, J.S. (1986) *Actual Minds, Possible Worlds*. Cambridge, Mass.: Harvard University Press.

Callan, E. (1994) Autonomy and alienation, *Journal of Philosophy of Education*, 28(1): 35–53.

Carr, W. and Hartnett, A. (1996) *Education and the Struggle for Democracy*. Buckingham: Open University Press.

Cather, W. (1980) *My Antonia*. London: Virago. First published in 1918.

Cockburn, C.K. (1987) *Two-track Training: Sex Inequalities and the YTS*. London: Macmillan.

Coffield, F. (1997) *Can the UK Become a Learning Society?* London: School of Education, King's College London.

Coles, M. (1985) The tender trap? Commitment and consciousness in entrants to teaching, in S.J. Ball and I.F. Goodson (eds) *Teachers' Lives and Careers*. Lewes: Falmer Press.

Cowie, H. and Rudduck, J. (1995) Cooperative Learning – Unit 5, Foundation Module: Learning, Teaching and the Curriculum. Division of Education, University of Sheffield (unpublished).

Dale, R., Bowe, R., Harris, D. *et al.* (1990) *The TVEI Story*. Buckingham: Open University Press.

Darling, J. and Glendinning, A. (1996) *Gender Matters in Schools*. London: Cassell.

Davies, B. (1979) Children's perceptions of social interactions in school, *CORE: Collected Original Resources in Education*, 3(1).

Dearing, R. (1996) *Review of Qualifications for 16–19 Year Olds: Summary Report.* London: School Curriculum and Assessment Authority.

Department for Education (DfE) (1994) *GCSE and GCE A/AS Examination Results 1992–3.* London: HMSO.

Department for Education and Employment (DfEE) (1997) *Excellence in Schools.* London: The Stationery Office.

Department of Education and Science (DES) (1988) *Advancing A Levels.* London: HMSO.

Department of Education and Science (DES) (1989) *National Curriculum: From Policy to Practice.* London: DES.

Dewey, J. (1910) *How We Think.* Lexington, Mass.: Heath.

Dewey, J. (1933) *Democracy and Education.* New York: Macmillan. Firat published in 1916.

Driver, R., Asoko, H., Leach, J., Mortimer, E. and Scott, P. (1994) Constructing scientific knowledge in the classroom, *Educational Researcher*, 23(7): 5–12.

Durkheim, E. (1993) *The Division of Labour in Society.* New York: Macmillan. First published in translation in 1933.

Edwards, A.D. and Furlong, V.J. (1978) *The Language of Teaching.* London: Heinemann.

Edwards, A.D. and Westgate, D.P.G. (1987) *Investigating Classroom Talk.* Lewes: Falmer Press.

Edwards, D. and Mercer, N. (1987) *Common Knowledge: The Development of Understanding in the Classroom.* London: Routledge.

Elliot, J. (1990a) Competency based training and the education of the professions. Conference paper presented to the British Educational Research Association Annual Conference, University of Nottingham, September.

Elliot, J. (1990b) Teachers as researchers: implications for supervision and teacher education, *Teaching and Teacher Education*, 6(1): 1–26.

Elliot, J. (1991) *Action Research for Educational Change.* Buckingham: Open University Press.

Ennis, R.H. (1982) Logical and critical thinking, in D.R. Nicola (ed.) *Philosophy of Education 1981.* Normal, Ill.: Philosophy of Education Society.

Equal Opportunities Commission and Office for Standards in Education (Ofsted) (1996) *The Gender Divide.* London: HMSO.

Flavell, J.H. (1979) Metacognition and cognitive monitoring, *American Psychologist*, 34(10): 906–11.

Ford, J., Mongon, D. and Whelan, M. (1982) *Special Education and Social Control.* London: Routledge & Kegan Paul.

Foucault, M. (1977) *Discipline and Punish: The Birth of the Prison.* London: Penguin.

Foucault, M. (1988) The ethic of care for the self as a practice of freedom, in J. Bernauer and D. Rasmussen (eds) *The Final Foucault.* Cambridge, Mass. and London: The Massachusetts Institute of Technology Press.

Fox Harding, L. (1996) *Family, State and Social Policy.* Basingstoke: Macmillan.

Fromm, E. (1971) *Man for Himself.* London: Routledge & Kegan Paul. First published in 1949.

Fullan, M.G. and Hargreaves, A. (1991) *What's Worth Fighting For? Working Together for Your School.* Toronto: Ontario Public School Teachers' Federation.

Further Education Unit (FEU) (1990) *The Core Skills Initiative.* London: FEU.

Further Education Unit (FEU) (1994) *Implementing GNVQs: a manual*. London: FEU.

Gewirtz, S., Ball, S.J. and Bowe, R. (1995) *Markets, Choice and Equity in Education*. Buckingham: Open University Press.

Giddens, A. (1991) *Modernity and Self-Identity*. Cambridge: Polity Press.

Giddens, A. (1992) *The Transformation of Intimacy*. Cambridge: Polity Press.

Giddens, A. (1994) *Beyond Left and Right*. Cambridge: Polity Press.

Gold, K. (1995) Hard times for Britain's lost boys, *New Scientist*, 145(1963): 12–13.

Goodson, I.F. (1994) *Studying Curriculum*. Buckingham: Open University Press.

Gore, J.M. (1993) *The Struggle for Pedagogies*. London: Routledge.

Gorman, T.P., White, J., Brooks, G., Maclure, M. and Kispal, A. (1988) *Language Performance in Schools: Review of APU Language Monitoring 1979–1983*. Department of Education and Science/Department of Education for Northern Ireland/Welsh Office. London: HMSO.

Green, A. (1994) Postmodernism and state education, *Journal of Education Policy*, 9(1): 67–83.

Green, A. (1997) Core skills, general education and unification in post-16 education. Paper presented to the Work and Learning Network Second Annual Conference, Sheffield, 12 November.

Greenhalgh, P. (1994) *Emotional Growth and Learning*. London and New York: Routledge.

Grumet, M. (1981) Restitution and reconstruction of educational experience: an autobiographical method for curriculum theory, in M. Lawn and L. Barton (eds) *Rethinking Curriculum Studies*. London: Croom Helm.

Habermas, J. (1979) *Communication and the Evolution of Society* (trans. T.A. McCarthy). Boston: Beacon Press.

Hadley, E. (1980) The conversation of the classroom, *English in Education*, 14(3): 34–40.

Hall, S. and Jacques, M. (1989) *New Times: The Changing Face of Politics in the 1990s*. London: Lawrence and Wishart.

Hall, S. and Jefferson, T. (1976) *Resistance through Rituals*. London: Hutchinson.

Hammersley, M. (1977a) School learning: the cultural resources required by pupils to answer a teacher's question, in P. Woods and M. Hammersley (eds) *School Experience*. London: Croom Helm.

Hammersley, M. (1977b) *Teacher Perspectives*. Units 9 and 10 of Open University course E202, *Schooling and Society*. Milton Keynes: The Open University.

Hannon, P. (1995) *Literacy, Home and School*. London: Falmer Press.

Hansen, D.A. (1993) The child in family and school: agency and the workings of time, in P.A. Cowan, D. Field, D.A. Hansen, A. Skolnick and G.E. Swanson (eds) *Family, Self and Society: Toward a New Agenda for Family Research*. Hillsdale, NJ: Lawrence Erlbaum Associates.

Hargreaves, A. (1989) *Curriculum and Assessment Reform*. Milton Keynes: Open University Press.

Hargreaves, A. (1994) *Changing Teachers, Changing Times*. London: Cassell.

Hargreaves, D. (1972) *Interpersonal Relations in Education*. London: Routledge & Kegan Paul.

Hargreaves, D. (1982) *The Challenge for the Comprehensive School: Culture, Curriculum and Community*. London: Routledge & Kegan Paul.

Harris, S., Nixon, J. and Rudduck, J. (1993) Schoolwork, homework and gender, *Gender and Education*, 5(1): 3–15.

Harvey, D. (1989) *The Condition of Postmodernity*. Oxford: Blackwell.

Haskey, J. (1991) Estimated numbers and demographic characteristics of one-parent families in Great Britain, *Population Trends*, 65: 35–47.

Hennessy, S., McCormick, R. and Murphy, P. (1993) The myth of general problem solving capability: design and technology as an example, *Curriculum Journal*, 4(1): 73–89.

Hodkinson, P. (1989) Crossing the academic/vocational divide: personal effectiveness and autonomy as an integrating theme in post-16 education, *British Journal of Educational Studies*, 37(4): 369–83.

Hopkins, D. (1995) Towards effective school improvement, *School Effectiveness and Improvement*, 6(3): 265–74.

Hyland, T. (1994) *Competences, Education and NVQs*. London: Cassell.

Irwin, A. (1995) *Citizen Science*. London: Routledge.

Irwin, A. and Wynne, B. (1996) *Misunderstanding Science? The Public Reconstruction of Science and Technology*. Cambridge: Cambridge University Press.

Jessop, G. (1990) *Outcomes*. Basingstoke: Falmer Press.

Johnson, T.J. (1972) *Professions and Power*. London: Macmillan.

Jonathan, R. (1990) State education service or prisoner's dilemma: the 'hidden hand' on a source of education policy, *Educational Philosophy and Theory*, 22: 16–24.

Jones, K. (1989) *Right Turn*. London: Radius.

Jones, M. (1988) Education and racism, *Journal of Philosophy of Education*, 19(2): 225–30.

Jones, R. (1989) Sex education in personal and social education, in P. White (ed.) *Personal and Social Education*. London: Kogan Page in association with the Institute of Education, University of London.

Jordan, B., Redley, M. and James, S. (1994) *Putting the Family First*. London: University College of London Press.

Joseph, K. (1991) *The Importance of Parenting*. London: Centre for Policy Studies.

Kelly, A. (1988) Towards a democratic science education, in H. Lauder and P. Brown (eds) *Education in Search of a Future*. Lewes: Falmer Press.

Kiernan, K. and Wicks, M. (1990) *Family Change and Future Policy*. York: Rowntree/Family Policy Studies Centre.

Kincheloe, J.L. and Steinberg, S.R. (1993) A tentative description of post-formal thinking: the critical confrontation with cognitive theory, *Harvard Educational Review*, 63(3): 296–320.

Kitwood, T. (1990) Psychotherapy, postmodernism and morality, *Journal of Moral Education*, 19(1): 3–14.

Kleinig, J. (1982) *Philosophical Issues in Education*. London: Croom Helm.

Klemp, G.O. (1977) *Three Factors of Success in the World of Work: Implications for Curriculum in Higher Education*. Boston: McBer and Co.

Kuhn, T.S. (1970) *The Structure of Scientific Revolutions*. Chicago: University of Chicago Press. First published in 1962.

Lash, S. (1994) Reflexivity and its doubles: students, aesthetics, community, in U. Beck, A. Giddens and S. Lash (eds) *Reflexive Modernization*. Cambridge: Polity Press.

Lave, J. (1988) *Cognition in Practice*. Cambridge: Cambridge University Press.

Layton, D. (1991) Science education and praxis: the relationship of school science to practical action, *Studies in Science Education*, 19: 43–79.

Layton, D., Jenkins, E., MacGill, S. and Davey, A. (1993) *Inarticulate Science?* Nafferton, Driffield: Studies in Education Ltd.

Lees, S. (1987) The structure of sexual relations in school, in M. Arnot and G. Weiner (eds) *Gender and the Politics of Schooling*. London: Hutchinson/The Open University.

Lees, S. (1993) *Sugar and Spice: Sexuality and Adolescent Girls*. London: Penguin.

Leonard, D. (1990) Persons in their own right: children and sociology in the UK, in L. Chisholm, P. Buchner, H. Kruger and P. Brown (eds) *Childhood, Youth and Social Change*. London: Falmer Press.

Levidow, L. (1997) Democracy and expertise: the case of biotechnology education, in R. Levison and J. Thomas (eds) *Science Today: Problem or Crisis?* London and New York: Routledge.

Lewis, T. (1994) Difficulties attending the new vocationalism in the USA, *Journal of Philosophy of Education*, 25(1): 95–108.

Licht, B.G. and Dweck, C.S. (1983) Sex differences in achievement orientations: consequences for academic choices and attainments, in M. Marland (ed.) *Sex Differentiation and Schooling*. London: Heinemann.

Lukes, S. (1973) *Individualism*. Oxford: Basil Blackwell.

Lukes, S. (1977) *Essays in Social Theory*. London: Macmillan.

Mac an Ghaill, M. (1994) *The Making of Men*. Buckingham: Open University Press.

MacEwen Scott, A. (1994) *Gender Segregation and Social Change*. Oxford: Oxford University Press.

MacIntyre, A. (1981) *After Virtue*. London: Duckworth.

Macmurray, J. (1961) *Persons in Relation*. London: Faber and Faber.

Maden, X. and Hillman, Y. (1996) Lessons in success, in Nation Commission on Education (eds) *Success Against the Odds*. London and New York: Routledge.

Marsh, P., Rosser, E. and Harré, R. (1980) *The Rules of Disorder*. London: Routledge & Kegan Paul.

Marton, F. (1986) Some reflections on the improvement of learning, in J.A. Bowden (ed.) *Student Learning: Research into Practice*. Centre for the Study of Higher Education, University of Melbourne.

Marx, K. and Engels, F. (1970) *The German Ideology*. London: Lawrence and Wishart. First published in 1846.

McFarlane, A. (ed.) (1997) *Information Technology and Authentic Learning*. London and New York: Routledge.

McPeck, J.E. (1981) *Critical Thinking and Education*. Oxford: Martin Robertson.

Mead, G.H. (1934) *Mind, Self and Society*. Chicago: University of Chicago Press.

Measor, L. and Woods, P. (1984) *Changing Schools*. Milton Keynes: Open University Press.

Menter, I., Muschamp, Y., Nicholls, P. and Ozga, J. with Pollard A. (1997) *Work and Identity in the Primary School*. Buckingham: Open University Press.

Millar, R. and Wynne, B. (1988) Public understanding of science: from contents to processes, *International Journal of Science Education*, 10(4): 388–98.

Millard, E. (1997) *Differently Literate: Boys, Girls and the Schooling of Literacy*. London: Falmer Press.

Miller, D. (1988) The ethical significance of nationality, *Ethics*, 98: 640–8.

Mortimore, P. (1991) The nature and findings of research on school effectiveness in the primary sector, in S. Riddell and S. Brown (eds) *School Effectiveness Research*. Edinburgh: HMSO.

Mouffe, C. (1993) Liberal socialism and pluralism, in J. Squires (ed.) *Principled Positions*. London: Lawrence and Wishart.

Mulkay, M. (1997) Review of Irwin and Wynne – Misunderstanding Science?, *Science, Technology and Human Values*, 22(2): 254–64.

National Commission on Education (1993) *Learning to Succeed*. London: Heinemann.

National Council for Vocational Qualifications (NCVQ) (1995) *Introducing GNVQs*. London: NCVQ.

National Curriculum Council (1991) *Education for Economic and Industrial Understanding*, Curriculum Guidance 4. York: National Curriculum Council.

Nisbet, J. and Shucksmith, J. (1986) *Learning Strategies*. London: Routledge & Kegan Paul.

Nixon, J., Martin, J., McKeown, P. and Ranson, S. (1996) *Encouraging Learning*. Buckingham: Open University Press.

Nixon, J., Martin, J., McKeown, P. and Ranson, S. (1997) Towards a learning profession: changing codes of occupational practice within the new management of education, *British Journal of Sociology of Education*, 18(1): 5–28.

Noon, M. and Blyton, P. (1997) *The Realities of Work*. London: Macmillan.

Noss, R., Goldstein, H. and Hoyles, C. (1989) Graded assessment and learning hierarchies in mathematics, *British Educational Research Journal*, 15(2): 109–20.

Ofsted (1993) *Boys and English*. Ref: 2/93/NS. London: Department for Education.

Ofsted (1994) *GNVQs in Schools 1993/4: Quality and Standards of General National Vocational Qualification*. London: HMSO.

Paul, R. (1987) Dialogical thinking: critical though essential to the acquisition of rational knowledge and passions, in J.B. Baron and R.J. Sternberg (eds) *Teaching Thinking Skills: Theory and Practice*. New York: Freeman.

Peim, N. (1993) *Critical Theory and the English Teacher*. London: Routledge.

Perkins, D.N. and Salomon, G. (1989) Are cognitive skills context-bound?, *Educational Research*, 18(1): 16–25.

Peters, R. (1966) *Ethics and Education*. London: Allen & Unwin.

Phizacklea, A. and Miles, R. (1980) *Labour and Racism*. London: Routledge & Kegan Paul.

Pinker, S. (1994) *The Language Instinct*. London: Penguin.

Polanyi, M. (1966) *The Tacit Dimension*. New York: Doubleday.

Pollard, A. (1985) *The Social World of the Primary School*. London: Holt, Rinehart and Winston.

Porter, E. and Smith, R. (1989) Autobiography: the thread and the mirror, in P. White (ed.) *Personal and Social Education*. London: Kogan Page in association with the Institute of Education, University of London.

Pring, R. (1976) *Knowledge and Schooling*. London: Open Books.

Pring, R. (1987) Implications of the changing values and ethical standards of society, in J. Thacker, R. Pring and D. Evans (eds) *Personal, Social and Moral Education*. Windsor: NFER/Nelson.

Purvis, J. (1981) Towards a history of women's education in nineteenth century Britain: a sociological analysis, *Westminster Studies in Education*, 4: 45–71.

Quicke, J. (1988a) The 'New Right' and education, *British Journal of Educational Studies*, 36(1): 5–20.

Quicke, J. (1988b) Using structured life histories to teach the social psychology and sociology of education, in P. Woods and A. Pollard (eds) *Sociology and Teachers: A New Challenge for the Sociology of Education*. London: Croom Helm.

Quicke, J. (1993) Social background, identity and political consciousness in the sixth form, in I. Bates and G. Riseborough, *Youth and Inequality*. Buckingham: Open University Press.

Quicke, J. (1994) Pupil culture and the curriculum, *Westminster Studies in Education*, 17: 5–18.

Quicke, J. (1995) Gender and GCSE results: what schools are doing. Paper presented to the Annual Conference of the British Educational Research Association, Bath University, September.

Quicke, J. and Winter, C. (1994) Teaching the language of learning: towards a metacognitive approach to pupil empowerment, *British Educational Research Journal*, 20(4): 429–45.

Quicke, J. and Winter, C. (1995) Best friends: a case study of girls' reactions to an innovation designed to foster collaborative group work, *Gender and Education*, 7(3): 259–81.

Ranson, S. (1993) Markets or democracy for education, *British Journal of Educational Studies*, 41: 333–52.

Rattansi, A. (1992) Changing the subject? Racism, culture and education, in J. Donald and A. Rattansi (eds) *'Race', Culture and Difference*. London: Sage/The Open University.

Riddell, S.I. (1992) *Gender and the Politics of the Curriculum*. London and New York: Routledge.

Roche, M. (1992) *Rethinking Citizenship*. Cambridge: Polity Press.

Rose, G. (1995) *Love's Work*. London: Chatto and Windus.

Samuel, R. (1995) The people with stars in their eyes. *The Guardian*, 23 September.

Sandel, M. (1984) The procedural republic and the unencumbered self, *Political Theory*, 12: 81–96.

Saunders, L., Stoney, S. and Weston, P. (1997) The impact of the work-related curriculum on 14 to 16-year-olds, *Journal of Education and Work*, 10(2): 151–67.

Schlechty, P. (1990) *Schools for the Twenty-First Century*. San Francisco: Jossey-Bass.

Schon, D. (1983) *The Reflective Practitioner*. London: Temple Smith.

Schutz, A. (1971a) *Collected Papers*, Vol. 2 The Hague: Nijhoff, pp. 72–3.

Schutz, A. (1971b) The stranger, in B.R. Cosin, I.R. Dale, G.M. Esland, D. Mackinnon and D.F. Swift (eds) *School and Society*. London: Routledge & Kegan Paul.

Sheeran, Y. and Barnes, D. (1991) *School Writing*. Buckingham: Open University Press.

Siegel, H. (1986) McPeck, informal logic and the nature of critical thinking, in D. Nyberg (ed.) *Philosophy of Education 1985*. Normal, Ill.: Philosophy of Education Society.

Smith, R.S. (1997) Parent education: empowerment or control? *Children and Society*, 11: 108–16.

Smyth, J. (1993) *A Socially Critical View of the Self Managing School*. London: Falmer Press.

Solomos, J. and Back, L. (1996) *Racism and Society*. London: Macmillan.

Spours, K. (1995) *The Strengths and Weaknesses of GNVQs: Principles of Design, Learning for the Future*. Working Paper 3. Post-16 Education Centre, University of London: Institute of Education.

Spours, K. (1997) Vocational specialization: the future of GNVQs, NVQs and traditional vocational qualifications. Paper presented to the fourth London Region Post-16 Network Seminar, February.

Spours, K. and Young, M. (1988) *Beyond Vocationalism*. Working Paper 4. Post-16 Education Centre, University of London: Institute of Education.

Stoll, L. and Fink, D. (1996) *Changing Our Schools*. Buckingham: Open University Press.

Sutton, C. (1992) *Words, Science and Learning*. Buckingham: Open University Press.

Swann, J. (1992) *Girls, Boys and Language*. Oxford: Blackwell.

Tawney, R.H. (1938) *Religion and the Rise of Capitalism*. Harmondsworth: Pelican.

Tawney, R.H. (1961) *The Acquisitive Society*. London: Fontana. First published in 1921.

Taylor, C. (1985) *Human Agency and Language: Philosophical Papers 1*. Cambridge: Cambridge University Press.

Taylor, C. (1989) *Sources of the Self*. Cambridge: Cambridge University Press.

Taylor, C. (1992) *Multiculturalism and 'The Politics of Recognition'*. Princeton, NJ: Princeton University Press.

Tolmie, A. and Howe, C. (1993) Gender and dialogue in secondary school physics, *Gender and Education*, 5(2): 191–209.

Walkerdine, V. (1990) *The Mastery of Reason*. London: Routledge.

Watts, A.G. (1983) *Education, Unemployment and the Future of Work*. Milton Keynes: Open University Press.

Watts, M. and Bentley, D. (1994) Humanizing and feminizing school science: reviewing anthropomorphic and animistic thinking in constructivist science education, *International Journal of Science Education*, 16(1): 83–97.

Weber, M. (1930) *The Protestant Ethic and the Spirit of Capitalism*. London: Allen & Unwin.

Wellington, J.J. (1994) *Secondary Science*. London and New York: Routledge.

White, Janet (1990) Questions of choice and change, in National Writing Project, *What Are Writers Made Of?* Walton on Thames: Nelson.

White, John (1990) *Education and the Good Life*. London: Kogan Page in association with the Institute of Education, University of London.

White, John (1996) Education and nationality, *Journal of Philosophy of Education*, 30(3): 327–43.

Whitebread, D. (1997) Developing children's problem-solving: the educational use of adventure games, in A. McFarlane (ed.) *Information Technology and Authentic Learning*. London and New York: Routledge.

Whitty, G., Rowe, G. and Aggleton, P. (1994) Discourse in cross curricular contexts: the limits to empowerment, *International Studies in Sociology of Education*, 4(1): 25–42.

Wilkinson, A. (ed.) (1986) *The Writing of Writing*. Milton Keynes: Open University Press.

Williams, R. (1961) *The Long Revolution*. Harmondsworth: Penguin.

Williams, R. (1976) *Keywords*. Glasgow: Fontana.

Willis, P. (1977) *Learning to Labour*. Aldershot: Saxon House.

Willis, P. (1990) *Moving Culture*. London: Calouste Gulbenkian Foundation.

Wood, J. (1982) 'Boys will be boys', *New Socialist*, May/June: 41–3.

Woods, P. (1983) *Sociology and the School*. London: Routledge & Kegan Paul.

Woods, P. (1990) *The Happiest Days? How Pupils Cope with School*. Basingstoke: Falmer Press.

Index

Abbot, P., 122
Adcock, J., 164, 165
agency, 5, 6, 30, 42, 60
Aggleton, P., 139
Aikenhead, G.S., 152, 153
alienation, 28, 29, 131–2, 136–7
Apple, M., 168
Arnot, M., 100, 109
Asoko, H., 150
Aspin, D.N., 158
assessment, 166–7
autobiography, 20–7
autonomy, 2, 7, 24, 28, 33, 40, 50, 53,
    58, 73, 123, 128, 140, 141
Aviram, A., 72, 126

Back, L., 9
Baker, D., 102
Ball, S., 13, 64, 53
Ballinger, M., 36, 39
Barnes, D., 31, 35, 43, 71
Barrow, R., 37
Beck, V., 11
Bentley, D., 106
Berger, B., 7, 18, 123–5
Berger, J., 66
Berger, P.L., 7, 18, 123–5
Bernstein, B., 12
'best friends', 75–80
Billig, M., 83, 87
Bishop, N., 31–2
Blagg, N., 36, 39
Blyton, P., 131

Bocock, R., 2
Bonnett, M., 167–8
Borkowski, J.G., 42
Bowe, R., 13, 53
boys' 'underachievement', 101–5
Brell, C.D., 38
Broadfoot, P., 167
Brooks, G., 103
Brown, G., 37
Bruner, J.S., 43, 150, 151
Buchner, P., 135
bureaucracy, 6, 7, 8, 51, 52, 156–8

Callan, E., 28
capitalism, 130–1, 132
Carr, W., 3
Cather, W., 161
Chapman, J.D., 158
Christian socialists, 131
citizenship, 81, 113, 128, 162, 164, 168
class, 6, 12, 15, 87–91, 122, 126, 127
'close relationships', 8, 110, 113, 123
Cockburn, C.K., 99
Coffield, F., 15
Coles, M., 33
collaboration, 51, 54–7, 60, 63, 66
collaborative group work, 68–80
collaborative self, *see* self
commitment, 12, 28, 29, 92
communicative competence, 68
communitarianism, 33
community, 3, 16, 53, 76, 88, 93,
    147–9, 155

computers, *see* information technology
  (IT)
Confederation of British Industry (CBI),
  140
conversation
  between paradigms, 152
  and collaboration, 62, 69–70
  and home learning, 120
  inter-cultural, 85, 86, 91
  intra-cultural, 85, 86
  interdisciplinary, 43, 48
coping mechanism, 22
core skills, *see* skills
Cowie, H., 70
critical metacognition, *see*
  metacognition
critical theory, 23
cross curricular themes, 139
culture
  belonging aspect of, 82–3
  collaborative, 54
  contradictions of, 87
  counter, 125
  minority, 93
  and pluralism, 8, 81–95
  pupil, 72–80
  and structure, 57
  working class, 88–91

Dale, R., 139
Darling, J., 103, 104
Davey, A., 175
Davies, B., 76
Dearing, R., 139
deconstruction, 23
democracy, 2, 3, 74, 81, 123, 125, 126,
  149, 158
democratic character structure, 133
democratic learning communities, 122
democratic learning society, 160, 162,
  169
Department for Education (DFE), 103
Department for Education and
  Employment (DFEE), 35, 56
Department of Education and Science
  (DES), 104, 140
deschooling, 122, 162
developmental model, 21

Dewey, J., 5, 39, 133–5
disability, 96
discourse, 5, 24, 43, 118, 119, 120
diversity, 17, 60, 110
Driver, R., 150
Durkheim, E., 51, 124
Dweck, C.S., 104

economic and industrial understanding,
  139
ecosystem, 106
Education Reform Act,1988, vii, 12
Edwards, A.D., 43, 69
Edwards, D., 43, 157
Elliot, J., 63, 58
Engels,F., 132
Ennis, R.H., 38
equality/inequality, 2, 52
equal opportunities, 96, 101, 105
Equal Opportunities Commission
  (EOC), 103
ethnography, 135
Excellence in Schools, 35, 114
exemplars, 148

false consciousness, 90, 132, 136–7
family
  bourgeois, 123, 124, 126
  breakdown of, 115
  contradictions of, 115, 128
  'dark side of', 122
  democratic, 125, 126
  nuclear, 127
feminism, 106, 125
Fink, D., 57–9
Flavell, J.H., 40, 41
Ford, J., 101
formal/informal curriculum, 61–2,
  135–7, 138–43
Foucault, M., 60–1, 64–5
Fox Hardling, L., 8
Freud, S., 132
Fromm, E., 31, 125, 132
Fullan, M.G., 59
fundamentalism, 13, 53
Furlong, V.J., 43
Further Education Unit (FEU), 140,
  141

Gardner, R., 36, 39
gender, 96–112
General Certificate of Education (GCSE), 96, 98, 102–4
General National Vocational Qualification (GNVQ), 141–2
genetically modifed organisms, 156
Gewirtz, S., 13, 53
Giddens, A., 7, 99, 111, 145
Glendinning, A., 103, 104
Gold, K., 102
Goldstein, H., 167
'good society', ix
Goodson, I.F., 12
Gore, J.M., 65
Gorman, T.P., 103
grand narratives, 10
Green, A.,10, 143
Greenhalgh, P., 70
Grumet, M., 29
The Guardian, 113

Habermas, J., 55, 68
Hadley, E., 69
Hall, S., 4, 76
Hammersely, M., 43,136
Hannon, P., 118,119
Hansen, D.A., 115, 116, 117
Hargreaves, A., 55, 59
Hargreaves, D., 43, 166
Harre, R., 48
Harris, D., 139
Harris, S., 102
Hartnett, A., 3
Harvey, D., 9
Haskey, J., 8
Hennesy, S., 37
Hillman, Y., 57, 59
HIV/AIDS, 111
Hodkinson,P., 141
homophobia, 100
Hopkins,D., 57
Howe,C., 108, 109
Hoyles, C., 67
Hyland, T., viii

identity, 21, 92, 110, 129
  see also self

ideology, 63, 98, 90, 125
individualism, 2, 107, 124, 131, 133
information technology (IT), 16, 36, 164, 167–8
instrumentalism, 12, 105
interactive professionalism, 59
interpretative repertoires, 126
intimacy, 110, 126, 161
Irwin, A., 145

Jacques, M., 4
James, M.,167
James, S., 126–7
Jefferson, T., 76
Jenkins, E., 175
Jessop, G., 140
Johnson, T.J., 52
Jonathan, R., 13
Jones, D., 102
Jones, K., 14
Jones, M., 83, 85, 86
Jones, R., 111
Jordan, B., 126–7
Joseph, K., 114

Kellner, 7, 18
Kelly, A., 106
key skills, *see* skills
Kiernan, K., 8
Kispal, A., 103
Kincheloe, J.L., 106
Kitwood, T., 7
Kleinig, J., 38
Klemp, G.O., 42
Kuhn, T.S., 106, 147–50

language of learning, 43–8
Lash, S., 5, 9
Lave, J., 37
Layton, D., 175
Leach, J., 150
learning
  active, 34
  collaborative, 76
    see also collaborative group work
  continuous, 14
  and curriculum, 35, 43
  home, 118–22

learning (*cont.*)
lifelong, 15, 113, 163
official/unofficial, 68
transfer of, 35, 37
learning organization, 5, 7
learning profession, 54
learning society *see* democratic learning
society
Learning to Succeed, 14
Lees, S., 98
leisure, 133
Leonard, D., 135
Levidow, L., 156–7
Lewis, T., 134
liberalism, 6, 24, 25, 26, 74, 82, 126,
128
liberty, 2
Licht, B.G., 104
limitations, 74, 79
love, 123, 125, 126, 161
Loveys, M., 139
Lukes, S., 2, 132

Mac an Ghaill, M., 99, 100
McCormick, R., 37
MacEwen Scott, A., 99
MacGill, S., 175
MacIntyre, A., 3, 4, 20, 26, 27
McKeown, P., 54
Maclure, M., 103
McMeeking, S., 167
Macmurray, J., 4
Maden, M., 57
managerialism, 55, 137
market, 3, 9, 13, 52–3, 165
Marsh, P., 48
Martin, J., 54
Marton, F., 38
Marx, K., 125, 131, 132
McPeck, J.E., 37
masculinity, 97, 98, 106, 107
Mead, G.H., 5
Measor, L., 76
Menter, I., 136–7
Mercer, N., 43, 157
metacognition, 39–43
middle-class, *see* class
Miles, R., 90

Millar, R., 150
Millard, E., 104
Miller, D., 92
misogyny, 98, 100
modernization, 13–16
Mongon, D., 101
Moore, R., 139
moral-political, 2, 92
Mortimer, E., 150
Mortimore, P., 57
Mouffe, C., 33, 81
Mulkay, M., 155
multi-cultural curriculum, 82
Murphy, P., 37
Muschamp, Y., 136–7
Muthukrina, N., 42

narcissism, 30–1, 125
narrative, 26–7
National Commission on Education
(NCE), 14
National Council for Vocational
Qualifications (NCVQ), 140
National Curriculum, vii, 12, 61–2,
138–9, 168
National Curriculum Council (NCC),
139, 140
nationalism, 91–4
neo-conservatism, 8, 122–3
neo-liberalism, 56, 123
new professionalism, *see*
professionalism
New Right, 13, 82, 123
'new times', 4, 6, 8, 17, 18, 28, 30, 51,
54, 67, 96, 113, 144
Nicholls, P., 136–7
Nisbet, J., 39
Nixon, J., 11, 54
Noon, M., 131
Noss, R., 167
Nuttall, D., 167

Office for Standards in Education
(Ofsted), 101, 103, 104, 141, 142
Ozga, J., 136–7

paradigm, 58, 147–9
parenting skills, 114, 115, 128

paternalism, 72, 74, 106
patriarchy, 6, 9, 97–9, 108, 125
Paul R., 38
Peim, N., 23–6
penetrations, 74, 77, 79
Perkins, D.N., 38
person/personal, 2, 3, 4, 5, 10, 12, 14, 20, 22, 27, 30, 32, 40, 41, 66, 67, 70, 110, 120, 136, 140, 161, 163, 164
personal effectiveness, 141, 143
Peters, R., 34
phenomenologist, 33, 145
Phizacklea, A., 90
Pinker, S., 68
pluralism, 8, 9, 81–95
Polanyi, M., 150
political education, 4
Pollard, A., 72, 75, 136–7
polymath teacher-tutor, 164–5
Porter, E., 30
postmodernism, 5, 54
power, 26, 34, 43, 49, 51, 55, 60–4, 72, 79, 94, 100, 111, 134
practice, 3, 11, 20, 64, 74, 75–9
prejudice, 82–7
Pring R., 19, 40
problem-solving *see* skills
professionalism, 50–67, 136–7, 154, 156
property, 126
psychology, *see* social psychology
pupil culture, *see* culture
Puritan, 131, 133
Purvis, J., 97

Qualifications and Curriculum Authority (QCA) vii, 140
Quicke, J., 33, 35, 44, 49, 63, 75, 80, 87, 102

racism, 9, 84, 86, 87–92, 94, 95
Ranson, S., 13, 54
Rattansi, A., 90
recontextualization, 108, 109
Records of Achievement, 166–7
Redley, M., 126–7
reflective practitioner, 58–9, 63, 64

reflexivity, 2, 5, 8, 10, 16, 17, 20, 33, 39, 43, 63, 65, 70, 82, 121, 154
reflexive modernity, 4, 5, 8, 11, 33, 68, 95, 146
Reformation, 130
reproduction, 6
resistance, 91, 118
restorationism, 8, 11–13, 115, 123, 169
Riddell, S. I., 106
risk society, 145–7, 159
Roche, M., 123
Rose, G., 125
Rosser, E., 48
Rowe, G., 139
Rudduck, J., 70, 102

Saint Thomas Aquinas, 130
Salomon, G., 38
Samuel, R., 28
Sandel, M., 28
Saunders, L., 138, 139, 140
Schlechty, P., 10
Schon, D., 64
Schutz, A., 87, 145–6
science, 11, 17, 145–59
Scott, P., 150
school effectiveness, 57, 60
school improvement, 57, 58, 60–4
Scottish Certificate of Education (SCE), 103
self
    actualization, 124
    centredness, 133
    discloser, 32
    evaluation, 23, 39, 40
    identity, 7, 17, 18–33, 129
    in-the-world, 63, 131
    love, 30, 31
    real, 20, 135
    reification, 29–30
    understanding, 7, 8, 22, 27, 39, 64, 65,
sex education, 111
sexuality, 100, 110–11
Sheeran, Y., 158
Shemilt, D., 35, 43
Shilling, C., 139
Shucksmith, J., 39

Siegel, H., 38
Sikes, P., 139
skills
-based curriculum, 15
cognitive, 36
core, 140, 142, 143
generalizable, 37, 38, 39
generic, 15
key, 140, 142, 143
personal, 140
problem-solving, 37, 39, 141
thinking, 35–8, 39, 43
Smith, R.S., 30
Smyth, J., 55
social justice, 2, 93
social psychology, 5, 131, 132, 133, 143
sociology, 38
Solomos, J., 9
Somerset Thinking Skills Course (STSC), 36
Spours, K., 138, 140, 141
Steinberg, S.R., 106
Stierer, B., 167
Stoll, L., 57, 58, 59
Stoney, S., 138, 139, 140
survival strategies, 136
Sutton, C.,150
Swann, J., 101

tacit knowledge, 150
Tate, N., 150
teachers
alienation, 137
and autonomy, 55–6
and collaboration, 54–6
concerns, 136
and families, 115–18
job satisfaction, 137
knowledge, 56
and pupil relations, 73
and reflection, 58–9, 62–3
Tawney, R.H., 50, 51, 130, 131

Taylor, C., 9, 19, 23
Technical Vocational Educational Initiative (TVEI), 139
Times Educational Supplement, 100
Todd, F., 71
Tolmie, A., 108, 109
Towards a Skills Revolution, 140
transfer, *see* learning
transformational, 6
Trevitt, J., 139
trust, 31–2, 123

Valsecchi, V., 139
virtues, 20
vocational education, 134–5
voice, 100

Walkerdine, V., 119–20
Wallace, C., 122
Watts, A. G., 106
Watts, M., 129
Weber, M., 52, 130
Wellington, J.J., 150
Westgate, D.P.G., 69
Weston, P., 138, 139, 140
Whelan, M., 101
White, Janet, 104
White, John, 92–4
Whitebread, D., 36
Whitty, G., 139
Wicks, M., 8
Wilkinson, A., 21
Williams, R., 132
Willis, P., 74–5, 88
Winter, C., 35, 75
Wood, J., 98
Woods, P., 76
work, 129–44
Wright Mills, C., 52
Wynne, B., 150

Young, M., 138